WHAT YOUR COLLEAGUES ARE S

"*School Counseling to Close Opportunity Gaps* addresses six key functions that should be proactively performed by school counselors across the nation. At its very core, it provides a blueprint on how culturally competent school counselors may actively address systemic and structural racism and oppression within our school systems.

"I applaud Cheryl Holcomb-McCoy's tenacity for social justice and this earnest attempt to connect culturally relevant research to culturally competent practice. This text is passionate and deliberately delivers a viewpoint that is both poignant and ferociously honest. The book delivers a profound understanding of the devastating impact that systemic racism has on OUR society, especially as experienced by marginalized and oppressed people of color. I am confident that the challenge put forth within this second edition will lead to action: game-changing, sustainable, and meaningful action. I love this book for our children, because they need us, the adults in the room, to step up our game. We are co-conspirators for positive change, and it is time for action. Let's accept the challenge and get to work!

"Dr. Holcomb-McCoy speaks truth and power to the overdue racial justice conversations and implores school counselors, and I add ALL counselors, to lean into discomfort and be an active part of the solution. The time is now for good people to do something; perhaps get into some good trouble, as posited by a great social justice advocate, John Lewis. As one of my favorite quotes states, 'the only thing necessary for the triumph of evils is for good [people] to do nothing' (Edmund Burke).

"The preface states that the book is a labor of love, long overdue, and a 'love letter to her beloved profession.' Dr. Holcomb-McCoy delivers a profound call to the profession to 'Wake UP.' I, too, echo this challenge! I implore readers to delve into the words and digest them well and with discernment so that they can come out of this on the right side of justice. For the established co-conspirators, the text will embolden you to step up your game and make a difference in your part of the world; for newcomers to the beautiful reality that is Dr. Cheryl Holcomb-McCoy, sit back, take a deep breath, and get ready to be encouraged by the words that make up this text. Let each syllable build upon the other and create within you a desire to be a staunch advocate for our children. The school counseling profession needs you, in fact it needs all of us, to take a bold stance for justice, a momentous stand that helps us to see each other. Envision it with Cheryl Holcomb-McCoy and me, how WE the people . . . together . . . doing the right thing . . . collectivistic in nature . . . can advocate and positively impact each and every school environment that we enter."

—**S. Kent Butler**
70th President of the American Counseling Association

"Cheryl Holcomb-McCoy's analysis of school counseling contexts is now more timely, incisive, and compelling than ever. For such a time as now, *School Counseling to Close Opportunity Gaps* provides school counselors with strategies to understand and dismantle inequitable systems using both antiracist and socially just frameworks in an effort to reduce the pernicious effects of oppression on Black and Brown students and their families."

—Norma L. Day-Vines
Professor, Associate Dean
Diversity and Faculty Development, Johns Hopkins University

"*School Counseling to Close Opportunity Gaps* is the book school counselors have needed for some time. School counselors are uniquely trained to identify and work to remove the social-emotional barriers to learning; however, first they must identify the role they have played in creating, enabling, or monitoring the barriers to academic success for some students. Cheryl Holcomb-McCoy courageously addresses the racial and social injustices that infiltrate the education system. She presents it clearly in this book: 'If school counselors focus on fixing access to opportunities, they aren't furthering racist ideas but providing resources and opportunities for student success.'

"Dr. Holcomb-McCoy pushes the reader to examine further the underfunding of schools that Black and Brown students disproportionately attend. She explores the economic and academic impact this has on the education of these students and the community. 'According to the Century Foundation (2020), the U.S. is underfunding public schools by nearly $150 billion annually, robbing millions of children—predominantly Black, Brown, and low-income children—of the opportunity to success.'

"In this book, Dr. Holcomb-McCoy does not allow the reader to focus solely on the challenges but encourages the school counselor to transform the way they think of their role in the school. She then provides the reader with tools needed to deconstruct the systems of oppression in place in education. This is the book that school counselors have needed for some time, and it is finally here. Now it is time for this book to be transformed into a course to train school counselors."

—Nikki Ham
President, Maryland School Counselor Association
Associate Director of Clinical Counseling, Bowie State University

"Cheryl Holcomb-McCoy brilliantly educates, inspires, and calls every school counselor to antiracist action, NOW. This is mandatory reading for everyone connected to the school counseling profession."

—Paul C. Harris
Associate Professor, Counselor Education
The Pennsylvania State University

"Once again, Cheryl Holcomb-McCoy lands a seminal read that is not to be missed! This second edition, a decade after her first, doesn't disappoint. Dr. Holcomb-McCoy calls for school counselors to actively address flawed racist policies, white-centered curriculum, and white supremacy culture in schools. One of the most significant shifts in the text is the focus on 'opportunities' rather than achievement gaps. Dr. Holcomb-McCoy implores school counselors to no longer be silent, but rather to commit to disrupting oppressive practices and policies in their schools. Throughout the text she pleads for counselors to rise up and restructure programs that continue to marginalize and oppress Black and Brown students. She calls for counselors to move the needle of the conversation in schools by identifying and describing racist policies, practices, and procedures and then be personally and collectively active in eliminating them. This is the proactive work of today's antiracist school counselor. Finally, Dr. Holcomb-McCoy introduces six key elements along with multiple scenarios and self-reflective activities for school counselors to draw from as they commit to addressing long-standing disparities in education by dismantling racism."

—Trish Hatch
President and CEO of Hatching Results, LLC

"Differential access to opportunities in life represents the primary issue in our society, and systemic discrimination does damage to a young person's sense of hope and possibility for the future. Discrimination represents a cancer transmitted by the power structure intent on controlling access to power, opportunity, resources, and influence. As the human development specialists in our schools, school counselors are called to be social-justice strategists—social-justice oncologists if you will—addressing this cancer and meeting students and stakeholders at the crossroads of what has been, what is, and what could be, pushing back against such discrimination. For our future to be the best that it can be for all students, we must engage in social justice and antiracist work. This is the call of this important book. It should be mandatory reading for all school counselors and educators."

—Spencer G. Niles
Professor and Dean Emeritus, The College of William & Mary

"Once again, Cheryl Holcomb-McCoy has written a critical and cutting-edge book that takes the reader on a comprehensive review of historical and current events that marginalize and harm Black, Brown, and Indigenous children. This edition builds on the author's prior work and utilizes student experiences to showcase the ways in which school counselors engage in oppressive and racist practices and serve as bystanders to policies that reinforce a deficit lens. This deficit lens unjustly places blame on the targeted group for the educational opportunity gaps the policies created. The author makes an urgent call for change and provides a six-step framework for school counselors and counselor educators to embed an antiracist and social justice approach to their work."

—**Laura Owen**
Executive Director, Center for Equity and Postsecondary Attainment
San Diego State University

"Cheryl Holcomb-McCoy has done it again! She has taken a book that once reformed the school counseling field and, with clarity and heart, has transformed it into a love letter to the entire school counseling community. In this contemporary and authoritative update, Dr. Holcomb-McCoy reminds us that simply claiming to be an antiracist educator is not the same as actively dismantling long-standing racism in schools. School counselors who are looking to make good on their commitment to support all students, rather than merely perpetuating the status quo, will need courage, tenacity, and a copy of this book."

—**Mandy Savitz-Romer**
Nancy Pforzheimer Aronson Senior Lecturer in Human
Development and Education
Harvard Graduate School of Education

"The updated edition of *School Counseling to Close Opportunity Gaps* revisits the lauded school counseling book more than 10 years later. The book serves as a reminder and a continued call to action, asking the simple question, 'Why haven't school counselors disrupted their students' uneven access to opportunity?'

"With a powerful foreword by Dr. Ibram X Kendi, challenging school counselors to shift their focus from the failures of their student to the negligence of the education system to our most marginalized students, the book servers as a spirited guide to continue to reimagine school counseling as a tool of equity and opportunity.

"This edition isn't a simple update of statistics and figures. The book structurally reworks school counseling through not only a social justice lens, but also an antiracist lens. Antiracist practices are highlighted, including defining opportunity, identifying affirming practices, and self-reflecting through the process. All these sound antiracist practices and more are highlighted while continuing to challenge the reader to Do the Right Thing. There are updated student stories showing the contours of opportunity and disparity. The new counselor snapshots create relevant and contemporary scenarios reflecting the increased complexity of modern education with practical guides and thought-provoking questions.

"More than other social-justice-in-education books, Dr. Holcomb-McCoy interweaves themes of empowerment and liberation, not just for students, but into the school counseling repertoire. The guides and self-assessments provide the foundation for counselors to transform themselves and their programs to instruments of liberation and opportunity for all students.

"*School Counseling to Close Opportunity Gaps* is a needed companion for school counselors of all experience levels to transform disparity to opportunity and bias to connectedness, and to build a foundation of hope in education as we move forward from the pandemic and the legacies of oppression in education."

—Stephen Sharp
School Counselor, Hempfield School District, PA

School Counseling to Close Opportunity Gaps

Second Edition

School Counseling to Close Opportunity Gaps

A Social Justice and Antiracist Framework for Success

Second Edition

Cheryl Holcomb-McCoy

Foreword by Ibram X. Kendi

FOR INFORMATION:

Corwin
A SAGE Company
2455 Teller Road
Thousand Oaks, California 91320
(800) 233-9936
www.corwin.com

SAGE Publications Ltd.
1 Oliver's Yard
55 City Road
London EC1Y 1SP
United Kingdom

SAGE Publications India Pvt. Ltd.
B 1/I 1 Mohan Cooperative Industrial Area
Mathura Road, New Delhi 110 044
India

SAGE Publications Asia-Pacific Pte. Ltd.
18 Cross Street #10-10/11/12
China Square Central
Singapore 048423

President: Mike Soules
Associate Vice President and Editorial
   Director: Monica Eckman
Publisher: Jessica Allan
Senior Content Development
   Editor: Lucas Schleicher
Associate Content Development
   Editor: Mia Rodriguez
Editorial Assistant: Natalie Delpino
Project Editor: Amy Schroller
Copy Editor: Erin Livingston
Typesetter: Hurix Digital
Proofreader: Dennis Webb
Cover Designer: Candice Harman
Marketing Manager: Olivia Bartlett

Printed in Canada

Library of Congress Cataloging-in-Publication Data

Names: Holcomb-McCoy, Cheryl, author.

Title: School counseling to close opportunity gaps : a social justice and antiracist framework for success / Cheryl Holcomb-McCoy.

Other titles: School counseling to close the achievement gap

Description: Second Edition. | Thousand Oaks, California : Corwin, [2022] | Includes bibliographical references and index.

Identifiers: LCCN 2021048772 | ISBN 9781071854914 (Paperback) | ISBN 9781071854921 (ePub) | ISBN 9781071854938 (ePub) | ISBN 9781071854945 (eBook)

Subjects: LCSH: Educational counseling—United States. | Student counselors—In-service training—United States. | Academic achievement—United states.

Classification: LCC LB1027.5 .H635 2022 | DDC 371.4/22—dc23/eng/20211208

LC record available at https://lccn.loc.gov/2021048772

This book is printed on acid-free paper.

MIX
Paper from
responsible sources
FSC® C103567

22 23 24 25 26 10 9 8 7 6 5 4 3 2 1

Contents

Foreword

When most students of color walk through their school halls, they are too often met with low expectations, hyper surveillance, lack of resources, racialized tracking, and a long-standing tradition of racist practices that linger in the walls silently. Because of class, race, ethnicity, ability, and language, students face invisible and visible barricades.

Districts with mostly white students receive more funding, and students are exposed to more internship opportunities and college preparatory classes. Districts with mostly Black and Latinx students experience punitive policies and practices that seek to push them out of school and into the criminal punishment system. These students are interacting with school resource officers when they should be interacting with school counselors.

School counselors are often the doors for students to higher education. But sometimes school counselors close doors on students. Sometimes school counselors have internalized the racist ideas that there is something academically or behaviorally wrong with Black, Latinx, and Native students; that Black caretakers don't value education; that Native people are not hard workers; or that Latinx parents don't care to spend time teaching their children. It is critical for school counselors to be antiracist, to realize there is nothing wrong or right with any group of students or parents, to individualize and encourage every single student, to standardize the opportunities that are available to students. Students need the emotional, social, and cultural support and resources to achieve.

Ten years after writing the first edition of this book, Cheryl Holcomb-McCoy returns and rightfully turns her attention to school counselors who have the power to disrupt the racist practices and policies in schools. School counselors must radically shift their attention from the failure of the students to the negligence of our education system to support students who are the most marginalized.

School counselors can and *must* intervene. If they are not increasing the opportunities for all students, then we are doing a disservice. School counselors—as people who engage with multiple stakeholders, including parents, students, teachers, administrators—must take advantage of their unique positionality to support the humanity of all students and fight for equal access.

I wish that we didn't need a book like this, that school counselors and teachers and all educators understood the significance of modeling antiracist practices and behaviors in schools. But the reality is that we need someone to lay out the foundational tools. Holcomb-McCoy wrote this purposeful and action-oriented volume, with deep concentration and care, with the intent for school counselors and educators to step into their roles as agents of change.

—Ibram X. Kendi, PhD
Andrew W. Mellon Professor in the Humanities and
Director of the Center for Antiracist Research, Boston University
Best-selling author, *How to Be an Antiracist*

Preface

Over 10 years ago, when I wrote the first edition of this book, I was a young mother of two and at the beginning of my career as a counselor educator. I had begun the complex and often tiring journey of training primarily white graduate counseling students to work in schools with a majority Black and Brown students. My recollections in the first edition were based on my experiences as a school counselor in the DC metropolitan area; my basic premise was that school counselors are well-positioned to be school equity strategists and leaders because they hear all narratives and work with a multitude of stakeholders—students, parents, teachers, and administrators. This is all still true. And addressing inequities is still at the core of school counselors' work. I'm just more convinced than ever before that school counselors are key players in education justice.

I wrote this second edition during one of the worst health crises this country has ever experienced—the coronavirus (COVID-19) pandemic. With a federal administration characterized by "small government," "anti-vaxxers," "school choice," and "anti-immigrant and anti-other" sentiments, the path forward for educators looked dim. However, the nation's public schools pivoted and adjusted to remote teaching and unheard-of work conditions. I watched and listened in amazement as school counselors across the country modified their programming to meet the needs of a country under attack by a deadly virus. Nevertheless, the COVID-19 virus killed over half a million people in the U.S. and millions worldwide. The grief and loss experienced during this period are insurmountable. Just think—more than 140,000 children lost a parent or grandparent caregiver to COVID-19 and this affected Black and Brown students disproportionately. Schools will surely be impacted in a multitude of ways, and school counselors will continue to adjust to meet the social, emotional, and academic needs of a grieving student population.

As I watched and experienced COVID-19 impact the nation and my family up close (I lost my mother-in-law to COVID-19), the pain was exacerbated by the brutal murder of George Floyd. Once again, an unarmed Black man was taken away from us and his family by a police officer—a police officer paid to serve and protect. George Floyd, like Breonna Taylor and countless others, was a victim to racial trauma and an untimely death. For nine minutes, Derek Chauvin, a white

Minneapolis police officer, kept his knee on the neck of the lifeless George Floyd, which symbolized to me the pain and slow death of many Black and Brown people at the hands of irresponsible and unaccountable police officers, educators, and other professionals who frame their work within an oppressive and racist framework. The large-scale protests that followed the death of George Floyd symbolized people's unwillingness to accept these deaths as the norm. It's time to act. My action was to write this long overdue second edition. It's a love letter to my beloved profession—wake up!

The questions that I kept coming back to as I wrote this new edition haunted me and still do: *Why haven't school counselors disrupted their students' uneven access to opportunities? Why do we continue to need a book like this to spell out to school counselors what they might already know?* The answer is simple—disrupting racist and oppressive policies and practices embedded in our schools is not easy. It's complicated and uncomfortable. School counselors, by nature, are well-meaning people. We want to believe that we are doing all that we can do. We also like others to like us! We want to be perceived as team players, so dismantling racist practices and policies doesn't always align with school counselors' typical personality profile. Thus, counselors aren't necessarily going to jump in and swim upstream to ensure equity for all students. Herein lies the internal challenge for school counselors—to act even when it's uncomfortable and unpopular. We need to find comfort in discomfort when it's the right thing to do. "Good and necessary trouble," as John Lewis described, is not comfortable trouble.

Two Stanford psychologists, Roberts and Rizzo (2021), provide a helpful framework for answering the above question of why school counselors haven't disrupted oppression. They outline seven factors, determined after an extensive review of interdisciplinary research, that contribute to American racism. I suspect that school counselors' willingness or unwillingness to disrupt racism in schools is based on several of these factors. The factors include (1) categories, which organize people into distinct groups by promoting essentialist and normative reasoning; (2) factions, which trigger in-group loyalty and intergroup competition and threat; (3) segregation, which hardens racist perceptions, preferences, and beliefs through the denial of intergroup contact; (4) hierarchy, which emboldens people to think, feel, and behave in racist ways; (5) power, which legislates racism on both micro and macro levels; (6) media, which legitimizes overrepresented and idealized representations of white Americans while marginalizing and minimizing people of color; and (7) passivism, such that overlooking or denying the existence of racism obscures reality and allows racism to fester and persist. I argue that school counselors, both white and nonwhite, often align with many of these factors but, most notably, *passivism* or *silence*. For many school counselors, doing nothing seems safe; unfortunately, silence actually perpetuates racist practices and beliefs.

Since 2007, when the first edition was published, national events have also shaped the current education landscape. It's important to consider that the context of education has changed but the inequities have not. Many of the events are cause for celebration while others are cause for despair. All in all, education progress has been made, but it hasn't changed the overall experiences of Black and Brown students in schools. Inequities persist. See the following events (in no particular order) in Box 0.1.

Box 0.1: Events That Have Shaped Education and Education Policy Since 2007

- *Termination of the No Child Left Behind Act (NCLB) and launch of Every Student Succeeds Act (ESSA)*

- *Launch of the Common Core Standards*

- *Election of Barack Obama as the first Black U.S. president*

- *Legalization of same-sex marriage*

- *Sylvia Mendez awarded the Presidential Medal of Freedom (Mendez's parents were lead plaintiffs in the historic civil rights case,* Mendez V. Westminster and the California Board of Education*)*

- *30th anniversary of the Americans with Disabilities Act (ADA)*

- *National recognition of school counselors by former First Lady Michelle Obama via her national movement, Reach Higher*

- *An economic recession that included significant cuts to state education budgets*

- *Mass shootings at K–12 schools occurred more frequently, including Sandy Hook Elementary School and Parkland High School*

- *The School District of Philadelphia cut nearly 4,000 employees, including 676 teachers as well as administrators and school counselors*

- *Minnesota and other states adopted policies allowing transgender students to join female sports teams*

- *The Civil Rights Project report,* Brown at 60: Great Progress, a Long Retreat, and an Uncertain Future *is published and shows a decline in non-Hispanic white students, a significant increase in Latinx students, and the growth of racial segregation*

- *In 2014, nationwide, students of color outnumber non-Hispanic white students*

- *President-elect Donald Trump appointed billionaire and school-choice advocate Betsy DeVos as Secretary of Education*

(*Continued*)

(Continued)

- *Thousands of students joined the March for Our Lives protest against guns/gun violence in Washington DC*

- *Hundreds of educators and former educators ran for office in the 2018 midterm elections; 2016 Teacher of the Year, Jahana Hayes from Connecticut, became a congresswoman*

- *Kamala Harris, a Black and Indian American woman, elected Vice President of the U.S.*

- *Alabama became the first state to "require public schools to check immigration status" of students*

- *President Joe Biden signed the $1.9 trillion COVID-19 relief bill into law. The bill provided $125 billion to help schools reopen.*

Again, the premise of the first edition continues because education disparities still plague our country. Well-meaning efforts to fix the gaps have been implemented but not on a large scale because educators haven't necessarily pushed for change locally. We need local policy change and educators who will not stop fighting.

Although I wrote this second edition out of frustration, I am incredibly proud of it. But it is indeed not perfect. I'm sure some will find that I didn't talk enough about certain racial, cultural, and/or identity groups or the intersectionality of those identities. I attempted in this book to address what I believe are six key functions of school counselors that will address systemic and structural racism and oppression in schools. I attempted to write so that school counselors will have more strategies to act on. Research citations are given, but the focus is on practice. The goal is to link research to practice.

As in the first edition, I am determined to dispel the myth that if students fail in school, they are unwilling to achieve. Unfortunately, it is not that simple. In many cases, schools fail students by implementing flawed policies, tolerating culturally incompetent and racist educators, utilizing white-centered curricula, and ignoring students' lived experiences. And the subtle—and sometimes overt—messages that educators relay to students matter. If we believe in, respect, and love all students, *they will respond*. Conversely, we must not tolerate educators who devalue and demean students.

The most significant change in this second edition relates to the magnification of access to *opportunities* rather than *achievement differences*. In no way do I want school counselors to infer that students of color are intellectually unequal to their peers. This is simply not the case and only further perpetuates white supremacist views. Access to opportunities that enable learning is the ultimate barrier. The problem is not the student; the problem is the opportunities afforded to students and the communities in which they live. Unfortunately, students' academic performance and school behaviors are often the culmination of generations of blocked opportunities based on racist ideas and policies.

Also, in this edition, I delve more into issues of racism, the multiple layered social identities of students (intersectionality), and the notion of student success. Although addressing racism is a component of my social justice framework for school counseling, I decided to highlight *antiracism* as a complementary construct on which school counselors should base their work. Hence, the book's title change. Given the painful and often overlooked history of racism in the U.S., I thought it was imperative to shine a light on the legacy of racism in the U.S. and to build on it as a place of strength. In this edition, I seek to bridge the painful legacy of colonialism and racism to the present-day experiences of students. I was struck by Nikole Hannah Jones's words in her 1619 essay when she reflected on the history of slavery and her current being. Her words exemplify the power of linking the past to current personal strengths:

> *At 43, I am part of the first generation of black Americans in the history of the United States to be born into a society in which black people had full rights of citizenship. Black people suffered under slavery for 250 years; we have been legally "free" for just 50. Yet in that briefest of spans, despite continuing to face rampant discrimination, and despite there never having been a genuine effort to redress the wrongs of slavery and the century of racial apartheid that followed, black Americans have made astounding progress, not only for ourselves but also for all Americans.*

What if America understood—finally, in this 400th year—that we have never been the problem, but we are the solution?

I feel incredibly blessed to have this platform to write about school counseling. I thank my colleagues and friends who shared with me their deep and personal thoughts about the future of school counseling.

Thank you for reading this book (my love letter!) and, more importantly, thank you for caring enough about children to give of your time and energy to read my thoughts and ideas on school counseling. And above all else, thank you for using this book to move forward overdue conversations about justice in counseling. We owe our students more than talk. They deserve real action. They deserve learning environments free of racism, discrimination, and oppression. We need to act now.

PURPOSE

The purpose of *School Counseling to Close Opportunity Gaps: An Antiracist and Social Justice Approach* is to introduce school counselors to six key elements of school counseling that will dismantle racism in schools and resolve long-standing education disparities based on race, gender, culture, and income. For many years, school counselors have been blamed for their biased advising, faulty assumptions, and discriminatory practices that ultimately block opportunities from students of historically marginalized communities. In many cases, school counselors are to blame for not disrupting racist and oppressive practices and policies in their schools. Although school counselors might unintentionally promote inequities, there is a benefit to their silence and maintenance of the status quo. With the status quo comes familiarity and no need to relearn or reeducate oneself. I am hopeful that after reading this book, school counselors will feel energized to act, to make changes in their approach to working with students, and to take a stand against "business as usual."

I would like to mention that even though a large part of this book is focused on the oppression experienced by Black and Brown students, the concepts can certainly be applied to any oppressed group of students. I believe that once counselors understand social justice and antiracism, they will begin to see inequities everywhere and across many diverse groups.

Acknowledgments

Writing this book was an emotional experience not only because it deals with a topic that is personal but also because I feel incredibly passionate about correcting injustices. The support of colleagues, students, friends, and family is priceless and has given me the will to complete it. Most of all, however, I would like to thank my family for their endless support and encouragement. My children—Niles and Nia—are my inspiration, for they represent the many vulnerable children who are affected each day by inequitable practices and policies in schools. Because of my love and hope for them and for all children, I wrote this book. I also want to thank my husband, Alvin, for his love and faith in my ability to convey a message that others would like to hear. I love you, Al.

And most importantly, thanks to my late mother, Colethia R. Holcomb, and my dad, Frederick Holcomb, for many years of validation, support, guidance, and love.

I dedicate this book to the souls lost to COVID-19 and to police violence/brutality.

The universe shrank
when you went away.
Every time I thought your name, stars fell upon me.

—Henry Dumas (poet, social activist, teacher)

PUBLISHER'S ACKNOWLEDGMENTS

Corwin gratefully acknowledges the contributions of the following reviewers:

Ileana Gonzalez
Assistant Professor
Johns Hopkins University
Baltimore, MD

Erik M. Hines
Associate Professor, Counselor Education Coordinator,
School Counseling Track Coordinator
College of Education
Florida State University
Gainesville, FL

Kara Ieva
Associate Professor, Counseling in Educational Settings
Rowan University
Glassboro, NJ

About the Author

Cheryl Holcomb-McCoy believes in the revolutionary power of school counseling. An American Counseling Association (ACA) Fellow with 30 years of experience as a former kindergarten teacher, elementary school counselor, family therapist, and (most recently) university professor and administrator, she has a wealth of knowledge, expertise, and wisdom.

Dr. Holcomb-McCoy is currently the dean of the School of Education and a professor at American University (AU). She is also the author of the best-selling book, *School Counseling to Close the Achievement Gap: A Social Justice Framework for Success* (Corwin) and has an upcoming edited book, *Antiracist Counseling in Schools and Communities* (ACA Publishing).

In her five years as dean, Dr. Holcomb-McCoy founded AU's Summer Institute on Education, Equity and Justice, and the AU Teacher Pipeline Project, a partnership with the DC Public Schools and Friendship Charter Schools. She is also actively working to develop an antiracist curriculum for teachers in training.

Prior to leading the School of Education at AU, she served as vice provost for faculty affairs campus-wide and vice dean of academic affairs in the School of Education at Johns Hopkins University. She launched the Johns Hopkins School Counseling Fellows Program and The Faculty Diversity Initiative. Dr. Holcomb-McCoy has also been an associate professor in the department of counseling and personnel services at the University of Maryland College Park and director of the school counseling program at Brooklyn College of the City University of New York.

A decorated scholar, she has written over 100 publications. From 2014 to 2016, she served as a consultant to former First Lady Michelle Obama's Reach Higher Initiative, a program dedicated to supporting first-generation students in making it to and through college. She also serves on the board of Martha's Table, a nonprofit group that supports health and wellness for children and families in the nation's capital.

Dr. Holcomb-McCoy's passion for school counseling, mental health, and wellness starts at home. As a proud mother of two, she knows firsthand the importance of systemic change to help students reach their full potential.

A proud member of Delta Sigma Theta Sorority, Inc., Dr. Holcomb-McCoy holds her bachelor's and master's degrees from the University of Virginia. In addition, she earned a doctorate in counseling and counselor education from the University of North Carolina at Greensboro.

She lives in Potomac, Maryland, with her husband and two children.

CHAPTER 1

Opportunity Gaps

Our Ultimate Challenge

Crystal, a ninth-grade Black student in an urban school district, wrote the following short essay in response to the question, "What do you want to be when you grow up?"

> *I'm not sure. One of my teachers says that I should go to a cosmetology school. She says that girls like me do well in cosmetology. But I don't know. I want money like Beyonce and I want to make a difference. My friends say that we can make videos and get lots of money. I'm good at videos. I get ok grades (3.0 average) in all of my classes and one teacher told me in 4th grade that I was smart. My cousin said that I should go to the community college so that I can get a job in a office. I thought about dropping out and just working on videos and stuff. I guess I just don't know what I want to be when I grow up.*

At Crystal's high school, there are three school counselors for 1,800 students (a 1 to 600 counselor-to-student ratio). Crystal's school is considered a high-minority/high-poverty school; thus, a majority of its students will be first-generation college students. Twenty percent of Crystal's classmates met ninth-grade reading/literacy standards on the state assessment and 10% of them met state mathematics standards, 4% met writing standards, and 3% met state science standards. There are few advanced (e.g., Advanced Placement [AP]) courses offered at her high school but students are heavily recruited by the local community college. Last year, the graduation rate at Crystal's high school was 72%; if Crystal is one of those 72% who graduate, chances are that she will not have the credits or skills necessary to get a job in her city nor will she have the required courses she needs to apply to the local four-year public university. Based on data,

Black women who graduate from her high school go on to either work or community college; even those with Crystal's grades do not apply for scholarships to four-year institutions. Unfortunately, Crystal's lack of options for career exploration and college information is not uncommon among her ninth-grade friends. Crystal has real potential, but she is unaware of options for her future. For snapshots of high school dropout rates by state, ethnicity, and gender, see Table 1.1 and Table 1.2 below.

Another ninth-grade student, Erin, attends a high school 25 miles from Crystal's school in a more affluent white suburban neighborhood. Her school, with an enrollment of 825, has three school counselors and a college counselor

TABLE 1.1   States in Which Status Dropout Rates for Black and Hispanic 16- to 24-Year-Olds Are Higher Than, Not Measurably Different From, or Lower Than the Status Dropout Rate for White 16- to 24-Year-Olds; 2013-2017

STATUS DROPOUT RATE FOR BLACK YOUTH			
Higher than the rate for white youth	Not measurably different from the rate for white youth	Lower than the rate for white youth	Not available/ does not meet reporting standards
AL, AZ, AR, CA, CO, CT, FL, GA, IL, IN, IA, KS, LA, MD, MI, MN, MA, MO, NE, NV, NJ, NY, NC, OH, OK, PA, SC, TN, TX VA, WA, WI	DE, KY, NM, OR, RI, SD, UT, WV	None	AK, HI, ID, ME, MT, NH, ND, VT, WY
STATUS DROPOUT RATE FOR HISPANIC/LATINX YOUTH			
Higher than the rate for white youth	Not measurably different from the rate for white youth	Lower than the rate for white youth	Not available/ does not meet reporting standards
AL, AZ, AR, CA, CO, CT, DE, FL, GA, ID, IL, IN, IA, KS, KY, LA, MD, MA, MI, MN, MS, MO, NE, NV, NH, NJ, NM, NY, NC, ND, OH, OK, OR, PA, RI, SC, SD, TN, TX, UT, VA, WA, WI, WY	AK, HI, ME, MT, WV	None	VT

NOTE: *Status dropouts* are 16- to 24-year-olds who are not enrolled in school and who have not completed a high school program regardless of when they left school. People who have received GED credentials are counted as high school completers. Status dropout rate gaps between white students and Black and Hispanic students in Washington, DC could not be calculated because the dropout rates for white students were suppressed in Washington, DC.

SOURCE: U.S. Department of Commerce, Census Bureau, American Community Survey (ACS), 2013-2017.

TABLE 1.2 Percentage of High School Dropouts (Status Dropouts) Among Persons 16-24 Years Old by Gender and Race, 2014-2019

YEAR	TOTALS				MALE			FEMALE		
	ALL RACES	WHITE	BLACK	HISPANIC	WHITE	BLACK	HISPANIC	WHITE	BLACK	HISPANIC
2014	6.5	5.2	7.4	10.6	5.7	7.1	11.8	4.8	7.7	9.3
2015	5.9	4.6	6.5	9.2	5.0	6.4	9.9	4.1	6.5	8.4
2016	6.1	5.2	6.2	8.6	5.8	8.2	10.1	4.6	4.3	7.0
2017	5.8	4.6	5.7	9.5	5.0	7.0	11.5	4.3	4.4	7.4
2018	5.7	4.5	5.8	9.0	5.1	6.0	10.4	3.8	5.6	7.5
2019	5.2	4.5	5.6	7.5	5.3	6.6	7.8	3.8	4.6	7.1

NOTE: *Status dropouts* are 16- to 24-year-olds who are not enrolled in school and who have completed a high school program, regardless of when they left school. People who have received equivalency credentials, such as the GED, are counted as high school completers.

SOURCE: U.S. Department of Commerce, Census Bureau, American Community Survey (ACS), 2013-2017.

(a 1 to 275 counselor-to-student ratio). Erin's school was considered a "blue ribbon school" last year because 50% of its senior class had taken at least two AP courses by graduation. Erin's uncertainty about the future is similar to Crystal's; however, Erin's aspirations are nurtured through internships and work experiences created by her teachers and counselors. Erin's chances for realizing her dreams are not as slim as Crystal's. At Erin's school, students receive in-school tutoring and test-taking support, and many of the parents provide college application support for their students, starting in tenth grade. Ninety-seven percent of Erin's ninth-grade class met reading standards and 96% met math standards. Eleventh-grade students in Erin's high school had an average ACT score of 24.3; 87% of the students met state standards in reading, 89% met standards in mathematics, 84% met standards in in writing, and 89% met standards in in science. The high school graduation rate was 98% last year. And 40% of last year's graduating class went to the local four-year public university. Although undecided about her career, Erin (also with a 3.0 grade point average [GPA]) will be well on her way to meeting her life's goals.

As Crystal enters tenth grade and prepares for her future, she will likely experience a trail of activities designed to help her *survive* high school, whereas Erin will experience activities designed for her to *thrive*. Crystal's high school journey is already characterized by roadblocks and mishaps while Erin's journey is full of joy and validating moments in which she is surrounded by people who believe in her abilities. That is not to say that Crystal will not succeed, but she will need educators who believe in her, and she will need to have fortitude, resolve, and a network of support, faith, and good fortune. She will certainly need more opportunities in school than she has now. Without additional intervention from the educational system, educators, and community, Crystal is far more likely to have a series of jobs but not a career. And, with the COVID-19 pandemic, the dramatic shifts in schooling have exacerbated prospects for opportunities for high school students like Crystal. She will likely have experienced personal loss, disrupted support networks, and inadequate academic support due to COVID-19.

The disparities between Crystal's and Erin's stories are all too familiar and can be echoed across the United States. Crystal's and Erin's disparate experiences represent what we think of when we think of *opportunity gaps*. The lack of opportunity creates gaps or extreme disparities among students of different racial groups, students who live in low-income, impoverished communities, and students who live in affluent, middle- to high-income communities. Education injustice is not new, and many educators have attempted to address it by tweaking school and classroom practices here and there. Nevertheless, the disparities persist because we fail to intentionally make bold changes to policies and practices that perpetuate the unevenness of how we educate children and, more importantly, to our uneven belief system about which groups of students matter!

School Counseling and Education Disparities

Most school counselors would say that they are doing all they can do to help students like Crystal. And there is no shortage of well-meaning school counselors. School counselors, by and large, report that they are concerned about education disparities and believe that they are doing everything they can to close gaps in opportunities. One missing link, however, is that many school counselors are not trained in nor have the knowledge of the root causes of racial injustices in education. In most cases, school counselors will know how to invite Crystal's parents/guardians to participate in school events, how to work with Crystal in a small group to develop resumés, and how to counsel Crystal about peer relationships. However, school counselors are rarely prepared to challenge Crystal's teachers regarding their low expectations of Black and Latinx students or to advocate for policy changes that will ensure that all students have access to academic support for college-track courses. These are the types of counselor activities that are needed to ensure Crystal's success and her ability to persevere and overcome obstacles to achieving her dreams. As a professional school counselor, counselor educator, and university administrator with extensive background in systems change, I believe that we will not move the "equity needle" until school counselors change the framework from which they work. This book is a plea to the school counseling profession to rise up and restructure school counseling programs to directly and intentionally disrupt systems and policies that have failed students like Crystal.

Identity Labels

Throughout history, dehumanizing names and refusal to manipulate language to refer to adults of color (e.g., Mr., Mrs., Dr., Professor) have perpetuated ideas about which groups are inferior and which are superior. For these reasons, the decision about the capitalization of Black and Brown in this book was essential to address. "*Black*" and "*Brown*" will be capitalized in the text and these terms will be used to describe the unified and shared oppression and political interests of people of African descent, Latinx and Hispanic origins, Asian origins, and Indigenous populations. In some places, *people of color* or *students of color* will be utilized to describe Black and Brown people. In June 2020, AP News changed its usage rules to capitalize the word *Black* when used in the context of race and culture but will continue its practice of not capitalizing "*white*." *The New York Times* followed suit and has now changed its policy to capitalize *Black*. In this book, the AP News standards will be utilized.

Where We Have Been, Where We Are, and Where We Are Headed

Systemic racism has a long history in U.S. public education, stemming from the country's long-standing history of racist practices, from the enslavement of Africans during the pre–Civil War period to overpolicing in Black and Brown communities in the 21st century. In the 1930s, the National Association for the Advancement of Colored People (NAACP) focused on dismantling racially segregated public schools, and *Brown v. Board of Education* (1954) became one of the most consequential legal judgments centering on school segregation. However, it would take many years and intense resistance before all public schools were desegregated.

In addition to desegregation resistance, many states enacted overt methods and policies that further segregated students. Black children in redlined neighborhoods were barred from accessing schools in white neighborhoods. And even though redlining was banned in 1968 by the Fair Housing Act, redlined neighborhood schools still experience segregation via less taxpayer funding for education as a result of lower property values. Today, two out of three Black, Latinx, and Native American students attend schools that are classified as "high minority," and those schools are funded well below their suburban counterparts. While *Brown v. Board of Education* was a landmark decision for education in the U.S., it was ultimately unsuccessful in fully integrating schools and creating equal education for all.

For many years, school counselors have, to some extent, been a part of the perpetuation of educational inequalities in schools by supporting damaging student discipline systems, harboring low expectations, denying the culture and history of oppressed populations, and most importantly, by denying students the opportunity to enter or remain in academic tracks that lead to successful postsecondary opportunities. Although the American School Counselor Association (ASCA) has professed a commitment to admonishing racism and bias in the profession, there is still an urgent need for school counselors to act on it.

ASCA's National Model recommends that school counselors organize their programming along four school counselor behaviors: define, manage, deliver, and assess (see the diagram in Figure 1.1 below). In its fourth edition, the current ASCA National Model emphasizes accountability, school counselor competence, mindsets and behaviors for student success, and ethical standards. Also included in the National Model are guidelines for the delivery of counseling services (e.g., direct student services, indirect student services) and an emphasis on program evaluation and assessment. Neither the National Model nor the recognition attached to the model (e.g., Recognized ASCA Model Programs [RAMP]) specifically require that school counselors dismantle and disrupt systems of oppression, such as structural racism, that ultimately cause long-standing gaps in student outcomes. Without a mandate, school counselors will continue to tweak their programs but avoid bold overhauls of their existing programs.

In recent years, ASCA has attempted to respond to racial injustice through the offering of additional resources for school counselors and a Standards in Practice statement. However, dismantling racist counselor practices is not explicit. While the mention of racism in ASCA materials is important, the absence of an intentional focus on correcting long-standing racist policies and practices is disheartening.

FIGURE 1.1 ASCA National Model Diagram

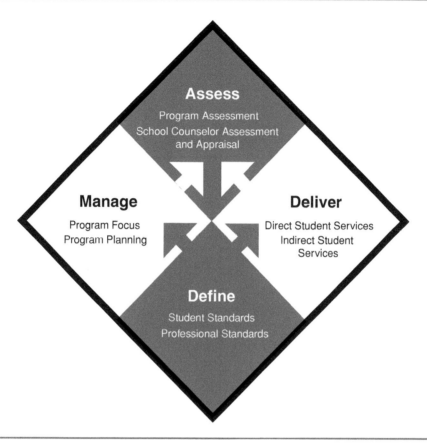

SOURCE: Reprinted with permission from the ASCA.

Students like Crystal who will not be adequately served by school counselors because of systemic and structural policies that subject Black girls to harsher discipline, low teacher expectations, and lack of educational opportunities will still be underserved. This is where this book will help. What else do school counselors need to do *beyond* the ASCA National Model to help all students achieve and thrive?

In this book, the emphasis on an antiracist approach to school counseling is offered as a complementary construct to social justice–focused school counseling. Amid the disproportionate impact of COVID-19 on communities of color and continued racial injustice in schools, taking stock of school counselors' roles in ensuring the development of antiracist schools is warranted. According to a recent survey conducted by EdWeek Research Center (2020), 84% of teachers want to teach from an antiracist perspective but only 14% feel they are well-equipped to do so. In a similar fashion, school counselors, by and large, want to serve and nurture all students from an antiracist perspective, yet they have few resources for improving their practice. This book offers an antiracist, socially just framework from which school counselors must work to fully see the humanity and potential of every student.

THE POWER OF SCHOOL COUNSELORS

School counselors must assume the power that they have in schools, power that enables them to either dampen the dreams of students or help them to realize their dreams. As evidence, I have heard the following statements from adults:

- "My counselor said that I would never get into college . . . that's why I never applied. I wish I hadn't listened to her."

- "My counselor really believed in my ability. If it hadn't been for him telling me that I was capable, I probably would have ended up like my friends—hanging out and getting into trouble."

These statements are evidence that school counselors have an enormous amount of power that, if channeled in the right direction, would help ensure that all students succeed. Research (e.g., Lapan et al., 2012) has indicated that students who have greater access to school counselors and comprehensive school counseling programs are more likely to succeed academically and behaviorally in school, particularly for students in high-poverty schools. And there's promising research to illustrate the power of school counselors with Black and Brown students. For instance, Leon et al. (2011) found that school counseling interventions designed to be culturally and linguistically appropriate can make a significant difference in increasing academic outcomes of Latinx students.

Of course, counselors are not the only people in a school who will make important decisions about students. However, school counselors can act as an advocate for change, a social justice and antiracist strategist, and an equity leader! Again, school counselors are in a strategic position to create change through their relationships with many stakeholders. This book will propose six key functions that will align with this strategic positioning.

OPPORTUNITY GAPS VERSUS ACHIEVEMENT GAPS

As mentioned previously, education disparities based on race and income continue to plague the U.S. On a variety of measures, such as high school completion, college participation, Advanced Placement course enrollment, and standardized achievement tests, Black and Brown students and low-income students have significantly lower rates of academic attainment. This gap has become more widely known as the "achievement gap" and denotes when groups of students with relatively equal ability don't achieve in school at the same levels.

The term *achievement gap*, however, doesn't accurately reflect the basis or reason for the gap. Actually, the term *achievement gap* is laden with deficit perspectives. For instance, some educators see the achievement gap as a result of something that Black and Brown students and parents didn't do. Statements such as "Native American students don't value school and education" and "If only Black parents cared more about their children's homework, they would do better in school" are common when discussing achievement gaps. However, there are larger structural issues, based on racist ideas, that deny students and their parents access to opportunities that result in varying attainment and achievement levels. For school counselors, it's important to focus on correcting accessibility to opportunities—gifted education, college-prep coursework, extracurricular activities, counseling services, and information about jobs and scholarships. If school counselors focus on fixing access to opportunities, they are not furthering racist ideas but are providing the resources and opportunities for student success.

Why focus on opportunity gaps at all? One reason for widespread concern over opportunity gaps across student groups is that it involves substantial social and economic costs. Low educational achievement is associated with a greater number of health disparities, higher unemployment rates, lower earnings, higher crime rates, and a greater dependency on social services. The social costs of these outcomes can be staggering. Another reason for the widespread concern over opportunity gaps is that the racial diversity of the U.S. population is steadily growing; new statistics project that the U.S will become "minority white" in 2045. During that year, whites will comprise 49.7% of the population, in contrast to 24.6% for Hispanics, 13.1% for Blacks, 7.9% for Asians, 3.8% for multiracial populations, and .9% who identify as "other." (Frey, 2018).

Opportunity gaps in schools are complex and parallel other societal gaps, such as income or wealth gaps, housing gaps, and criminal justice gaps. Although it is impossible to discuss the education opportunity gap without discussing these other societal disparities, opportunity gaps seem to be most prevalent in those schools that are not attending to issues of racism and racial equity.

Ever since racial categories were developed to facilitate slavery and colonial expansion in the 15th century, racism has been about building structures of unequal resource and power on notions of human difference (i.e., skin color). Social justice in education refers to a commitment to challenging social, cultural, and economic inequalities imposed on individuals arising from racism and dynamics that create differential distribution of power, resources, and privilege. Racism in schools involves the unequal measurements of intelligence, potential, and human worth based on static racial lines and accepting the distribution of unequal opportunities and the production of racially based disparities as normal. Antiracism, on the other hand, requires that educators make strategic, intentional everyday decisions to counter these ingrained tendencies. Acquiring an awareness and acknowledgment of antiracism and social justice is a logical goal in decreasing opportunity gaps. That is the focus of this book.

A Closer Look at the Gaps

Although schools may have little influence over community factors, what goes on in schools could lessen their negative effect. For decades, policymakers, researchers, and school reformers have sought ways in which schools could address opportunity gaps. Strategies have focused on school funding, teacher quality, student motivation, school organization and management, school climate, and school accountability. More recently, however, some conservative political groups have challenged school districts to omit any activities related to racism, equity, diversity, or inclusion in schools. Essentially, these groups want to ignore the gaps. The following pages offer a look at where education inequities and opportunity gaps exist.

AVAILABILITY OF RESOURCES

The U.S. educational system is one of the most unequal in the world, and students routinely receive dramatically different learning opportunities based on their race, social status, or location. In contrast to European and Asian countries that fund schools centrally and equally, the wealthiest 10% of U.S. school districts spend nearly ten times more than the poorest 10% of school districts.

Resource disparities limit schools. Predominately white schools tend to be much better funded and have all-around better resources than predominately Black, Latinx/Hispanic, or Native American schools. The same relationship holds true for schools in low-poverty versus high-poverty areas. According to The Century Foundation (2020), the U.S. is underfunding public schools by nearly $150 billion annually, robbing millions of children—predominantly Black, Brown, and low-income children—of the opportunity to succeed.

There is persuasive evidence that this factor contributes to opportunity gaps. For example, in the 1990s, variation in education spending largely overlapped with variation in student outcomes. In general, where states invest more in public schools, students tend to achieve higher scores and perform better (Education Trust, 2001).

HARSH DISCIPLINE AND OVER-SURVEILLANCE OF STUDENTS

Black, Latinx, and other non-white students overwhelmingly experience what is called the "school-to-prison pipeline," a trend in which overly punitive school discipline policies push students out of school, criminalize them, and then push them into the criminal justice system. For instance, Black students make up 15% of grade school students, yet account for 31% of law enforcement referrals (U.S. Department of Education, 2018). Recent data revealed that more than 1.5 million students across the nation attend a school with a school resource officer (SRO) or police officer but without a school counselor! In these schools, students who have disagreements or typical problems with friends are more likely to be reported to law enforcement rather than a helping professional. Sadly, these referrals have disproportionately impacted Black and Brown students.

Research (e.g., Nance, 2017) has also shown that public schools serving primarily Black and other non-white students rely on more restrictive security, including metal detectors, locked gates, security cameras, random sweeps, and school police. The extent to which the increased security is related to race and ethnicity, rather than grounded in legitimate safety concerns, is further proven in research studies. Interestingly, the overwhelming majority—some 62%—of the occurrences of major school violence happens in schools that serve primarily white students.

STANDARDIZED TESTS

Despite the move to decreased standardized high-stakes testing, standardized tests are still utilized by many districts and higher education institutions. The gaps between Black, Latinx, and Native American students' scores when compared to their white and Asian peers remain wide. For instance, on the 2019 fourth-grade reading test of the National Assessment of Educational Progress (NAEP), the average score of white students was 230, Latinx/Hispanic students' average score was 209, African American students' average score was 204, Asian students' average score was 237, American Indian students' average score was 204, and multiracial students' average score was 204. Among racial/ethnic groups, white and Black fourth-grade students scored lower in reading in 2019 compared to 2017; however, the 2019 average scores for white and Black fourth-graders were not significantly different from their scores a decade ago. Compared to 1998 and to 1992, average scores were higher in 2019 for all reportable racial/ethnic groups (white, Black, Hispanic, and Asian/Pacific Islander students). In essence, the difference in standardized test scores and participation rates has remained, although students' scores have increased overall (see Figure 1.2).

College admission standardized tests have a long history of perpetuating racial inequities. Geiser and Atkinson (2013) indicated that irrespective of the quality or type of school attended, high school GPA proved the best predictor not only of freshman grades in college but also of long-term college outcomes such as cumulative GPA and four-year graduation rate. Nevertheless, the SAT and ACT are still highly utilized for college admissions, even though test-optional university admissions has become more popular and effective.

Here are examples of the racialized college admission test gap: In 2020, the average SAT score was 523 on the math section, slightly below the College Board's college readiness benchmark score of 530. The average scores for Black (454) and Latinx/Hispanic students (478) are significantly lower than those of white (547) and Asian

FIGURE 1.2   SAT Participation and Performance by Race Class of 2020

RACE ETHNICITY	NUMBER	PERCENT	TOTAL MEAN SAT SCORE
American Indian/Alaska Native	14,050	1%	902
Asian	223,451	10%	1217
Black/African American	261,326	12%	927
Hispanic/Latino	569,370	26%	969
Native Hawaiian/Other Pacific Islander	5,107	0%	948
White	909,987	41%	1104
Two or More Races	89,656	4%	1091
No Response	125,513	6%	996

SOURCE: The College Board (2020). Copyright © 2020. Reproduced with permission.

students (632). The proportion of students reaching college readiness benchmarks also differ by race. Over half (59%) of white and Asian test takers met the college readiness math benchmark compared to less than a quarter of Black students and under a third of Latinx/Hispanic students. There are similar patterns for other sections of the SAT as well as for the ACT. For too long, these test scores have been taken as a proxy for individual intellectual merit when they have always correlated more highly with demographics than with academic performance. Over the last decade, race has become a higher predictor of SAT/ACT test scores than parent education or family income. With regard to income, a 2015 analysis found that students with a family income of less than $20,000 scored lowest on the test, and those with a family income above $200,000 scored highest—and we're not talking about a couple of points. The average reading score for those students whose family income is below $20,000 is 433, but the average for those with an income of above $200,000 is 570.

The College Board, in response to the gap in SAT scores, created an "adversity score" to level the playing field. In doing so, the College Board treated adversity as a handicap to be accommodated while missing an opportunity to address a myriad of factors that make SAT scores either lower or higher than they should be for different racial and ethnic groups and socioeconomic statuses. While the adversity score effort was good, it missed the mark by not acknowledging the adversity of racism and ignoring the impact of social privilege on test score gaps. As a result of backlash, the College Board dropped the adversity score.

An example of social privilege is the recent college admissions scandal in which parents paid for test proctors, hired test stand-ins, and paid for the right psychologists to sign off for their students to receive more time on the test. For wealthy parents with significant social capital, boosting their students' SAT and ACT scores is not difficult.

HIGHER EDUCATION

Higher education in the U.S. has a long history of perpetuating racism and the systematic reproduction of white racial privilege. For hundreds of years, college/university enrollment trends have illustrated unevenness based on race. For instance, in the paper, *Separate & Unequal: How Higher Education Reinforces the Intergenerational Reproduction of White Racial Privilege* (Carnevale & Strohl, 2013), the researchers found that since 1995, 82% of new white enrollments have gone to the 468 most selective colleges, while most enrollments for Latinx/Hispanics (72%) and Blacks (68%) have gone to two-year and four-year open-access schools.

For many years, the conversation about equity in higher education has focused on the serious gaps in access for Black and Brown students. Awareness has also been growing that getting into college is not enough; Black and Brown students are also much less likely to graduate (college persistence). There are serious inequities even among students who do graduate from college. Using federal data on the type of credentials students earn and the majors they study, research has found that compared with white students, Black and Latinx graduates are far more likely to have attended for-profit colleges and less likely to have attended four-year public or nonprofit institutions. Black and Latinx/Hispanic graduates are significantly underrepresented in STEM (science, technology, engineering, and mathematics) fields such as engineering, mathematics and statistics, and the physical sciences.

According to a study last year by the Institute for College Access and Success (2019), 54% of Black, Latino, American Indian/Alaska Native, and Pacific Islander students who attended public colleges in 2016–2017 were enrolled at two-year institutions. In comparison, 23% of those attending institutions that offer master's degrees that year were people of color.

COURSE-TAKING PATTERNS

Disparities exist in high school students' course-taking patterns. Data from the U.S. Department of Education's National Center for Education Statistics (NCES)'s High School Longitudinal Study (2016) indicate that Asian students earned more high school credits in math than students of every other racial/ethnic group. Additionally, white students earned more credits (3.7 credits) than Latinx/Hispanic students (3.5 credits) and students of two or more races (3.5 credits). Asian students earned more credits in science (3.9 credits) than white students (3.4 credits), and both Asian and white students earned more credits in science than students in any other racial/ethnic group. There were no measurable differences in the number of credits earned in computer and information sciences by racial/ethnic group. White students earned more credits in engineering and technology (0.2 credits) than students in any other racial/ethnic group.

A higher percentage of white students earned their highest math credit in precalculus (22%) than Latinx/Hispanic students (17%), students of two or more races (16%), and Black students (16%). The percentage was also higher for Asian students (22%) than students of two or more races and Black students. A higher percentage of Asian students (45%) earned their highest math course credit in calculus than students of all other racial/ethnic groups. The percentage earning their highest math course credit in calculus was also higher for white students (18%) than students of two or more races (11%), Latinx/Hispanic students (10%), and Black students (6%).

Nationwide, admissions officers at selective colleges look for students who have challenged themselves academically. But not all students get the chance to build a stellar transcript. Black, Latinx/Hispanic, and Native American students are less likely to attend high schools that offer advanced courses, such as physics and calculus, and they're less likely to participate in those courses when they are offered. Black and Brown students are less likely to go to high schools that offer a college-prep curriculum. About one-quarter of high schools that serve the highest percentage of Black and Latinx/Hispanic students don't even offer a second year of algebra, even though two years of algebra are usually required for college-level courses in math and science. Fewer AP courses are available to non-Asian students of color in aggregate, and even when courses are available, non-Asian students of color are less likely to take them (Quinton, 2014). Furthermore, research suggests that many students of color would have found success in AP coursework based on subsequent standardized test data (Barnard-Brak et al., 2011). Thus, equitable access to AP course offerings is an important issue and is impacted by the informal pathways to AP related to identification criteria, teacher expectations, and counseling behavior (Theokas & Saaris, 2013).

The news is not all bad. Today, there are more Black and Latinx/Hispanic students taking academically rigorous courses than in the past. But researchers have found that schools in racially and linguistically diverse or high-poverty areas often offer fewer college-preparatory courses (particularly advanced-level math) to begin with. This is a problem because research has shown that student enrollment in higher-level math courses and challenging courses overall—in topics such as calculus, algebra, trigonometry, chemistry, and advanced English—in high school has strong, positive effects on a host of postsecondary educational outcomes and is associated with higher wages in adulthood, both directly and indirectly through its impact on educational attainment (Long et al., 2012; Rose & Betts, 2004).

TEACHER DIVERSITY, EXPERIENCE, AND EXPECTATIONS

A growing body of literature (e.g., Holt & Gershenson, 2015) suggests that student outcomes are impacted by the demographic match between teachers and students. Studies have also indicated that white teachers expect significantly less academic success from Black students than do Black teachers. Findings from an American University and Johns Hopkins University study (i.e., Gershenson et al., 2018) found that when a Black teacher and a white teacher evaluate the same Black student, the white teacher is about 30% less likely to predict that the student will complete a four-year college degree. White teachers are also almost 40% less likely to expect their Black students to graduate high school. By setting low expectations, teachers run the risk of perpetuating education disparities because they do not encourage Black and Brown students to follow a rigorous curriculum. On a related note, the teacher workforce is overwhelmingly white and female. The number of Black and Brown teachers is declining, whereas student diversity is increasing. See Figure 1.3 below:

Teaching experience is also an important factor when examining opportunity gaps. Low-income students and Black, Latinx/Hispanic, and Native American students are more likely to be taught by less-experienced teachers than are white students. Researchers have cited this factor as one of the most critical variables for explaining opportunity gaps. There is a correlation between higher teacher certification scores and higher student achievement scores. Teachers in districts where there are high percentages of Black or Latinx students tend to have lower scores on their certification tests. For instance, in an examination of 30 studies over 15 years, Kini and Podolsky (2016) found the following:

1. Teaching experience is positively associated with student achievement gains throughout a teacher's career. Gains in teacher effectiveness associated with experience are most steep in teachers' initial years but continue to be significant as teachers reach the second (and often third) decades of their careers.

2. As teachers gain experience, their students not only learn more, as measured by standardized tests, but they are also more likely to do better on other measures of success, such as school attendance.

3. Teachers' effectiveness increases at a greater rate when they teach in a supportive and collegial working environment and when they accumulate experience in the same grade level, subject, or district.

4. More-experienced teachers support greater student learning for their colleagues and the school as a whole as well as for their own students.

CULTURAL RESPONSIVENESS AND COMPETENCE

Educators' lack of cultural responsiveness and competence can negatively impact the education of students. Educators who lack cultural knowledge, awareness, and skills to work with diverse students are less equipped to nurture their academic and social/emotional development. Recent research findings (Larson et al., 2018;

FIGURE 1.3 Percentage Distribution of Teachers in Public Elementary and Secondary Schools by Race/Ethnicity: School years 1999-200 and 2017-2018

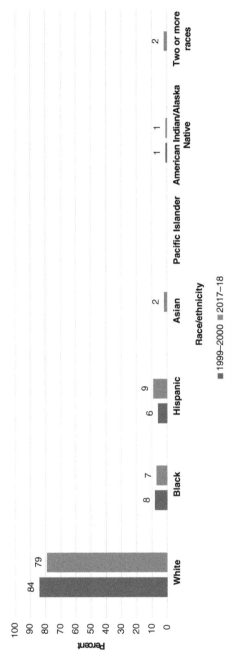

1999–2000: data not available for Asian, Pacific Islander, and Two or more races
2017–18: Pacific Islander percentage rounded to zero

■ 1999–2000 ■ 2017–18

SOURCE: U.S. Department of Education (2000). NCES, Schools and Staffing Survey (SASS), Public School Teacher Data File, Charter School Teacher Data File, Public School Data File, and Charter School Data File, 1999-2000; National Teacher and Principal Survey (NTPS). Public School Teacher Data File, 2017-2018. See also Table 209.22.

NOTE: Data are based on a head count of full-time and part-time teachers rather than on the number of full-time-equivalent teachers. Separate data on Asians, Pacific Islanders, and persons of Two or more races were not available in 1999-2000. In 1999-2000, data for teachers who were Asian included those who were Pacific Islander, and teachers of Two or more races were required to select a single category from among the offered race/ethnicity categories (White, Black, Hispanic, Asian, and American Indian/Alaska Native). Although rounded numbers are displayed, the figures are based on unrounded data. Detail may not sum to totals due to rounding.

Mackay & Strickland, 2018) suggests that there is a positive relationship between teacher cultural responsiveness and student outcomes (e.g., behavior, belongingness). Howard and Terry (2011) found in their research that overall student outcomes, graduation rates, and college attendance rates increased when culturally responsive pedagogical practices were used with Black students in Oakland, CA.

In addition to the cultural responsiveness of teachers, there is also the impact of counselor cultural responsiveness and competence. With rising mental health concerns among students of racially diverse backgrounds, the lack of culturally responsive counselors is profoundly unjust. For instance, Native American children have traditionally reported the highest depression rates of any racial group, and the suicide death rate for those between the ages of 15 and 19 is more than double that of their white peers. Yet, Native American children lack access to mental health services from highly trained, culturally responsive counselors. The National Tribal Behavioral Health Agenda, a blueprint for tribal behavioral health needs and proposed policy solutions, identified a lack of culturally competent care as a key barrier to effective treatment for mental health problems among Native teens. Indian Health Service hospitals, which are more likely to provide culturally competent care, are not easily accessible; most are built on tribal lands, but only 22% of Native Americans live on reservations.

SPECIAL EDUCATION AND GIFTED EDUCATION

Racial disparities in special education, including gifted education, are widespread. For decades, research has documented that Black students are disproportionately identified as having disabilities, particularly behavioral and emotional disturbances. In 2016, 12% of Black children in the U.S. received disability services, whereas 8.5% of white children received those services. The disability rate for Latinx/Hispanic students was 9.4% nationally. Conversely, a couple of recent studies have found that Black, Latinx/Hispanic, and Native American students are actually less likely than similar white students to be identified as having disabilities and to obtain special education services at schools. Morgan et al. (2015) purports that his research illustrates stronger evidence that there may be bias, and white students are more likely to be identified with a disability and receive services. Hence, there are more Black and Brown students who are not receiving services.

The relationship between special education and harsher discipline is another pervasive problem in today's schools. Nationally, among secondary students with disabilities, 24% of Black students, 15% of Native American students, and 11% of white students were suspended at least once in 2017–2018. These disparities are even greater in many large districts, where the risk for suspension for Black secondary students with disabilities was well above 40% and 33% for Native American students. The disparities widen when discussing different categories of disabilities. For example, students with "emotional disturbance," a category in which Black students are overrepresented, have a 37% risk for being removed for discipline and the highest risk for being educated in a correctional facility.

In addition, Latinx and Asian American students are underidentified in cognitive disability categories compared to white students, raising questions about whether the special education needs of these children are being met (Losen et al., 2014). Once identified, most students of color are significantly more likely to be removed from the general education program and educated in a more restrictive environment.

Losen and Orfield (2002, pp. xv–xxxviii) report even more disturbing statistics:

- Among high school youth with disabilities, about 75% of African American students, as compared with 47% of white students, are not employed two years out of school. Three to five years out of school, the arrest rate for African Americans with disabilities is 40%, as compared with 27% for whites.

- The identification of African American students for mental retardation is pronounced in the South. Southern states constituted nearly three quarters of the states with unusually high incidence levels, where between 2.75% and 5.41% of the African Americans enrolled were labeled as mentally retarded. The prevalence of mental retardation for whites nationally was approximately 0.75% in 2001, and in no state did the incidence of mental retardation among whites rise above 2.32%.

- Poverty does not explain the gross racial disparities in mental retardation and emotional disturbance, nor does it explain disparities in the category of specific learning disability or any medically diagnosed disabilities.

Like special education, gifted education in the U.S. has embedded racial disparities. Black students make up nearly 17% of the total student population nationwide. Yet less than 10% of students identified as gifted are Black. A shocking 53% of remedial students are Black, however. This disparity across tracks is what educators call *racialized tracking*, in which Black and Brown students get sorted out of educational opportunities and are relegated to a pathway to lower socioeconomic possibilities. Sixty percent of students in gifted education are white, according to the most recent federal data, compared to 50% of public school students overall. Black students, in contrast, made up 9% of students in gifted education, although they make up 15% of the overall student population.

Many factors contribute to this gifted education disparity. Gifted education has racism in its roots. Lewis Terman, the psychologist, who in the 1910s, popularized the concept of IQ that became the foundation of gifted testing, was a eugenicist. And admissions for gifted programs tend to favor children with wealthy, educated parents, who are more likely to be white. Black students are regularly excluded from schools' conceptions of what it means to be gifted, talented, or intellectually advanced.

What is the process for identifying students for special education and gifted education at your school? Are there a disproportionate number of students of color in special education programs and underrepresentation of Black and Brown students in gifted education? If so, has your staff discussed what to do about it? What are the possible racist and biased beliefs that are driving special education and gifted education identification processes?

THE GAPS ACROSS THE EDUCATIONAL CONTINUUM

Although opportunity gaps are typically seen as a problem affecting school-age children, gaps in opportunity happen early on. Consider, first, that not all mothers in this country have the same odds of making it through their pregnancy alive. In some places in the U.S., Black women are as much as 12 times as likely to die from childbirth as white women are (Creanga et al., 2015). Also, consider that nationally, the infant mortality rate for Black babies is more than twice as high as it is for white babies. And we know that children who grow up in poverty face disadvantages that hamper healthy development. A gap in early vocabulary development between children in poverty and their higher-income peers is evident as early as 18 months of age. Research shows that these differences have lasting effects on a child's academic success later in life.

Nationwide, early childhood education is more segregated than kindergarten and first grade, even while enrolling a similar number of students. Early childhood programs are twice as likely to be nearly 100% Black or Latinx/Hispanic, and they are less likely to be somewhat integrated (with a 10% to 20% Black or Hispanic enrollment share; Urban Institute, 2019). Studies also consistently show that low-income and Black, Latinx/Hispanic, and Native American children have already fallen behind well before they enter kindergarten. These children, as young as three years old, already perform far below average on tests of school readiness.

Early childhood education, particularly when it is high quality, is associated with higher levels of school readiness and subsequent academic achievement. Historically, children from low-income families have been less likely than their more-affluent peers to be enrolled in such high-quality programs, leaving federal government and state and local governments to invest in early childhood education options, particularly for low-income families (Magnuson & Waldfogel, 2005). Preschool is expensive, typically costing far more than other informal care arrangements. A report by Child Care Aware of America (2014) found that the average annual cost for center-based care for an infant was higher than a year's tuition and fees at a four-year public college in 31 states. Costs for center-based care vary across states and with child age. In 2013, for example, the average cost of full-time center-based care for a four-year-old ranged from $4,515 in Tennessee to just over $12,320 in Massachusetts. Given the high costs, it is not surprising that the use of center-based care increases with family income.

Also, preschool attendance differs by race. For instance, Hispanic and American Indian 3- to 4-year-old children have lower enrollment rates (43% and 45%, respectively), while Asian, white, and Black children are enrolled at higher rates (56%, 50%, and 53%, respectively). These differences in early childhood educational experiences may contribute to longer-term educational and health inequities (U.S. Department of Commerce, 2019). Black children are less likely to attend amply equipped preschools with small classroom sizes and trained teachers. State budget cuts in the wake of the coronavirus could make it that much harder for children of color to enroll in quality early education programs.

■ ■ ■ Thinking About Barriers to Learning

Think about the challenges that many low-income families experienced during the COVID-19 pandemic and subsequent lockdown (e.g., loss of family members to COVID-19, lack of healthcare, unemployment, lack of childcare, lack of internet connectivity). How do these challenges impact the education of students immediately and over time? What are some of the factors and policies that led to a disproportionate number of Black and Brown families being impacted by COVID-19? What is the role of school counselors during crisis situations when low-income and Black and Brown families are disproportionately impacted?

COMMUNITY AND HOME FACTORS

Although school counselors have less control over what takes place in the community than in the school, there are certain factors we need to be aware of in order to do our work most effectively. If low-income students are not thriving in school, it may be due to a variety of community-based factors, such as food scarcity, lack of housing, overpolicing, and unemployment. These conditions influence students' ability to learn.

Another community factor is the legacy of racism and racist ideas that plague many communities and affect the belief that one can or cannot succeed. The belief that some children cannot learn at high levels persists, and when children believe that society does not expect them to succeed, or when they themselves believe they cannot succeed, they do poorly in school.

In general, Black, Latinx/Hispanic, Native American, and low-income children are less likely than affluent white children to have parents with high levels of educational attainment. Combined with lower family income and parents' hectic work schedules, the extent to which parents can foster positive opportunities for learning at home is limited. Opportunities such as having access to books and computers may be more limited for racially diverse and low-income children. Finally, a family speaking a language other than English at home can also affect a child's learning opportunities.

STUDENT FACTORS

There has been some research to indicate that students' emotional and social development contributes to their academic outcomes. For instance, research has suggested that Black students can become anxious about displaying negative racial stereotypes in their academic work. The result, researchers say, is a kind of vicious cycle in which Black students can be so worried about seeming stereotypically ungifted academically that their anxiety actually makes them perform worse than they could normally. This phenomenon has been called *stereotype threat* (Steele, 1997).

Peer pressure and identity issues have also been cited as contributing to the academic outcomes of minoritized youth. Peer pressure related to academic success has been correlated with ridicule or demeaning behaviors. However, peer pressure has been correlated with motivating students to get better grades, too. There is some dispute as to the effects of peer pressure on Black students. Some researchers (e.g., Ogbu, 1994), for example, have pointed to a phenomenon in high-minority schools whereby Black students who perform poorly actually criticize their academically successful peers for "acting white." Researchers have charged that Black students tend to idolize a youth culture that scorns academic achievement. However, other researchers (Connell et al., 1994) have argued that such a culture exerts no special power on Black students in particular; instead, they claim that Black students are no more likely to dislike or scorn school than are white students. Peer relationships and academic outcomes is an area of research that needs to be examined more deeply, given the emergence of the Black Lives Matter movement and other social movements that uplift the voices of minoritized youth.

The mental health of Black, Latinx/Hispanic, Native American, and other students of color is a critical factor that should not be underestimated in impacting student outcomes. Amid concentrated job losses and financial insecurity, disproportionate rates of contracting and becoming seriously ill from COVID-19, and centuries of racial injustice and anti-Black racism, the disparate mental health needs of many Black, Latinx/Hispanic, Indigenous, and nonblack people of color are exacerbated.

Anxiety, depression, and suicide are all on the rise, and victims of suicide are getting tragically younger. There has been nationwide divestment from mental health programs and many remaining programs are more punitive than restorative. Laws such as the Florida Mental Health Act, also known as the Baker Act, can even subject students to involuntary institutionalization simply for disruptive behavior in class. The Baker Act allows law enforcement officers, school counselors, and medical personnel to petition for someone who is perceived as being a danger to themselves or others to be institutionalized for 72 hours. In Florida, the Baker Act has been invoked more than three times every school day, but little policy or practice change has been done to prevent the growing use of the Baker Act unevenly across race, gender, and income (Southern Poverty Law Center, 2021).

From education to income to environment, structural racism undergirds many risk factors for mental illnesses. As a result, there are racial disparities in rates of diagnosis, treatment access, and prognosis. According to the Agency for Healthcare Research and Quality (2017), not only are Black and Brown people in America less likely to have access to mental health services, but when they do receive care, it is often of lower quality than the care their white peers receive. In schools, Black and Brown students are less likely than white students to say they could reach out to a counselor if they needed mental health support (Craft et al., 2020).

Many Black and Brown students who are most at risk of COVID-19–related trauma are in schools and districts that already lacked full mental health services prior to the pandemic and risk being hardest hit by cuts due to state budget shortfalls (Education Trust, 2020). This is especially true for tribal populations, which have some of the highest rates of coronavirus cases and some of the lowest education funding. There is no one way to address Black and Brown students' mental health because there is no one mental health need for all Black and Brown students. Across racial groups, there can be vast differences in underlying causes of mental illness, social stigmas, and access to effective treatment. Understanding these differences is critical to ensure that resources are allocated in a way that will improve mental health outcomes for all students.

WHAT DO WE KNOW ABOUT CLOSING OPPORTUNITY GAPS?

The Education Trust took an initial look at student data from high-poverty schools and was able to verify that there were, in fact, schools where low-income students were significantly outperforming schools containing students from middle- to high-income backgrounds (Parrett & Budge, 2012). This analysis by the Education Trust led to numerous efforts geared toward learning about high-performing, high-poverty (HP/HP) and high-minority schools and how other schools with similar characteristics could improve.

According to the research of Parrett and Budge (2012), there are hundreds of public schools across the United States that enroll large numbers of underachieving students who live in poverty and these schools have successfully reversed the long-standing traditions of low achievement and high dropout rates. High-poverty schools do not become high performing by chance. Chenoweth and Theokas (2011) state, "These schools do, however, have something that helps explain their success: They all have excellent school leaders." (p. 57). Although this is not the only trait found by researchers among HP/HP schools, it is by far the most common trait that contributed to the overall success of the school. In fact, one study conducted by Leithwood et al. (2004) concluded that up to one-quarter of all school effects on achievement can be contributed to leadership.

In 2000, the North Central Regional Education Laboratory (NCREL) published a study of HP/HP schools in Wisconsin (Manset et al., 2000). They found that these schools had some common characteristics. Each had more than one of the following:

1. purposeful and proactive leadership,

2. data-based decision making and program monitoring,

3. a sense of community,

4. high expectations for students,

5. staff-initiated professional development,

6. opportunities for staff interaction,

7. curriculum aligned with state standards,

8. use of local and state assessment data,

9. parent and community involvement, and

10. alternative support programs.

In addition, several other studies have identified commonalities among successful schools. One of the federal Comprehensive School Reform models, Success for All (Slavin et al., 1998) identified the following characteristics of schools that were instrumental in closing the gap:

1. leadership,

2. commitment of the entire staff,

3. extensive professional development,

4. early literacy support, and

5. data-driven instructional decision making and student monitoring.

Though this research is helpful, it is unclear how these school reform components translate to school counselor practice. In 2003, the Education Trust and MetLife Foundation established the National Center for Transforming School Counseling (NCTSC) to ensure that school counselors were trained and ready to help all groups of students reach high academic standards. The Center's initiative—the Transforming School Counseling Initiative (TSCI)—has been one of a few school reform initiatives focused on school counselors. Based on the work of the TSCI, a small number of school counselor education programs modified their training protocol to include more of an equity perspective, and aspects of their training curricula (e.g., data-driven practice, accountability, equity) were integrated into the ASCA National Model. See elements of Transformed School Counselors in Figure 1.4.

After the TSCI, the National Office of School Counselor Advocacy (NOSCA) was formed by the College Board to advance the equity work of school counselors, particularly related to college readiness and college going. NOSCA, with partners such as the ASCA and the National Association of Secondary School Principals (NASSP), tapped distinguished researchers and practitioners to gather information from surveys, case studies, in-depth interviews, and data analysis. The staff of NOSCA's most significant contribution was the distribution of the *Eight Components of College Readiness and Counseling*, which focused on developing college readiness of those students historically underrepresented on college campuses. NOSCA ended in 2012–2013.

Although the TSCI and NOSCA provided some movement in the school counselor profession to address issues of equity, social justice, and racism, there is still much to be done. And given the recent shift in the education landscape due to the

FIGURE 1.4 Elements of Transformed School Counselors

Counseling
Coordination of Services
Consultation
Leadership
Advocacy
Collaboration and Teamwork
Managing Resources
Use of Data
Technology

SOURCE: Education Trust (1997).

COVID-19 pandemic and the country's attention to racial justice, it is time for school counselors to be more intentional and bolder in their actions to disrupt racist and oppressive policies and practices in schools. The antiracist and social justice–focused functions offered in this book will hopefully begin to fill a void in the literature and in the work of school counselors.

Counselor in Action

Download data from your state's Department of Education website. Choose a school in an urban, suburban, and rural district. Examine accessible student and community data, including attendance, graduation rates, college-going rates, and so on. Also search for data about each school's community. Community and district data might include district school segregation data, special education data, gifted/talented data, unemployment rates, deaths due to COVID-19, poverty index, number of high-quality preschools, number of health care facilities, homelessness rates, and so on. Discuss the school and community data with your colleagues and uncover opportunity and access gaps as well as policies that perpetuate and maintain these gaps. What would you do to correct the gaps?

Questions to Consider

1. Why do you think school counselors and school counseling professionals have been absent from the table when instituting new initiatives pertaining to school and policy change, particularly during the COVID-19 pandemic?

2. How do you explain the lack of a gap between Asian American students and white students in reading and math? What does the model minority myth mean to you? How does the model minority myth influence inequities and injustices in schools?

3. In your community, what efforts are being made to close opportunity gaps between students? Write down a few efforts that come to mind. Are these efforts successful? Why or why not? Is there community resistance to overcoming opportunity gaps? Why and how does this resistance impact your school community?

CHAPTER 2

School Counseling Within the Context of Social Justice and Antiracism

I can't breathe.

—George Floyd

Questions regarding how to fix schools to be more equitable and "just" have become commonplace in education reform discussions. Systemic racism is evident in all aspects of schooling, from early childhood education options to college readiness and preparation. The racist ideas and beliefs inherent in school counseling programs impact students as well as schools and are often especially punishing for students of color who are also marginalized along other social identities, such as gender, ability, socioeconomic status, and sexual orientation.

Counseling, as a profession, has recently attempted to address the question, "What should professional counselors do to address systemic and structural racism in schools?" The American Counseling Association (ACA) created a toolkit for being an antiracist advocate and put forth recommendations for dealing with racial trauma. The American School Counselor Association (ASCA) put forth two position statements on cultural diversity and equity. And, in 2020, the ASCA created a Standard of Practice document to give more clarity regarding school counselors' role in ending racism in schools. But what does an antiracist school counselor do that is different from the traditional approach to school counseling? And, better yet, what should school counselors *stop doing* in order to create antiracist schools and learning communities?

Exhibit: ASCA Standard of Practice

Eliminating Racism and Bias in Schools: The School Counselor's Role

Racism and bias in the U.S. impede its citizens from achieving success and the nation from reaching its highest potential. Racism and bias manifest themselves overtly through verbal and physical harassment of people of color, tragically culminating in outcomes such as decreased mental well-being, joblessness, homelessness, and senseless and deadly violence against individuals, including Black, Latinx, Asian, and Indigenous people. They manifest themselves subtly through unconscious bias, denial of access to privileges and benefits, and low expectations. The systemic and institutional racism that underlies violence toward people of color and relegates them to generations of poverty permeates every facet of American society, including the educational system. Progress has been made in many school districts, but there is still much work to be done.

All educators have an obligation to end racism and bias in schools. School counselors have a unique opportunity to be an important part of the solution. Through implementation of an inclusive and antiracist school counseling program, school counselors promote equity and access for all students and make a significant impact on creating a school culture free from racism and bias.

School counselors have specific training to recognize signs of racism and bias *that harm students and ultimately impede our nation from reaching its full potential, including the following:*

- *gaps in achievement, opportunity, and attainment*

- *disproportionate rates of discipline and suspension of students of color*

- *self-destructive behavior*

  o *acting out*

  o *withdrawal and lack of engagement in learning*

  o *nonparticipation in school activities*

- *disproportionate numbers/rates of Black, Latinx, and Indigenous students in gifted education and college-preparation courses such as honors, Advanced Placement, and International Baccalaureate courses*

- *lower participation of Black, Latinx, and Indigenous students in higher education*

Exhibit

ASCA Position Statement on Cultural Diversity

School counselors demonstrate cultural responsiveness by collaborating with stakeholders to create a school and community climate that embraces cultural diversity and helps to promote the academic, career, and social/emotional success for all students.

ASCA Position Statement on Equity for All Students

School counselors recognize and distinguish individual and group differences and strive to equally value all students and groups. School counselors are advocates for the equitable treatment of all students in school and in the community.

REDEFINING SCHOOL COUNSELING TO SERVE DIVERSE GROUPS

Over 15 years ago, Lee (2005) emphasized that schools must be willing to redefine traditional counseling models in order to serve diverse groups of students. Bemak and Chung (2005) and Green and Keys (2001) also reinforced the view that school counselors should be guided by (a) the acknowledgment of broad, systematic societal inequities and oppression and (b) the assumption of the inevitable, if unintentional, location of every individual (and the profession) within this system. In turn, this assumption leads the school counselor to take responsible action that contributes to the elimination of systematic oppression in the forms of racism, sexism, heterosexism, classism, and other biases. As such, school counselors who believe in creating socially just school environments must also work within an antiracist framework. Social justice and antiracism are complementary and expand the profession's commitment to multiculturalism and cultural competence. I propose an expanded role of school counseling that includes the dismantling of unequal systems and policies based on a long-standing history of white supremacy and consequential structural and systemic racism.

FOCUSING ON ANTIRACISM AND SOCIAL JUSTICE

After the murder of George Floyd in May of 2020 by a white Minneapolis police officer, the discussion of police brutality, systemic racism, white supremacy, and racial justice became popular discussion topics in mainstream media. Mr. Floyd is not the first Black person whose death in police custody sparked protest. But his death was particularly gruesome and was recorded on video. The police officer, Derek Chauvin, kept his knee on Mr. Floyd's neck for nearly nine minutes—even as Mr. Floyd repeatedly said, "I can't breathe." The world watched as Derek Chauvin murdered a Black man, unarmed and not posing a threat to his surroundings.

Protests following the Floyd murder sparked emotion and an urgent call for policy change in law enforcement and other systems plagued by racial injustices. *Antiracism*, a concept used to describe the process of challenging and dismantling racism, also became the answer to solving the nation's history of racism. The concept of antiracism, however, is not new. It has been utilized by many social scientists, educators, historians, and scholars who have studied racism for years. Essentially, there has been an impassioned struggle against racism as far back as John Brown's white antislavery protests in the 1800s to Dr. Angela Davis's championing of antiracism and anti-industrial complexes (prison systems) in the 1960s to the writing of "How to Be an Antiracist" by Dr. Ibram X. Kendi in 2019. At the Aspen Ideas Festival in 2019, Dr. Kendi profoundly stated, "The only way to undo racism is to consistently identify and describe it—and then dismantle it. That is the essence of antiracism." Essentially, being an antiracist is an action-oriented stance in which one recognizes and works to eliminate racist ideas, practices, structures, policies, and beliefs in all levels of society and its institutions. It is much more than being "not racist."

Educators, including school counselors, have been receptive to the idea of integrating an antiracist perspective to their work. Jamilah Pitts (2020), an author and education consultant, makes the case that antiracist practice in schools is "the exercise of hope, the practice of undoing and dismantling systems of oppression, the practice of freedom and of truth-telling. Antiracist work is the practice of healing and of restoring; it is a practice of love." Dr. Bettina Love, a prolific writer and educator, coined the term *abolitionist teaching* as a form of antiracist education. Similar to Pitts, she views antiracism and abolitionist teaching as restoring humanity in schools. Her abolitionist framework for teaching borrows from the work of Dr. Angela Davis, who wrote that abolition of slavery didn't end with the removal of chains. Instead, abolition begins with the development of institutions that allow for the incorporation of previously enslaved people into a democratic society.

Conceptually, antiracism is the school counseling profession's social justice foundation. To be socially just, one must also be an antiracist. The same is true of cultural competence: One must be antiracist in order to be truly culturally competent.

A broad definition of *social justice* would be the way in which human rights are manifested in the everyday lives of people at every level of society. Whereas equal opportunity and human rights are applicable to everyone, social justice targets those groups of people who have been historically oppressed in society. Social justice recognizes that there are situations in which application of the same rules to unequal groups can generate unequal results. Social justice and antiracism provide a framework to assess the impact of policies and practices.

Multicultural counseling, on the other hand, refers to counseling in which the counselor and client take into account their cultural and lived experiences (Lee & Richardson, 1991). The focus of multicultural counseling is on the counseling process between two or more individuals who have different and distinct perceptions of the world. Typically, counselors who engage in effective multicultural counseling will promote social justice and will attend to the human rights of their clients.

After studying the work of scholars in counselor education (Kiselica & Robinson, 2001; Lee, 1995), counseling psychology (e.g., Cokley, 2006; Neville & Carter, 2005; Utsey & Ponterotto, 1996), education (Freire, 1970; Ladson-Billings, 1998; Love, 2019), history (Anderson, 2016; Gordon-Reed, 2009; Kendi, 2017), law (Bell, 1992; Crenshaw, 2017), psychology (Spencer, 2019), and cultural studies (Gates, 2019; West, 1994), I believe the following set of assumptions are important to keep in mind when developing an antiracist foundation to school counseling:

- The status quo is characterized by inequitable distribution of power and resources based on race.

- Racism and other external sources (e.g., community, health, income, housing) influence behavior and attitudes.

- We all have internalized racist and biased attitudes, ideas, understandings, and patterns of thought that allow us to function in systems of oppression.

All forms of oppression, such as racism, classism, ableism (prejudice against those with disabilities), sexism, and heterosexism, clearly undermine the emotional and interpersonal well-being of students and thus potentially result in student underachievement and mental and emotional distress. Social justice and antiracist perspectives acknowledge the role that the status quo and dominant cultural values have in shaping the educational success and failure of youngsters, as evidenced by subsequent opportunity gaps. Recognition, then, of the cultural and racialized outcomes of traditional school counseling practice and theory encourages counselors to consider ways in which societal structure and the status quo either privileges them and their students or puts them at a disadvantage. Essentially, a social justice and antiracist approach to school counseling is centered on dismantling the status quo and creating new ways in which to affirm students and to ensure equitable and equal opportunities for all students. Table 2.1 presents differences between what might be considered traditional school counseling and an antiracist and social justice approach to school counseling.

OPPRESSION AND ANTI-OPPRESSION EDUCATION

Oppression refers to a social dynamic in which certain ways of being in this world—including certain ways of identifying or being identified—are normalized or

TABLE 2.1   Traditional versus Antiracist and Social Justice Approaches in School Counseling

TRADITIONAL SCHOOL COUNSELING	ANTIRACIST AND SOCIAL JUSTICE APPROACH TO SCHOOL COUNSELING
Dependence on counseling theories and approaches with little to no regard for the racial or cultural background of students	Dependence on strengths-based counseling, proactive coping strategies, spirituality and racial healing, and decentering "whiteness" in counseling theories. Major focus of counseling is on highlighting the strengths of students
Emphasis on individual student factors (e.g., unmotivated, depressed, angry)	Emphasis on sociocultural and environmental factors (e.g., racism, poverty) that influence students' and educators' behaviors
Little to no emphasis on racism and oppression and its influence on students	Major goal of school counseling program is to dismantle racist and oppressive practices and policies in schools
Emphasis on equality only	Emphasis on equality *and* equity
School counseling activities are typically implemented during the school day	School counseling activities are implemented during the school day *and* outside of school hours (e.g., advocating for policies, resources in the community)
Reliance on labels to identify students (e.g., defiant, aggressive)	Avoidance of labeling. Students are described by their strengths and positive characteristics
Little to no use of data to guide programming or to evaluate services	Dependence on data to highlight unevenness of student outcomes and to evaluate existing interventions
Focus on maintaining the status quo	Focus on creating antiracist, justice-oriented policies
Focus on providing student services to those students who are expected to achieve (student support is based on racist, stereotypical ideas about student demographic groups)	Focus on providing student supports and opportunities based on need and to increase equality and equity among student groups

privileged while other ways are oppressed or marginalized. Forms of oppression include racism, classism, sexism, heterosexism, anti-Semitism, and ableism, among others. More specifically, oppression occurs in situations in which people are exploited, marginalized, or rendered powerless (Zutlevics, 2002). A faulty belief that people tend to subscribe to is that those who are oppressed are somehow less than or inferior to those who are not oppressed. *Internalized oppression* is the manner in which an oppressed group ironically comes to use the methods of the oppressor against itself.

Anti-oppressive education encourages us to critically analyze our common methods of educating to see if those methods contribute to the perpetuation of oppression. Common methods of educating include ability grouping, student exclusion for bad behavior, and providing more opportunities for students who score higher on standardized tests rather than supports for those that don't. Anti-oppressive education results in a deep commitment to changing how we think about and engage in many aspects of education, from curriculum and pedagogy to school culture and activities to institutional structure and policies. Ideally, educators will make a commitment to exploring perspectives that do not conform to what has become common sense in the field of education. Anti-oppressive education aims to challenge the status quo at the risk of being controversial and causing discomfort.

CRITICAL RACE THEORY

Critical race theory (CRT), a legal framework, has become a highly politicized, catchall term used by conservative politicians to denote educational activities that address issues pertaining to race and racism. According to CRT critics, the underlying premise of CRT is anti-white education. This is not true. CRT was developed in the 1970s and 1980s by legal scholars as a means to address the law's role in producing and facilitating the role of racism, according to those who are marginalized, in the legal system. The school of thought—founded by academics including Derrick Bell, Alan Freeman, Richard Delgado, Kimberlé Crenshaw, and others—builds on critical legal studies and radical feminism. CRT examines the interconnected relationships among race, power, and the law. These concepts are not taught by pre-K–12 teachers and counselors.

The CRT debate in the U.S. is manufactured and is merely a political tactic to create fear, divide people by race, and maintain the status quo. While CRT is aligned with social justice and antiracist perspectives, these concepts are not synonymous. Many state legislators have proposed bills to bar educators from teaching about race and racism, including historical facts about colonialism, slavery, and other global atrocities (e.g., the Holocaust). The proposed anti-CRT policies mimic former President Donald Trump's Executive Order to stop funding for any type of training on CRT for federal employees, calling it a "propaganda effort." Anti-CRT critics also condemned the *1619 Project*, a Pulitzer Prize–winning report that tells the history of the first enslaved people who were brought to the American colonies. Nikole Hannah-Jones, the reporter who led the 1619 Project, has been branded as "controversial" because she challenges the founding date of United States—July 4, 1776—by pointing out that August 20, 1619, is when a ship arrived at Point Comfort in the British colony of Virginia, bearing a cargo of 20–30 enslaved Africans. Their arrival marked the beginning of chattel slavery that would last for the next 250 years.

So, what does CRT mean for school counselors? There are several core concepts of CRT that enhance the work of school counselors. First, school counselors must embrace historical facts and the consequences of historical events on the current lives of their students. Second, CRT encourages the development of counter-narratives of minoritized people, and these narratives are utilized to counter dominate educators' understanding of students and communities. In schools, antiracist school counselors should encourage storytelling as a means to validate the experiences of those students who are not often heard, including students of color, women/girls, LGBTQ (lesbian, gay, bisexual, transgender, and queer/questioning) students, and low-income students. And finally, antiracist school counselors expand the repertoire of their strategies and become skilled in strategies borne out of the experiences of Black and Brown people, such as African/Black-centered psychology (Akbar, 1996), Indigenous/Native therapeutic approaches (Hartmann & Gone, 2012), and strengths-based approaches (Arredondo, 2005).

 Counseling Snapshot

Before Doug, a school counselor, could give his beginning of the year presentation to his middle school's Parent-Teacher Association (PTA), chants of "No CRT!" echoed in the board room only to be countered by a teacher shouting out, "Stop whitewashing history!" Middle school parents packed the routine PTA meeting that quickly transformed into a tense setting. Conservative legislators, including the local mayor, had recently signed on to new state legislation aimed at keeping CRT out of classrooms. Although many of the parents who attended the PTA meeting were vocal critics of CRT, others were pushing for honest conversations about the country's painful racist history (e.g., slavery, Jim Crow laws) and more opportunities for teachers and counselors to learn about culturally responsive strategies in schools. The school's student enrollment is 55% white, 25% Black, 10% Asian, and 10% Latinx/Hispanic. Racial equity is one of the school's core values. Doug courageously gave remarks at the meeting; he addressed the following:

- The goals of school counseling are to serve all students equitably and equally and to ensure that all students have opportunities for success, including opportunities to learn U.S. historical facts about colonialism, immigration, slavery, and more.

- The school counseling program's core values include respect, honesty, equity and equality, and inclusion.

- Antiracist education and school counseling are means to achieve inclusion and true equality for all students.

EQUITY VERSUS EQUALITY

Arthur Levine, former president of Columbia University's Teachers College, stated in the school's 2004 annual report that "the equity issue should be as important to education schools as AIDS or cancer is to medical schools" (Teachers College Columbia University, 2004, p. 3). I agree with Dr. Levine's statement and firmly believe that equity is at the core of a social justice approach to school counseling. At its most fundamental level, equity is an orientation toward doing the right thing by students (Marshall, 2002), which does not mean treating students equally regardless of their different needs. Imagine communities in which one's race, ethnicity, or culture is not the most powerful predictor of how one fares. In a racially equitable community, some children excel in school and some struggle—but race isn't the factor that makes the difference. Some families are wealthy and some are poor—and there are people of every race at both ends of the wealth spectrum and in the middle. A racially equitable community is one in which individuals and groups have racial/ethnic and cultural identities but those racial and ethnic identities do not predict whether an adolescent goes to college or jail or which groups are healthiest and how long they are likely to live on average.

Equity requires that school counselors treat students differently on the basis of aspects of the students' cultures, including race, ethnicity, gender, and economic class. However, decisions to treat students differently should always be based on students' specific needs. Equity demands that school counselors resist using aspects of culture or external factors (e.g., poverty, family status, disability) as excuses for not setting high standards and demanding the best of students. In short, equity forces school counselors and educators to focus on students' strengths, not their deficits.

Equality, in contrast, urges counselors and educators to enforce formal school policies in a consistent manner. Equality focuses on impartiality and retaining policies without regard to student differences or unique circumstances. Ideally, counselors and other educators should seek a balance between equity and equality in their school practices because both are critical to promoting success for all students. However, it is important to remember that school policies that are grounded in equity bring about different results than those that are based on equality. For example, a school may enforce their zero-tolerance discipline policy in terms of equality. However, when examining the data regarding the students who have been expelled because of the policy, school officials may realize that the policy is more detrimental to, say, Native American boys when executed equally. From an equity perspective, the school would then need to reevaluate its discipline policy and the core issues (e.g., low teacher expectations, tardiness) that are at the root of discipline problems among Native American boys. It could then develop a new discipline policy and train the staff to use a new discipline curriculum that includes more culturally appropriate discipline strategies.

The Resource section of this book features a list of questions that should be discussed by a school's leadership team to assess whether or not equity is being addressed by the school.

Counseling Snapshot

Scenario 1 (EQUITY)

During the COVID-19 pandemic, schools in Parish School District were required to move to all-remote classes. Many of the district students (about 25%) didn't have consistent access to internet service nor computers. There are communities with limited or unstable Wi-Fi capabilities. A majority of the students who had limited connectivity were also English language learner (ELL) students. The School Counseling Association pointed out the inequities in access to internet and computers across the district. As a result, the school board purchased loaner computers for students who needed them and provided communities with Wi-Fi trucks so that students could connect for service.

Scenario 2 (EQUALITY)

Jamal, a high school counselor in an urban district, realized that students in the magnet program at his school were not being held to the same discipline standards as the students in the general population. He collected data that showed that—for the same offense—students in the magnet program were not issued the same punishment as students in the general population. As a result of Jamal's presentation of this data, the administration developed a new districtwide discipline policy for all students—including magnet and gifted students.

Ask Yourself

Does the following scenario present an equity or equality issue?

At your high school, 62% of graduating seniors are offered admission to a four-year college or university. The most recent data indicate that only 5% of the students offered admission to four-year colleges and universities are Black or Latinx (Black and Latinx students make up 43% of the school's population). After further review of data, you discover that Black and Latinx students are disproportionately underrepresented in courses that are required for college admission, such as calculus and Advanced Placement English.

Is this an equity or equality issue? Why or why not? What would you do to ensure equity and equality in this case?

KEY FUNCTIONS OF SCHOOL COUNSELING BASED ON SOCIAL JUSTICE AND AN ANTIRACIST APPROACH

The following section outlines what I believe are six key functions (the six *C*s) of school counselors who employ an antiracist and social justice approach in their work. (See Figure 2.1 on page 37.) The key functions include

1. counseling and intervention planning;

2. consultation;

3. connecting schools and communities;

4. collecting and utilizing data;

5. challenging bias and racism; and

6. coordinating student success and support.

COUNSELING AND INTERVENTION PLANNING

This function includes implementing counseling and interventions that acknowledge and integrate students' racial, cultural, and familial experiences. The importance

FIGURE 2.1 Six Key Functions of School Counselors Using an Antiracist and Social Justice Approach

of school counselors being able to identify and recognize both the academic and social/emotional needs of Black, Latinx/Hispanic, Indigenous, and other minoritized youth is critical. It's imperative that school counselors utilize interventions and strategies that align with students' cultural and racial norms around healing.

Within the counseling process, antiracist school counselors acknowledge the intersectionality and multitude of contextual factors that impact students' development. For instance, in actuality, in any given year, more than 90% of Black youth over age eight will experience racial discrimination (Pachter & Coll, 2009) but many will also experience issues related to their gender, sexual orientation, and other social identities. School counselors, therefore, must utilize strategies for addressing the social and emotional effects of multiple identities and discriminatory issues. Black, Latinx, Native American, Asian American, and other minoritized youth will likely experience the ill effects of being subjected to not only the overt use of racist epithets by other students but also more subtle forms of discrimination, such as being omitted from consideration for advanced courses by teachers and staff, disproportionate scrutiny of their behavior, and the omission of their cultural and racial representation in the curriculum. For Black youth in particular, the negative physical, psychological, physiological, and academic effects of racism include traumatic symptoms (e.g., hypervigilance about potential acts of racism), diminished self-esteem, symptoms of depression, impaired academic self-concepts, decreased school engagement, and lower academic performance, to name a few (Chavous et al., 2008; Jernigan & Daniel, 2011; Wang & Huguley, 2012; Wong et al., 2003). And while racial trauma is not yet widely recognized as one of the diagnostic criteria for psychological problems, these intermediate symptoms likely result in not only individual difficulties but also population-level challenges, such as academic achievement gaps and a high (and growing) suicide rate among Black children (Saleem et al., 2019). Racialized stress among youth is a real phenomenon (Utsey, 1999) and has been documented.

Socially just, antiracist school counselors must place more emphasis on students within their environment, sometimes referred to as the *person-in-environment approach*. This focus takes into account students' background experiences, their interaction with others in their families and immediate community, the resources in their environment, and—most importantly—their adaptive and maladaptive interactions with other people in their environment. When using this approach to counseling interventions, a school counselor should consider giving special consideration to students' particular cultural values. By doing so, counselors will be better able to identify student problems within environmental and personal contexts and better able to refer students to specific community assistance programs, if relevant.

Counseling and intervention planning is ideally carried out by school counselors who are culturally competent and responsive. Cultural competence, broadly speaking, involves combining cultural awareness and sensitivity with a skill set to bring about effective cross-cultural and multicultural practices (Moule, 2012). To assess your cultural knowledge, awareness, and ability to work with culturally diverse students and staff, turn to the School Counselor Multicultural Counseling Competence Checklist in the Resource section of this book (Holcomb-McCoy, 2004).

 Counseling Snapshot

Eric is a sixth-grade Black student at your school. In a recent class presentation by a local police officer, Eric yells out "I don't trust the police! The police kill Black people." Eric is immediately sent to the principal's office. Later, the teacher and counselor learn that Eric's older brother was involved in an altercation with local police after an incident in his neighborhood and he was arrested. Media coverage has depicted Eric's brother as "a thug" who deserved to be arrested. The school counselor and principal decide to work with Eric rather than discipline him. The school counselor meets with the teacher to discuss differing views of police officers. The school counselor shares data regarding overpolicing in Eric's community. Believing that Eric could be suffering from anxiety and depression, the school counselor also consults with a local therapist specializing in racialized stress and depression in Black adolescents.

CONSULTATION

The consultation function involves school counselors' work with parents and teachers to resolve students' problems and concerns. Consultation, unlike counseling, is an indirect service delivery approach and can be used to influence change in an entire classroom, school, or family. Counselors can use consultation as a means to support parents, teachers, and students most appropriately so that counselors can better assist larger numbers of students. It is through the consultation function that a school counselor can serve as an advocate for students who are being either treated unfairly or who are unable to speak for themselves. Consultation also provides space for large-scale teacher consultation and professional development with aims of changing school culture, climate, and policies. Important roles include

- identifying school or student inequities during the consultation process with teachers, parents, and other educators;

- ongoing consultation with teachers and community members to educate them about how they can best support all students;

- attention to the cross-cultural, cross-racial nature of student–teacher interactions in teacher consultation; and

- attention to teacher and parent self-awareness in the consultation.

Counseling Snapshot

A young female teacher has a reputation for sending at least one Latinx student to the office every day for discipline purposes. The principal addresses the matter with the teacher and asks the counselor to work with the teacher in order to reduce office referrals. Through several consultation sessions with the teacher, the counselor becomes aware of additional teachers' negative stereotypes and assumptions about Latinx students. The counselor works with the school leadership to design teacher professional development opportunities focused specifically on evidence-based strategies to increase Latinx students' academic and social emotional development. Consultation with the school leadership about discipline policy change is also a step in the counselor's plan of action.

CONNECTING SCHOOLS AND COMMUNITIES

Time is a precious commodity for all school-based educators. To the extent that they are able, antiracist and socially justice–focused school counselors must spend as much time as possible listening to and working in partnership with community organizations (e.g., nonprofit organizations, places of worship) and families to improve support services offered in the school. When working in this role, it is beneficial for counselors to be unbiased, flexible, and collaborative. By conducting culturally relevant and antiracist community programming, counselors can empower community members to advocate for policies and legislation that will improve and enhance opportunities for students. School–family–community partnerships have proven to be effective in raising the test scores of racially, culturally, and linguistically diverse and low-income students (Bohan-Baker & Little, 2002).

Counseling Snapshot

A middle school community has experienced a series of hate crimes targeting the influx of gay couples and transgender youth in one of its neighborhoods. The hate crimes have generated fear and the prevalence of homophobic and transphobic attitudes among students and families. Some community members talk as if pedophilia and homosexuality are the same. Many parents of transgender students worry about the safety of their children. The counselor initiates a work group of concerned parents, community members (including gay couples in the community), and school personnel. The committee's goal is to develop a plan for ceasing the hate crimes and educating the community on school policies and hate crime legislation in the city.

COLLECTING AND UTILIZING DATA

Data help us make critical decisions related to inequities and social injustices that occur in schools. Data collection increases a school counselor's ability to monitor student progress and to understand which students may need more guidance or intervention. Counselors can better highlight social injustices and advocate for students and families by collecting, analyzing, and presenting data to colleagues. We can collect data pertaining to student test scores, attendance, dropout rates, suspension, expulsion, and grades. By analyzing the results, we are better able to discover achievement and opportunity gaps categorized by grade, race, immigration status, income, gender, disability, or any cultural specification.

 Counseling Snapshot

One of the school counselors at Saint Francis High School collected data indicating that 12% of eleventh-grade students drop out before graduation. Further analysis of the data showed that those who dropped out were primarily made up of Native American (42%) and Latinx (50%) girls. The counselor presented her data to the administration and her school counseling colleagues. After much discussion, they decide to present the data to the entire high school staff to spark a discussion of the root causes of the high dropout rate of girls of color.

CHALLENGING BIAS AND RACISM

One of the most important functions of a school counselor within a social justice and antiracist framework is to challenge racism and bias in the school setting and community. Clearly, racism and bias can inhibit student achievement and influence the behavior and perceptions of educators. For this reason, we need to be diligent about identifying and challenging our own biases and racist ideas and those of others. We can then help to shape new policies that focus on providing students with equal and equitable experiences and opportunities. We can also incorporate social justice and antiracist education into the work we do with students.

 Counseling Snapshot

Tim, an elementary school counselor, is a member of the site-based leadership team at his school. During the selection process of a parent committee member, several committee members mentioned that the committee should choose a parent who is a stay-at-home

(Continued)

(Continued)

mother because she would be available for meetings and would understand the mission of the school. Tim opposed this idea and challenged the committee's ideas about who should participate on the leadership team. He felt that the committee was not giving all parents, particularly working parents who tended to be Black or Brown, an opportunity to participate in an important and powerful aspect of the school.

COORDINATING STUDENT SUCCESS AND SUPPORT

The research suggests that far too often, low-income and racially and linguistically diverse students encounter watered-down curricula and unchallenging academic environments. Providing students with additional academic and social/emotional opportunities and supports to encourage and enhance their learning is important. Counselors can collaborate with organizations and institutions (e.g., local universities, civic groups) to provide these extra supports for students' academic and social/emotional development. School counselors who work from an antiracist and social justice framework focus on providing support for students who often have fewer high-quality academic services. Also, school counselors can use scheduling and other counselor activities (career and job fair coordination, individualized education program meetings, etc.) to advocate for increased access to opportunities that would further all students' potential for postsecondary opportunities.

 Counseling Snapshot

Dawn, a high school counselor, developed a partnership with a local university's admissions office and career center. She and university personnel developed a series of student experiences for juniors and seniors from underrepresented groups (e.g., Black, Latinx, Native American) at the university. The university provides free credit-bearing opportunities (e.g., dual enrollment) and college application and preparation support for students. Dawn manages the partnership and receives time and support from her school's leadership to maintain the partnership.

Questions to Consider

1. How would you handle a situation where you want to challenge a particular bias that your fellow counselors are not willing to recognize?

2. Jot down a job description that could be used for your next school counselor opening. You want to ensure that the successful candidate is an antiracist and will help your team address gaps in students' opportunities. List interview questions you will ask the candidates.

3. In your own words, describe *student success*. Is your definition of success different from your friends' and colleagues' definitions? Who and what should define student success?

4. Social justice is often defined as providing fairness and equality for all. Do you think it is possible for all students to be treated equally in a school?

5. Antiracism is often misunderstood as being anti-white. What would you tell your colleagues if they have this opinion of your declaration of being an antiracist?

CHAPTER 3

Counseling and Intervention Planning

It is easier to build strong children than to repair broken men.

—Frederick Douglass

At a district-level meeting to discuss anticipated mental health needs of children reentering schools after the COVID-19 lockdown, one educator said, "Who will provide mental health support during the school day—and better yet, who will coordinate community mental health services for students and their families? Should we invest in school social workers?" This question struck me as odd. What? There are school counselors already in schools. This district has hundreds of school counselors. I responded to this question in a calm but firm manner: "School counselors are well-equipped to provide emotional and mental health support to students. They can coordinate counseling services for children who are in need of services from external sources." The educator looked at me and said (with a solemn face), "I've never seen a school counselor implement counseling or take on that kind of a role. You think they can do it?" I said, "Absolutely!"

Counseling is what school counselors are trained to do! No doubt about it. Counselors can provide counseling services for students. However, counselors in high-need schools are often not able to conduct enough counseling sessions to cover the magnitude of students' needs. Hence, I believe school counselors in many school settings should work from a triage model, which is a process for assessing the severity of the mental health needs of students and then coordinating support services for them. Through community partnerships, a school counselor can help parents and families find mental health supports outside of the school day and the appropriate services given the student's problem.

Since counseling skills, both individual and group, are at the core of school counselors' work, those skills can be transferred to many other roles in the schools. For instance, it's not uncommon for school counselors to use their counseling skills to help mediate staff problems or to help a group of teachers problem solve. Counseling skills are needed everywhere in a school. However, counselors often use culturally inappropriate strategies and interventions that perpetuate injustice or stereotypical perspectives about students. Antiracist and social justice–focused school counselors use counseling strategies that enhance students' sense of self-worth and academic and personal self-efficacy and ultimately improve students' feelings of purpose and value. The role of antiracist and social justice–focused school counselors is to initiate counseling services with a mixture of the following: a justice mindset, a keen understanding of environmental factors that hinder child/student development, a knowledge of the barriers to effective cross-cultural counseling, and an ability to build on the strengths of students and their families.

After I explained that school counselors are equipped to lead efforts to address students' social and emotional needs upon reentry, the educator in the scenario above was intrigued by the potential of school counselors in that district. However, the question of whether counselors would provide counseling services that align with the increasingly diverse student population was still unknown. In addition, there is no cookbook for how to implement counseling that will empower or create the change necessary for students to be successful. However, I told the educator that school counselors and all educators must start with the following questions:

- What are the strengths of students?

- What survival skills have been used by students and families to get to this point?

- What environmental barriers need to be removed to help this student be successful? How can I—or we—alter that environment?

This chapter offers ways to take an antiracist and social justice approach to counseling and intervention planning. Because counseling is the cornerstone of school counseling programs, it is often this area in which counselors feel most comfortable. Part of delivering effective counseling services is developing cultural competence and working with students sensitively, creatively, and responsibly. This also includes taking into account the societal and environmental factors that influence students' success.

CRITICAL FACTORS THAT AFFECT SCHOOL COUNSELING AND THE COUNSELING RELATIONSHIP

CULTURE

What is culture? Unfortunately, there is no fixed or universal understanding of what culture entails. Across many disciplines, including education, culture is discussed broadly to include three fundamental human activities: what people think, what people do, and what people make. Put simply, a cultural group is a collection of individuals who share a core set of beliefs, patterns of behavior, and values. The groups may be large or small, but their ways of thinking and behaving identify them.

Assimilation—the degree to which cultural groups can blend into the norm—was once the expectation for culturally diverse people in the United States. As a result, assimilation involved hiding or even rejecting one's cultural uniqueness. For instance, many immigrants would adopt new, Americanized names to fit into the norm culture. Today, our society is increasingly recognizing and appreciating the value of cultural diversity and the importance of helping students navigate social, academic, and career ladders while retaining their cultural uniqueness. Because this was not the case for many years, however, many who identify as Black and/or Brown students, LGTBQ (lesbian, gay, bisexual, transgender, and queer/questioning) students, religious minority students (e.g., Muslim students), and others from culturally diverse backgrounds still feel that school systems do not value their culture. We see this particularly in how many students avoid voluntarily meeting with or opening up to school counselors.

The multilayered lived experiences of students and the intersections of their various cultures must be addressed in counseling. Salient dimensions of cultural identity, including race, ethnicity, class, gender, sexual orientation, socioeconomic status, and religion/spirituality and how these aspects of identities intersect to reconstruct new meanings for students, are paramount to counseling within the context of social justice and antiracism. Examination of these dimensions is critical to fully understanding the intersectionality of students' cultural identities.

Cultural differences, cultural group membership, and cultural identities can significantly influence how a counselor perceives a student and how a student perceives a counselor. In many cases, school counselors think that when they treat all students equally, they are fair and culturally sensitive. Although the intention is correct, this practice is problematic because all students are not the same. Students, particularly those from historically oppressed groups, have different needs, experiences, and perceptions. Therefore, students' cultural backgrounds will likely determine how they approach counseling, perceive their counselor, and react to the content of what a school counselor says. For instance, a 14-year-old Muslim student may become agitated and anxious when the counselor assumes that all students go to church on Sunday. Or a Black female student in a predominately white school could become angry and resistant to counseling if a white counselor described beauty as "fair skin with keen features" in a group counseling session. Or a gay male eleventh-grader may feel left out when his counselor assumes that he is dating a girl. Being sensitive to cultural differences and multilayered cultural identities during counseling is imperative and forms the basis for students' perceptions of school counselors.

RACISM, DISCRIMINATION, AND OPPRESSION

To someone who has not experienced racism, prejudice, discrimination, and oppression, it is difficult to convey the insidious, pervasive, and lifelong impact these experiences can have. In addition to affecting how a person perceives themself, these experiences also influence how a person relates to others, to organizations (e.g., schools), and to the counseling process.

According to the Anti-Defamation League (2021), *racism* is the marginalization and/or oppression of people of color based on a socially constructed racial hierarchy that privileges one race (i.e., white people) over others. Throughout U.S. history, opportunity, freedom, and prosperity have been largely reserved for white people through the intentional exclusion and oppression of Black and Brown people. The deep racial inequities in education that exist today are a direct result of *structural racism*: the historical and current policies, practices, and norms that create and maintain white supremacy. At the core of racism is a belief in white supremacy. *White supremacy* refers to the systematic marginalization or oppression of people of color based on a socially constructed racial hierarchy that privileges people who identify as white.

Over fifty years ago, in response to the racist climate in the U.S., Allport (1954) defined *prejudice* as beliefs based on faulty and inflexible generalizations. Attitudes originating from these beliefs may be directed toward a group as a whole or toward an individual because they are members of that group. The group or individual who becomes the object of prejudice most often experiences a position of disadvantage.

The potential to experience the social stressors of racism, prejudice, and discrimination exists for culturally and racially diverse students. Many students may report that they experience what we call *microaggressions* targeted at them based on their racial and/or cultural background. *Microaggressions* are defined as the everyday, subtle, intentional (and often unintentional) interactions or behaviors that communicate some sort of bias toward historically marginalized groups. The difference between microaggressions and overt discrimination (macroaggressions) is that people who commit microaggressions might not even be aware of them. In the school setting, racism, prejudice, and overall oppressive acts occur every day. For example, Malik, age 10, reported to his counselor, "My teacher doesn't like Black people; that's why I don't do her work. She never calls on Black kids, and I heard her say that kids from the projects don't learn well." Sam, age 16, reported to a teacher, "My counselor told me that I could never go to that university because no kids from my neighborhood have ever been accepted there." Sam's teacher nodded and agreed with the counselor, thus sending Sam the message that he should not apply to that college based on where he lived and possibly his racial background. Other culturally diverse groups share the brunt of similar comments.

School counselors who want to build a relationship of trust and openness with students need to acknowledge the effects of racism, prejudice, and discrimination and broach the counseling relationship mindfully. Day-Vines et al. (2007) offered a framework for differentiating among five broaching styles: avoidant, isolating, continuing/incongruent, integrated/congruent, and infusing. According to Day-Vines et al., broaching "functions as one facet of therapeutic responsiveness that places the onus of responsibility on the counselor to initiate race-related dialogues; otherwise, such dialogues might remain unexamined, reflecting, in large measure, the taboo nature of race within a racially charged society" (p. 402). The goal is for school counselors to have a well-developed understanding of the extent to which sociocultural and sociopolitical concerns take shape in the lives of students.

Discomfort and Fear

Not only should counselors assess the impact of other people's prejudiced and racists beliefs on students' success, but they must also be cognizant of their own racist and prejudiced beliefs that cause them to fear and feel uncomfortable with specific groups of students and topics related to issues of racism, discrimination, and oppression. Without a doubt, a counselor's fear and discomfort will interfere with the counseling relationship. The following examples illustrate this point:

> William, a 16-year-old Black student, went to the school counselor to discuss the painful experience of coming out as queer. As the counselor listened, however, she had difficulty suppressing her surprise that William was queer and refused to acknowledge any pronoun change (from *him* to *they*). In a nervous manner, the counselor said, "Oh, I didn't know you were gay. When did that happen?" William, in turn, was put off by her comment and sat silently, unresponsive. The counselor waited for a response while shuffling papers. Finally, after a few minutes, William walked out and never spoke to the counselor again.

> Shanique, an 11-year-old biracial student, approached the school counselor about creating a Black Lives Matter club for fifth- and sixth-graders. The school counselor responded by saying, "All students

matter. I'm not comfortable promoting a group that promotes Black students only." Shanique looked down, left the counselor's office, and never returned.

The counselors in both examples would have done better to simply ask William and Shanique more about their feelings at the moment. Also, it's apparent from the counselors' behaviors and responses that they have misunderstandings and biases about the students' concerns or requests. But even if a student does not come to the counselor to talk about a cultural or racial issue specifically, counselors should ask themselves the following questions about their treatment of culturally and racially diverse students in all of the work they do:

- Am I equally comfortable working with all students (e.g., LGBTQ [lesbian, gay, bisexual, transgender, and queer/questioning] students, students from different religious groups, students of various racial backgrounds)?

- If not, are there certain services I may have denied to students because of my level of discomfort?

- How might my fellow counselors or I reach these students so that they have access to the services to which all students are entitled?

Some counselors may hold an unrecognized fear of the potential dangerousness of the student based on stereotypes and a lack of familiarity with the students' racial and/or cultural background. Norris and Spurlock (1992) reported that counselors with limited contact or direct experience with people of a specific race or culture might initiate counseling with fears that stem from racist ideas and cultural stereotypes. School counselors may even distance themselves from students by passively accepting a student's refusal to meet or talk with them. It's essential, then, for counselors to separate the student from the stereotype and put fears aside in favor of doing right by all students. In the Suggested Readings at the end of the book, I recommend some resources that will help school counselors delve into the influence of racism, prejudice, discrimination, and oppressive practices on the counseling process and counselor/client behavior. I encourage reading as many of these books as possible, either individually or in a study group with other school counselors.

POVERTY

Child poverty affects more than 11.5 million children in the United States. And, according to estimates by UNICEF and the World Bank, more than 387 million children around the globe live in extreme poverty. In 2019, 14.4% of all children under 18 in the United States were living below the official poverty measure. About 6% were living in deep poverty, defined as 50% of the federal poverty measure. Almost one-quarter were living in poverty or were at risk, defined as 150% of the official measure. Children of color across most racial categories are more likely to experience poverty than their white counterparts. Black, Latinx/Hispanic, and American Indian and Alaskan Native (AIAN) children have the highest poverty rates. And while the broader category of Asian American and Pacific Islander children have lower poverty rates, disaggregated data from past years show that grave disparities based on ethnicity persist with significantly higher rates for Bangladeshi, Pakistani, Burmese, and Hmong children.

Growing up in poverty can affect a child's access to education, proper nutrition, and comprehensive healthcare. In addition, many reside in inner cities or relatively isolated rural areas, compounding existing obstacles to equal educational opportunities and academic success. Yet, studies consistently document that most educators, including school counselors, come from middle-class backgrounds, making it difficult for them to relate personally with students who live in poverty (Zeichner, 2003).

Among the many factors that impact access to opportunities and student success, socioeconomic status is at the top of the list. For example, children who live in poverty are more likely to suffer early nutritional deficiencies that have a lifelong impact, are less likely to receive a quality education, are more likely to experience neglect and abuse, and have a significantly shorter life expectancy. All in all, it's well-documented that poverty impacts child development in general and school readiness in particular.

For school counselors, reversing the effects of poverty and preventing poverty is key to an antiracist and social justice counseling program. Decreasing the risk factors in a child's environment increases a child's potential for educational attainment. Counseling and intervention programs that target health concerns (Stonerock & Blumenthal, 2017), parent–child relationships (Chao & Willms, 2002), and parental involvement (Hango, 2007) are associated with better educational outcomes for low-income children and result in increased cognitive ability. A list of readings on the effects of poverty and promising strategies for addressing poverty can be found in the Suggested Reading section at the back of the book.

IMMIGRATION AND ACCULTURATION

Many culturally and racially diverse students are immigrants, either recently or in the past, or are the children of parents who immigrated. The United States has more immigrants than any other country in the world (Krogstad & Gonzalez-Barrera, 2021). Today, more than 40 million people living in the U.S. were born in another country, with almost every country in the world represented among U.S. immigrants. Of the 40 million people who were foreign born, 53.1% were from

Latin America and the Caribbean, 28.2% were born in Asia, and 12.1% originated in Europe. The remaining 2% were from other countries. School counselors in urban, suburban, and rural areas have increasing numbers of immigrant children as part of their caseloads (Groce & Johnson, 2021).

Immigrant students and families face many challenges that will undoubtedly bring them to the counselor's office. They are more likely than nonimmigrants to live in poverty and be uninsured. About 5 million children have a parent who is undocumented. While children of immigrants make up less than a quarter of the nation's population of children, they account for 30% of those from low-income families. Many immigrant parents/guardians have limited English proficiency, so higher-paying jobs are not accessible to them and they are therefore not eligible for some services and are fearful of completing federal forms such as the Free Application for Federal Student Aid (FAFSA), a required form for college scholarships and financial aid.

As one can imagine, the process of adapting to a new language and culture is stressful for any immigrant family. Additionally, parents and children often enter the country at different times, which causes added stress in their relationships. There are differences in how quickly parents and children adapt to the new culture, affecting family roles. In addition, many immigrants, mainly if they are refugees or come from crime-ridden countries, experience trauma either in their home country or before they arrived in their new country. Finally, undocumented immigrant families face the added stress related to the fear of apprehension and deportation.

For undocumented immigrants, the fear of deportation can cause significant stress. Additionally, those in the country with documentation are concerned about their legal status and increased racism and discrimination. Cost is always a significant barrier for low-income immigrant families. And when an immigrant family can afford services, there are often no services available in their native language. Depending on the culture, there may be a stigma attached to receiving mental health services. Some cultures believe these types of problems are a private family matter, are a sign of weakness, or can be dealt with by the church or other faith practice.

For those who have recently migrated, it is helpful for school counselors to understand the reasons and circumstances for the migration, which family members came and which didn't (and why), and the level of disruption this caused in the child's support system. For some, the process may have been voluntary. The families have chosen to come for better educational and job opportunities in a receptive host community. For other families, who may have escaped war-torn countries where they have experienced the loss of their loved ones and the chronic disruption of other supportive networks such as their extended families and schools, this process may be different. The Suggested Readings at the back of the book offers information on numerous resources that address migration and acculturation to help school counselors understand these critical factors.

LANGUAGE DIFFERENCES

Language differences present another perceived obstacle or barrier in school counseling. If the counselor is not bilingual or has limited proficiency in the student's primary language, the language barrier can affect the student–counselor relationship. If the counselor does not clearly understand what the student is trying to communicate, they may unintentionally recommend an inappropriate intervention. It is also possible that the student may spend so much time trying to say words correctly to be understood that they may not accurately reflect their feelings and behaviors to the counselor (Gopaul-McNicol & Thomas-Presswood, 1998). Therefore, counselors of bilingual students should achieve some level of proficiency in the student's primary language. Short of this, they should do their best to bring another trusted person into the counseling session who can interpret the idiosyncrasies, subtle nuances, and idiomatic expressions in the student's primary language. Ideally, another counselor or a school professional could serve in this position. School counselors working to achieve equity for all should admit their limitations in working with bilingual students and do their best to find a solution that will work for both them and the students being served. The best educational environment for English language learners (ELL) and bilingual speaker (BLS) students are in dual-language schools where they can continue to develop both languages simultaneously (Thomas & Collier, 1997). Children who are learning a second language need continued development of their first language to become proficient speakers, readers, and writers in English. For school counselors to carry out their mandate to develop students' social and emotional lives for their academic success, counselors in these schools must understand language development and its influence on learning.

ANTIRACIST AND CULTURALLY APPROPRIATE COUNSELING INTERVENTIONS

In the previous sections of this chapter, I introduced how various factors impact students' school experiences and thus influence the counseling process. In this section, I will explain methods to help school counselors provide culturally appropriate and social justice–focused counseling for students.

HELPING STUDENTS PROCESS THEIR BEHAVIOR, ATTITUDES, AND FEELINGS

Beyond acknowledging their uncertainties, fears, fixed notions, and stereotypes, counselors are responsible for recognizing students' negative feelings and attitudes. Helping students process their behavior, attitudes, and feelings about counseling and school-related issues is something school counselors can do to show respect for students and demonstrate that they genuinely accept students for who they are, even if they must work together to improve a particular behavior or attitude. In addition, if school counselors address issues that they recognize may affect the counseling relationship, difficulties will be avoided. The following story illustrates this point:

> Elissa, a 16-year-old student, went to her counselor to discuss her schedule for the next semester. Since arriving at the high school the previous year, Elissa had never been to her counselor's office. Because Elissa's grades were average to the above-average range, the counselor had never requested to speak to her. However, when Elissa signed up for Honors Trigonometry, the counselor wanted to make sure that she was aware of the challenging nature of the course.
>
> In the conference with the school counselor, Elissa was quiet and reserved. She did not look at the counselor, and her arms were crossed throughout the conference. She nodded in agreement with everything that the counselor said. The counselor finally asked, "Elissa, I detect that you are a bit nervous talking to me. Is this true?" Elissa nodded in agreement, so the counselor continued, "What makes you nervous about talking to me?" Elissa didn't speak, but the counselor went on to acknowledge that it's sometimes scary to come to the guidance office. She reassured Elissa that she wanted to help her have a positive school experience and would be open to listening to any of her concerns. Elissa smiled and left the office. The following week, Elissa returned, wanting to talk with her counselor about changing a course.

This type of simple exchange between a counselor and student can be compelling. Building trust and respect between the counselor and student is critical to counseling programs that take a social justice approach. The example with Elissa nicely demonstrates the early stages of the three components of the effective counseling relationship: working alliance, transference–countertransference, and real relationship (Terrell & Cheatham, 1996).

The *working alliance* is the alignment that occurs between the counselor and student. The counselor acts as a positive mirror for the student, reflecting the student as a unique and valuable individual. This positive reflection allows the student to see himself as an individual *with* an issue (such as a concern or problem) rather than simply *as* an issue. More importantly, the counselor is an ally or advocate who can help the student resolve external and internal conflicts. For example, a low-income fourth-grade student whose father was recently incarcerated and whose mother is struggling to support five children is acting out in class and not turning in homework. His school counselor realizes that he may not need study skills or anger management but instead needs to discuss his struggles at home in a safe, nonjudgmental environment. This culturally sensitive and appropriate intervention places the counselor in the role of a trusted advocate.

Transference is the unconscious process by which students' negative feelings, attitudes, and behaviors associated with discriminatory practices are transferred onto the counselor. Similarly, *countertransference* or *counselor transference* is the counselor's response to the student that stems from the counselor's past relationships and experiences. Elissa, for example, may have associated going to the counselor's office with being in trouble and, for that reason, was closed-off and quiet. Counselor transference could have occurred if the counselor had a preconceived notion about students like Elissa (say, those who seemed shy or resistant) and assumed that Elissa would be the same. Using the example above, countertransference might play out if the counselor validates her faulty perceptions (based on past experiences with low-income fourth-grade students) by stating, "If you would only listen to your teachers and do your work, everything would get better. Stop being lazy." School counselors must recognize transference and countertransference because both are important to understanding the counseling dynamics, and both are essential to the counseling relationship.

The *real relationship* is authentic and operates from genuineness, respect, and openness that both counselor and student have established. Unfortunately, these positive relationship qualities may be hampered by misconceptions, racist and prejudiced beliefs, lack of cultural knowledge, and lack of self-awareness. The school counselor who genuinely wants education justice must obtain historical and current knowledge regarding different cultures and diverse communities. In addition, the school counselor should be willing to participate in different environments that provide a working knowledge and awareness of culturally diverse people. Thus, counselors who examine their culturally based attitudes and beliefs and who are self-aware can develop a real relationship with all students. Listening, interpreting, appreciating students' differences through appropriate verbal and nonverbal responses, and identifying pertinent student issues amplifies the school counselor's ability to form real relationships. Please refer to the Suggested Readings later in this book for a list of titles on cultural counseling relationships that I strongly recommend that counselors read and digest.

STRENGTHS-BASED COUNSELING

Strengths-based counseling assesses and recognizes students' inherent strengths and then builds on those strengths to create change (Dixon & Tucker, 2008). Strengths-based counseling is highly effective when working with Black and Brown students or students with a history of marginalization in schools. Essentially, strengths-based counseling builds on the concept of "mattering" (Dixon, 2006).

The focus of counseling when using a strengths perspective is not on "fixing" a broken student. Instead, the focus is on determining student strengths and emphasizing those strengths to resolve or at least reduce the frequency of the problem that brought the student to the counselor's attention. The strengths-based approach reduces the power structure between the student and the counselor, and it instills hope that the student has something positive to offer and achieve.

The effective strengths-based practice may require that school counselors acknowledge that they are not necessarily significant in students' lives—that is, *the counselor* will not produce the change in students' lives. Instead, school counselors act as a resource and a guide for students as they strive to change their lives themselves using their innate abilities. School counselors who use a strengths-based approach do not use stigmatizing labels and behavior descriptors to describe students. The following terms should never be used about students because they only further alienate students and negatively shape their realities:

- noncompliant
- bad/bad news
- stupid/dumb
- resistive
- dysfunctional

- unwilling
- oppositional
- unmotivated
- defiant

A strengths-based approach requires that school counselors use students' strengths when discussing or describing student concerns. It also requires that school counselors point out their perceptions of students' strengths or ask students to identify their strengths. In the following exchange, the school counselor reflects the student's concern in a way that highlights her existing strengths without trying to change her negative feelings.

| *Student:* | I stayed in the advanced math class even though I hate math. I hate math, and I hate that class! |
| *Counselor:* | It sounds like you dislike math, which makes me admire your perseverance. |

School counselors and students might also collaborate to give meaningful labels to the identified strengths, as demonstrated in the conversation here between a school counselor and a fifth-grade student:

| *School counselor:* | Yesterday, your friends were making fun of you, yet you remained calm. What was it about you that helped you stay calm? |

Student:	I was furious at my friends, but I didn't want to get in trouble again. So, I just walked away.
School counselor:	That ability you had to walk away when you were angry, can you give it a name? What would you call that?
Student:	*[Thinks for a minute]* I'll call it my "no trouble strength" because I'm tired of going to the office and getting in trouble.
School counselor:	Tell me more about when you use your "no trouble strength."

School counselors working from a strengths-based perspective must avoid referring to students by a label or a diagnosis. It is essential to employ an asset-based framework when thinking about supporting students, particularly students who have historically been marginalized. To accomplish this, school counselors must first disrupt and supplant the tendency to describe everything wrong with students. For example, when asking people who work with Black males in educational settings to describe their students' neighborhoods, phrases such as *crime-ridden*, *broken homes*, and *drug-infested* are often used. And describing a student as *hyper* or an *ADHD student* identifies the student as their diagnosis rather than as a person with a physical, emotional, or psychological difficulty. It is better to use what is called *person-first language*, which would mean that a school counselor works with *a student with ADHD* rather than *an ADHD student* or *a child with a reading disability* as opposed to *the reading-disabled kid*. Recognizing the person first helps dissociate them from the diagnosis or problem and makes it easier to shift the focus to strengths. Counselors can use inherent character strengths to great success as a starting point for counseling and further growth.

 ## Counseling Snapshot

Shameka, a Black seventh-grade student, went to the counselor with concerns about a failing math grade and complaints about her math teacher. Shameka has a label among teachers of being a troublemaker. Teachers have written on her report cards that she talks back, does not respect authority, and is too aggressive in her tone. Shameka receives grades in the C range, but she scored extremely high on intelligence and gifted placement tests.

In the counselor's office, Shameka opens up about her home life. Born and raised in a low-income, inner-city neighborhood, Shameka is the oldest of five children, and she currently

(Continued)

(Continued)

lives with her grandmother in a two-bedroom apartment. Shameka's mother is in and out of her life, and she has had no contact with her father since she was five years old.

Because Shameka's grandmother is diabetic and very ill, Shameka is responsible for getting her younger siblings to school. Shameka says that she often thinks about her life as if her mother and father were together. Shameka admits that she is angry with her parents because they are not around, and she wishes that she had another life. The school counselor expresses empathy for Shameka and focuses their time on identifying the strengths she has relied on to survive and cope with her difficulties. The counselor identifies Shameka's intelligence, perseverance, and maturity. Shameka determines her major strength as her unwillingness to take "stuff" from other people. The counselor calls it *assertiveness*. Shameka and her counselor continue to spend significant time planning how Shameka can use her strengths to work on her problems at school.

EMPOWERMENT-BASED AND LIBERATION COUNSELING

Although traditional counseling theories and approaches (e.g., person-centered, rational emotive) can be modified and applied to counseling with most students, they still lack a focus on students' struggles with their environment or the impact of the environment on the students. Students and families who struggle to overcome decades of oppression and marginalization require more than what these traditional theories offer. Students of color and low-income students benefit from school counselors who can apply traditional counseling approaches and are also skilled in advocacy and empowerment.

Empowerment and advocacy are not new to the counseling field. In the 1970s, the growth of community counseling brought advocacy and community organizing to the attention of the counseling profession (Toporek & Liu, 2001). In 2009, Ratts and Hutchins (2009) introduced a set of advocacy competencies for the American Counseling Association. The movement toward integrating advocacy competencies in the practice of counseling signaled the need for counselors to advocate for the removal of environmental factors that impede clients'/students' development. As a result, advocacy is now an essential skill for all school counselors, particularly in the context of social justice and antiracism.

Antiracist and social justice–focused school counselors take on two complementary roles in the counseling process. The first role is to explore or broach with students the environmental, sociopolitical, community, and economic forces at play in their lived experiences. This role requires counselors to advocate for their students. The second role is to reverse the process of self-disempowerment or internalized oppression. The counselor helps students recognize and modify any ideas, values, feelings, and behaviors that contribute to their oppressive situation or how they perceive themselves. This is empowerment-based counseling. Empowerment is characterized by the counselor helping the student achieve goals, with the outcome being to enable the student to act independently in the future. As a general definition, *empowerment* can be defined as a process of increasing personal, interpersonal, or political power so that individuals, families, and communities can take action to improve their situations. It is a process that fosters power (that is, the capacity to implement) in disenfranchised and powerless groups of people for use in their own lives, their communities, and in their society by acting on issues that they define as necessary.

When counseling, critical consciousness can be used to move students to a point at which they feel a sense of personal power (empowerment). *Critical consciousness* involves three psychological processes:

1. *group identification*, which includes identifying areas of shared experiences and concern with a particular group;

2. *group consciousness*, which consists in understanding the differential status of and power of groups in society; and

3. *self- and collective efficacy*, which is described as perceiving one's self as a subject (rather than object) of social processes and as capable of working to change the social order.

For students to understand that their problems stem from a lack of power, they must first comprehend their group's status in society and the overall structure of power in society. At the individual level, counselors can help students gain empowerment by facilitating discussions about one's group identification and helping them understand how their group membership has affected their life circumstances. Equipped with this greater understanding and with new confidence in themselves, students can develop new life strategies that better meet their needs.

 Counseling Snapshot

Edward, a Native American tenth-grader, is told to see the counselor because of recent confrontations with teachers. Edward tells the counselor that he is tired of being told what to do by "these f—g white teachers. They want to tell us what to do. . . . They are the problem. They go back to their nice families and nice houses and leave us here . . . with

(Continued)

crappy houses and nothing. I hate white people." The counselor recognizes Edward's anger and frustration with the oppression of his people. He validates Edward's anger, "I hear your anger and frustration with white people."

Ask Yourself:

1. What could the counselor say next for Edward to explore his group's history of oppression?

2. How might you link his group's history to future empowerment? Practice what you would say with a friend or colleague.

BLACK PSYCHOLOGY AND LIBERATION

The Association of Black Psychologists (ABPsi) was founded on September 2, 1968, in San Francisco, California, in response to the American Psychological Association's (APA) failure to address the mental health needs of the Black community. This revolutionary idea was borne out of the efforts of Black early career psychologists and student activists from across the United States. ABPsi, as the first national, ethnic psychological association, and the Association for Multicultural Counseling and Development (AMCD) have led the field of counseling and psychology in the areas of racial/ethnic identity, cultural psychology, multicultural competencies, positive psychology, and social justice.

The very formation of the ABPsi provided the road map for considering and confronting justice and mental health issues of people of African descent. White (1980) asserted that "it is tough if not impossible to understand the lifestyles of black people using traditional psychological theories developed by white psychologists to explain white behaviors" (p. 5). Thus, African/Black psychology set out to provide culturally relevant and consistent explanations, analyses, and theories of the behavior of people of African descent based upon a Black frame of reference. Over the years, African/Black psychology has shifted to a more African-centered approach grounded in African culture, spirituality, philosophy, and history.

Social justice–focused and antiracist school counselors draw from the research and literature written by Black psychologists, many of whom are ABPsi members. Members of ABPsi have amassed a body of literature that has had a profound impact on counseling and psychology as a whole. *The Psychology of Blacks: Centering Our Perspectives in the African Consciousness* (Parham et al., 2000), *Counseling Persons of African Descent: Raising the Bar of Practitioner Competence* (Parham, 2002), and the *Handbook of African American Psychology* (Neville et al., 2009) are some of the most definitive introductory textbooks for learning about African/Black psychology.

ETHNIC AND RACIAL IDENTITY DEVELOPMENT
AND THE COUNSELING PROCESS

Research articles on ethnic and racial identity development have grown rapidly in the past several decades (Schwartz et al., 2014) and are increasingly being considered central to ethnic and racial minority youth (Williams et al., 2012). The terms *racial identity* and *ethnic identity* are often used interchangeably, but the research on the two constructs has differed. For example, *racial identity* is used when the groups being investigated are considered racial (e.g., Black) or if the measure used is labeled as racial (e.g., Multidimensional Inventory of Black Identity; Sellers et al., 1997) and *ethnic identity* is used when the group is deemed to be ethnic (e.g., Latinos) or if the measure used is labeled as ethnic (e.g., Multigroup Ethnic Identity Measure; Phinney, 1992). Unsurprisingly, there is considerable empirical and conceptual overlap (e.g., Casey-Cannon et al., 2011). Studies (e.g., Quintana, 1998) have demonstrated that the development of children's and youth's conceptions of ethnicity and race follow similar trajectories. Moreover, ethnic identity development is stimulated by processes typically considered racial (Pahl & Way, 2006). Conversely, racial identity attitudes are associated with embracing cultural traditions (Cokley, 2005).

For Black and Brown adolescents, their racial and ethnic background can play an essential role in their identity development. Phinney (1990) proposed a three-stage model of ethnic identity development that includes a progression from an unexamined ethnic identity through a period of exploration to an achieved or committed ethnic identity. According to her model, early adolescents who have not been exposed to ethnic identity issues are in the first status, *diffused ethnic identity*. This early stage is characterized by an adolescent's lack of active exploration of ethnic problems. A lack of interest or concern regarding ethnic issues manifests in a diffused identity level. Phinney purported that early adolescents may simply not be interested in ethnicity and may have given it little thought. Alternatively, some adolescents may have committed to an ethnic identity without exploration based on inherited ethnic attitudes from parents or other influential adults. That is, their attitudes represent a *foreclosed status*. Adolescents with diffused and foreclosed statuses are at risk of accepting and internalizing negative and faulty stereotypes and beliefs. Therefore, Phinney encourages the active exploration of one's ethnicity (*moratorium*) before reaching an *achieved identity*.

Antiracist and social justice–focused school counselors are aware of the importance of adolescent racial and ethnic identity development. Therefore, they make enhancing students' ethnic and racial identity development a significant priority when counseling. To do this, school counselors recognize that the failure of an adolescent to examine ethnic issues and their ethnic identity creates risks for poor psychological and educational adjustment. In his clinical work, Zayas (2001) found that ethnic minority youth benefit from discussing their struggles with racism and ethnic identity. In addition, he found that adolescents' struggles with their ethnic identity were made salient when issues related to peer-group relations, family relations, and achievement were elicited. In this respect, providing students the opportunity to clarify, actively explore, and examine ethnic issues and their ethnic identity would enhance student development. Finally, ethnic racial identity is an interaction between maturation and context, and thus takes different forms and has different meanings across the life span.

In addition to racial and ethnic identity, racial socialization is an important related construct. *Racial socialization* refers to the process in which individuals are taught specific cultural values and beliefs that pertain to their racial group membership (Berkel et al., 2009). Although there has been much debate in the literature regarding how race and ethnicity (and therefore racial identity and ethnic identity) may overlap as well as differ from one another (Cokley, 2007), Brondolo and colleagues (2009) argued that each of these constructs is important to consider in the literature on coping with racism, as they all "focus on shared history, values, and a common heritage" (p. 68). All three variables (racial identity, ethnic identity, racial socialization) can buffer racial discrimination on mental health. Thus, students who are socialized and more strongly identify with their race and/or ethnicity are protected from the adverse effects of racial discrimination. It provides these individuals with the knowledge that discriminatory experiences result from societal injustice rather than personal deficits.

The development of racial identities and racial consciousness was limited to the study of Black and Brown people for many decades, and it was not until the late 1980s that the idea of white racial identity became a topic of interest in psychological research. White persons also have an identity development process. According to Helms (1990), the racial and ethnic identity development of students is often influenced by the racial identity development of teachers and educators that they interact with at school. Helms describes white racial identity as involving the abandonment of racism and a nonracist white identity development. She outlines six ego schemas (formerly known as *stages* or *statuses*) in her model: contact, disintegration, reintegration, pseudo-independence, immersion/emersion, and autonomy. The *contact* schema is characterized by a lack of awareness of cultural and institutional racism, fear of people of color based on stereotypes, and lack of understanding of white privilege. Individuals in this stage have identities based on perceptions of their traits and their adoption of family and social group beliefs. School counselors in this schema are not likely to perceive cultural differences and oppression among students because they "do not see color" and have little awareness of diverse people.

The *disintegration* schema begins when the white individual has a new understanding of cultural and institutional racism. The individual may experience guilt, shame, and sometimes anger at recognizing one's advantage because of being white (i.e., white privilege). Whites in this schema become conflicted over racial moral dilemmas that are frequently perceived as opposites. For instance, a counselor may believe she is not racist, yet she refuses to acknowledge racist practices at her school. School counselors in this stage may attempt to develop cross-ethnic relationships with students and colleagues, but these relationships are likely to be superficial (Marshall, 2002). Also, school counselors in this stage may experience dissonance and conflict in choosing between own-group loyalty and challenging oppressive practices in schools.

The following schema, *reintegration,* is characterized by the white individual regressing or reverting to a dominant ideology associated with race and one's own socioracial group identity. There is a firmer and more conscious belief in white racial superiority, and racial/ethnic minorities are blamed for their problems. A school counselor in both disintegration and reintegration statuses will acknowledge differences in their students but fail to institute new practices and challenge policies that hinder the success of marginalized and oppressed youth. School counselors in the reintegration status will tend to be angry about professional development or training related to diversity because they believe that they have no role in remedying oppression or the problems of ethnic or cultural minorities.

A person is likely to move into the *pseudo-independence* schema after a painful or insightful encounter or event that moves the person from the reintegration schema. In this schema, the person attempts to understand cultural differences and may reach out to interact with culturally and racially different persons. However, the choice of culturally diverse persons is based on how similar they are to them. Persons in this schema tend to conceptualize racial and cultural issues intellectually. For example, school counselors in this schema may reach out to culturally different colleagues but not culturally diverse parents or others outside of the school setting. Pseudo-independent counselors understand white privilege and the sociopolitical aspects of race and issues of prejudice and oppression, but their understanding is from an intellectual perspective only.

The *immersion/emersion* schema is characterized by the white individual engaging in self-exploration as a racist being. The person becomes more aware of what it means to be white and how they benefit from white privilege. There is a willingness to confront one's own biases and become more of an activist in combating racism and oppression. The school counselor in the immersion/emersion schema is ready for a social justice approach to school counseling. They can recognize oppressive practices in schools, are willing to confront and challenge overt and covert racist actions, and are honest about their own biases and white privilege.

And finally, the *autonomy* schema involves the white individual's increased awareness of their whiteness, reduced feelings of guilt, acceptance of one's role in perpetuating racism, and a renewed determination to abandon white entitlement. A school counselor in this schema is knowledgeable about racial, ethnic, and cultural differences; values diversity; and is not fearful, intimidated, or uncomfortable with the reality of race. The final list in the Suggested Readings section at the end of the book offers a short selection of titles that will help counselors understand and address racial and ethnic identity development issues.

School counselors using a social justice approach are also prepared to work with students who lack an interest in exploring their racial and ethnic background (i.e., diffused or foreclosed identities). White students, in particular, may show little interest in their ethnicity because they do not see themselves as having an ethnic background. However, it is just as important for white adolescents to examine their white identity development (as outlined above). Proweller (1999) stated, "the conflicts that white students experience when asked to talk openly about whiteness as a location of racial identity reflect a profound resistance to examining their positionality, lived experience, and racial histories of domination and oppression" (p. 808). Proweller further indicated that many white students do not avoid active engagement with race but selectively engage in "race talk" within the parameters of a polite and public discourse. For this reason, school counselors should provide safe but challenging environments for white students to openly discuss their racial identity and beliefs about race relations in this country. Safe environments include settings in which students are expected to respect one another, different opinions are valued and challenged, and students are open about their identity development.

It is important to note that an individual may operate from more than one identity status at a time, and which status predominates may vary with particular situations. However, as one's cross-racial experiences increase and understanding about racism deepens, the latter statuses are more likely to be the ones shaping an individual's behavior. Because the ideology of white racial superiority is so deeply embedded in our culture, the process of unlearning racism is a journey we need to continue throughout our lives. Antiracist and social justice school counselors are aware of racial and ethnic identity development and racial socialization on student and counselor responses during the counseling process.

 ## Counseling Snapshot

Russell, a white school counselor at Kennedy High School, was asked to counsel a white male student who has recently been acting out in class. During a counseling session, the student discloses that he's frustrated that teachers look at him differently because he is dating a black girl. Russell immediately states, "That's not true. Your teachers wouldn't have a problem with you dating a black girl. They don't see color or race. Therefore, you must be imagining that they are treating you differently." The student says, "They see race, and I know they do." The counseling session ended, and Russell never returned for counseling.

Group Counseling

Group work is one mode of counseling that has been indicated in the literature as a viable means to nurture adolescents' racial and ethnic identity development

(Baca & Koss-Chioino, 1997; Malott et al., 2010). Racial and ethnic exploration groups in which students research their racial and ethnic heritage, talk with others about their racial and ethnic backgrounds, and learn new information about other cultures and ethnic groups can be implemented by school counselors to enhance students' racial and ethnic identity development. For example, an activity for a small group of eighth-grade Korean American middle school students might include completing the following statements: "Being Korean American in this community means . . ." and "Being Korean American in this school means. . . ." The counselor might also include other aspects of students' identities: "What is it like being Korean and male?" "What is it like being Korean and lesbian?" These activities can act as a catalyst for students' exploration of the meaning attached to their race and ethnicity and, in turn, enhance their overall development.

In group work, counselors might also help early adolescents process others' negative perceptions about race and ethnicity (Holcomb-McCoy & Moore-Thomas, 2001). A Mexican American male group member, for example, complains to the counselor that students are teasing him because of his Mexican name and heritage. The counselor might encourage the student to discuss his feelings about the encounter and his feelings about experiencing racism. Other group members should also have the opportunity to share similar experiences or share how they would feel in a similar situation. These group discussions can ultimately lead to an exploration of students' feelings related to their ethnic membership. The counselor in this example might also guide the group in problem-solving activities and help students determine ways to handle this situation or similar situations in the future. For example, role-playing could be implemented to help students select appropriate solutions to problems related to their ethnic group membership.

 Counseling Snapshot

J'Nita, a Black eighth-grader from Jamaica, is an honors student at Frederick Douglass Middle School. Because J'Nita is a student leader and has scored exceptionally well on gifted and talented tests, she has been selected to attend a special three-week gifted and talented summer camp. J'Nita is not excited and has told her counselor that she does not want to go. She is concerned about what the other girls (who are Black) will say about her going to a camp for three weeks with a bunch of white girls. She would rather stay home. However, J'Nita's Jamaican parents are distraught and tell the counselor that J'Nita must go to the camp.

What would you, the school counselor, say to J'Nita? To her parents? How does J'Nita's dilemma relate to her racial and ethnic identity? What might be a good solution for J'Nita's problem?

Offering Diverse and Representative Resources

Considering the importance of race and ethnicity in students' identity development, school counselors must examine counseling resources for antiracism, social justice, cultural sensitivity, and appropriateness. For instance, implementing bibliotherapy (i.e., therapy using books with characters experiencing a circumstance similar to the student in counseling) with books that include only white characters reinforces a lack of racial and ethnic exploration and acceptance. Therefore, school counseling offices should offer books, videos, and other resources with representation of people of color and various cultures to promote students' exploration and acceptance of their racial and ethnic heritages. Also, school counselors must provide opportunities for positive acknowledgment of students' racial and ethnic group membership in classroom guidance lessons, small groups, and any other school counseling activity. See the following resources that counselors can use to discuss racial/ethnic identity, antiracism, and social justice issues with students:

- *This Book Is Anti-Racist* by Tiffany Jewell

- *Stamped: Racism, Antiracism, and You* by Jason Reynolds & Ibram Kendi

- *Ghost Boys* by Jewel Parker Rhodes

- *The Hate U Give* by Angie Thomas

- *An Indigenous Peoples' History of the United States for Young People* by Roxanne Dunbar, adapted by Jean Mendoza and Debbie Reese

- *Not My Idea: A Book About Whiteness* by Anastasia Higginbotham

- *Front Desk* by Kelly Yang

- *One Crazy Summer* by Rita Williams Garcia

- *Before We Were Free* by Julia Alvarez

- *Harbor Me* by Jacqueline Woodson

- *A Good Kind of Trouble* by Lisa Moore Ramée

Racial and Ethnic Identity Questions for Students In a group, have students write brief statements in which they confidentially describe how they feel about (a) their own racial and ethnic identity, (b) members of other racial and ethnic groups, and (c) members of the dominant group (white Americans). Then have students confidentially exchange these statements, so they don't know who they came from. Then see if class members can identify which stage of racial and ethnic identity development is represented in the statements.

Assessing School Counselors' Cultural Competence

Perhaps one of the most significant challenges confronting the antiracist and social justice–focused school counselor is acquiring cultural competence. According to Ponterotto and Casas (1987), cultural competence is achieved when a counselor possesses the necessary skills to work effectively with clients from various cultural backgrounds. Hence, a counselor with high cultural competence acknowledges client–counselor racial and cultural differences and similarities as significant to the counseling process. On the other hand, a counselor with low cultural competence provides counseling services with little or no regard for the counselor's or client's culture and race.

Over the past four decades, the literature regarding cultural counseling competence has focused on three main areas or dimensions: awareness, knowledge, and skills (Sue et al., 1992). The first area, *awareness*, stresses the counselor's understanding of their worldviews and how they are the products of their cultural conditioning. The second area, *knowledge*, reinforces the importance of counselors having a sense of their clients' worldviews. Finally, Sue and colleagues pointed out that counselors must understand and respect their clients' worldviews. Traditionally, counseling, similar to other disciplines, has accepted culturally different persons if they were willing to become acculturated and reject cultural distinctiveness. However, this "melting pot" philosophy creates negative consequences if counseling techniques designed for the dominant culture are misused with clients of ethnically dissimilar backgrounds.

Finally, the *skills* area covers the counselor's ability to use culturally appropriate intervention strategies. Counseling effectiveness is improved when counselors use techniques and interventions consistent with their clients' life experiences and cultural values.

In addition to the three-dimensional framework of cultural competence, other perspectives regarding cultural competence have been offered. Holcomb-McCoy and Myers (1999) suggested that there could be more than three dimensions to cultural competence. They proposed that one must also know cultural terminology and racial identity development theories. Pope-Davis et al. (1994) suggested that cultural competence in counseling is "an appreciation of and sensitivity to the history, current needs, strengths, and resources of communities and individuals who historically have been underserved and underrepresented by psychologists" (p. 466).

As the United States becomes more culturally and economically diverse, the need to understand school counselors' multicultural self-efficacy becomes imperative

(Holcomb-McCoy et al., 2008). *The School Counselor Multicultural Self-Efficacy Scale* and *The School Counselor Cultural Competence Checklist* can be found in the Resource section at the end of the book and can be used by professional school counselors to determine additional training areas.

THE INFLUENCE OF CULTURE AND RACE ON INTERVENTION PLANNING

As stated previously, there is a critical need for antiracist and social justice–focused school counselors who can take culture into account when assessing and planning interventions for students. Culture and race determine, to a large extent, how a student experiences, identifies, interprets, and communicates a problem in school. At the same time, counselors' cultural misunderstandings or reliance on stereotypes can lead to faulty conceptualizations and interventions. School counselors need to be able to differentiate between the nuances of normal and dysfunctional patterns. This section of the chapter describes essential components of culturally appropriate problem assessment and intervention planning.

1. DETERMINING THE PROBLEM

It is the school counselor's responsibility to gather sufficient information about the student's presenting problem and then negotiate the appropriate intervention with the student. The school counselor's first task is to clarify the nature of the problem that brings the student in for help from the student's perspective. Ideally, the counselor is aware that it is inappropriate in some cultures, particularly for strangers, to ask personal questions. However, the school counselor should also keep in mind that some necessary information may have special cultural meaning. For instance, some cultures view talking directly and frankly to parents as disrespectful.

Reasons for Referral

In addition, the counselor should inquire about the primary reasons for the referral and the specific situations of the complaints. Differences in opinion on parents, caregivers, teachers, other referral sources, and the child about the severity or frequency of behavior should be identified. Misunderstandings about the reason for the referral should be addressed with the student and the individual who referred the student. For example, an evaluation of a student who may be viewed as racially and culturally different requires the counselor to explore possible racial and cultural influences that may have precipitated the referral. The following vignette is illustrative.

> Sam, a 10-year-old Black boy, was referred to the counselor for disrespectful behavior in the classroom. Described by his teacher as

confrontational, aggressive, and too autonomous, Sam demanded more freedom and challenged his teacher on classroom rules and practices. His parents' child-rearing had promoted assertiveness and independence.

The differences in Sam's parents' and teacher's perceptions of Sam were apparent. His teacher perceived him as an aggressive and angry young man. She regarded his behavior as a possible indication of an emotional disturbance or deviance. On the other hand, Sam's parents viewed his behavior as a sign of strength and as that of an independent young man.

The school counselor learned that Sam's parents sent him to a progressive, Afrocentric school to achieve their goal of a good, cultural education for their son. At that school, Sam had been told to speak up, know his mind, question authority, and be independent. The school counselor arranged a meeting between the teacher and the parents to clarify the mixed messages given to Sam. After a series of discussions led by the counselor, the teacher became more aware of her perspectives based on her racial experiences and cultural beliefs. As a result, the teacher changed her approach and focused on Sam's assertiveness as a strength.

The Contexts of Environment and Family

Details on the duration and degree of a student's problem should be explored within the context of their environment. From the onset of the first symptoms to the characteristics of the presenting problem, chronological elements of the problem behavior should be identified and recorded. The school counselor should try to determine how the behavior is reactive to recent events in the child's environment. For instance, a student is referred to the school counselor for excessive fighting. The counselor examines the cumulative folder and realizes that the student has no history of fighting and that his excessive fighting started two months ago. The counselor discovers that the student's family recently moved into a hotel because they are homeless. The counselor realizes that the fighting is a reaction to the recent stress of moving and feeling lost.

It is critical to make determinations about students' behaviors in the context of their family's culture and to examine its meaning to the child and the community. Information should be gathered about any previous counseling or mental health treatment for the presenting problem (e.g., the frequency of sessions, the length of treatment, and the child's and family's response to treatment). Suppose no formal treatment was sought or provided. In that case, the school counselor should inquire whether the family approached others within the community for help—for example, religious leaders, community leaders, godparents, or healers. This type of information provides a good sense of the family's help-seeking behavior and previous experience in resolving their problems.

2. DEVELOPMENTAL HISTORY

Obtaining a student's developmental history is a critical component in determining the most appropriate intervention. The school counselor's goal in getting developmental history is to review behavioral patterns of childhood. For example, when discussing the pregnancy and delivery of the child, the counselor must inquire about the parents' sociocultural attitudes about pregnancy, motherhood, and fatherhood and then evaluate the influence of those attitudes on the development of their child. In addition, data should be obtained about any special diets, medications, feelings about prenatal health care, and cultural attitudes regarding diet and food cravings. Sample questions might include the following:

1. Who in the immediate community supported and advised the mother about ways to ensure a safe pregnancy?

2. Did the mother and father understand the risks of smoking, taking drugs, or drinking alcohol before and during pregnancy?

3. Was the child's father available and supportive? If not, who was available to provide support?

4. Was the mother exposed to any stressful life events during the pregnancy?

5. Were there any complications in the delivery?

Despite its sensitive nature, there is a need to ask about previous infant losses. The counselor can then address the impact of such losses on maternal and paternal attitudes toward other children. School counselors should also determine whether the parents had a preference for the sex of the baby, how the baby's name was selected, what process was followed in naming the child, and whether the mother experienced any period of postpartum depression. Cultural attitudes toward weaning practices, physical arrangements in the household, decisions about the primary caregiver, and feeding should all be discussed when assessing students' problems. The importance of eliciting a student's early developmental history is demonstrated in the following example:

> Victor, a six-year-old child from El Salvador, was referred to the school counselor with school phobia and immature behavior. However, when the school counselor talked to his parents, it was learned that the child still slept with his parents and was not yet weaned from the mother's breast.

> The parents informed the school counselor that in their culture, the decision to leave the parental bed was always made by the child. However, after further questioning, it was learned that the older children in the family had made this decision at a much earlier age.

Before Victor's birth, the mother lost two infant children. When the parents first arrived in this country, the parents were still mourning, and Victor was born not long after their arrival.

3. CHILD BEHAVIOR AND DEVELOPMENT

Expectations concerning children's development and behavior vary across cultures and must be assessed in a culturally sensitive manner. Attributes such as passivity, dependence, and language and motor skills acquisition have different meanings and symbolism in different cultures. For instance, one culture may tolerate delayed motor development but not delayed verbal acquisition. Likewise, a child with learning difficulties may be shown more tolerance in some cultures than a child who demonstrates anxious behavior.

Language and communication must be assessed within a student's cultural community. For example, some cultures highly value and reinforce early verbalization and fluency. Others show primary concern about early socialization skills and affective expression. School counselors should also pay special attention to a family's view of bilingualism.

4. CHILD-REARING PRACTICES

The school counselor needs to frame child-rearing practices within the context of a student's immediate home environment and the child's stage of development. It is particularly important to compare and contrast a family's attitudes with those of the community and larger society. Counselors should pay close attention to a student's views on sex and gender-role expectations because opinions about sex education and gender-role behavior vary among cultures. For example, some cultures and families use humor and short stories to teach their children about sexuality, whereas others teach nothing about sexuality. Some cultural groups grant men greater and earlier independence than women.

For a student whose family immigrated to the United States, gender expectations in a student's home culture may differ significantly from those in the new culture. A change in gender roles as a result of immigration creates considerable conflict in some families. It is also important to understand the particular role of gender and age in a student's culture. For example, the firstborn son may be expected to assume tremendous responsibilities, regardless of his age, if the father is absent.

The school counselor should also assess a family's attitudes toward authority and their ability to determine an adequate punishment for rule infractions. Cultures vary in their discipline styles, which may involve physical punishment, embarrassment or shame, withdrawal of love, suspension of social and recreational activities, or deprivation of toys and other forms of entertainment. Physical punishment has become a highly charged issue in communities where physical abuse is prevalent and has to be reported. The school counselor must assess when the cultural norm of physical punishment becomes abusive and dangerous and must help parents find alternative and practical approaches that are culturally sensitive. Furthermore, in some cultures, families may use disciplinary styles that are inconsistent. For example, boys are punished differently than girls and adolescents differently than elementary-age children.

5. ROLE OF THE EXTENDED FAMILY

For many culturally diverse groups, extended family functions as a source of support and means by which cultural and religious values are communicated. For instance, for many Latino subcultures (e.g., Mexican Americans), the family structure is characterized by formalized kinship relations to the godparent system and loyalty. Often, the extended family takes priority over other social institutions. Native American families include parents, children, aunts, uncles, cousins, and grandparents in an active kinship system. The extended family in Black culture is quite significant. Boyd-Franklin (1989) states, "Many Black families function as extended families in which relatives with a variety of blood ties have been absorbed into a coherent network of mutual emotional and economic support" (p. 43). An assessment of extended families might arise in such cases as the following:

> Jamal Simpson, a 12-year-old student, was referred to the school counselor for fighting at recess. When the counselor met with Jamal's mother, she discovered that the family lived with Ms. Simpson's mother (Ms. Brown) and her two youngest children (ages 24 and 25). Ms. Simpson was forced to move Jamal and his younger sister to Ms. Brown's house after Jamal's father died of COVID-19. Ms. Brown's apartment has two bedrooms, a living room, a kitchen, and a bathroom. Ms. Simpson was given the smallest bedroom, which she shares with Jamal and his sister. Ms. Brown's youngest children sleep in the living room.
>
> Ms. Simpson described the living arrangement as a nightmare, and she was emotional when discussing the influence of COVID-19 on her family. She discussed how tired she is and the pressure on Jamal to be strong. Jamal, his sister, and Ms. Brown's children are grieving and fearful of more loss.

Questioning the student about their family structure and asking them to identify those members with whom they get along best and least is an excellent way to obtain information about a student's extended family. After drawing a picture of the family, counselors may ask students to indicate the family member they love, fear, and dislike most as well as the one they worry about most and the one they have the most tension with. Counselors may ask similar questions about peers and teachers.

6. SCHOOL HISTORY

Once a counselor has gained the student's trust and information from the student's family, they should gather information regarding their school history. A school history should include a list of the different schools that the child has attended, attendance rates, and documented reasons for each school change. School counselors need to address the following when assessing a student's school history:

1. student achievements

2. grade trends

3. special class placements (including special education, gifted/talented placement)

4. attendance at other types of schools (e.g., boarding schools, private schools)

5. disciplinary actions

6. out-of-school activities

7. presence of mental health diagnoses

8. history of truancy

The student should be asked which teachers, subjects, and classmates they like most and least. If the student has attended several schools, the school counselor can ask about the school the child liked the most (and least) and why. In addition, the student's answers to questions about their participation in and reaction to extracurricular activities, bilingual programs, and enrichment programs should be noted. The student might also be questioned about any experiences that singled him out for ridicule or praise.

7. INSIGHT, JUDGMENT, AND COPING SKILLS

The school counselor should also address a student's understanding of the reasons for the referral and the basis of their problem and how it might be corrected. To elicit information about the child's insight, judgment, and coping skills, the counselor might ask how they themselves would feel or what they would do. See the following scenarios.

Scenario 1: You are the only Black person in your class. Your classmates tease you and call you dumb. How would you feel? What would you do?

Scenario 2: A 16-year-old girl and her family emigrated from Thailand a year ago. The girl now wants to be identified as a typical American girl, but her parents object to her dating outside of her ethnic group. In addition, they are angry about her disregard for the customs of their homeland. If you were this girl, what would you do?

Scenario 3: Seventeen-year-old Breonna, the oldest of five children, has grown afraid to go to school because of the hate crimes against transgender people in her neighborhood and school. Breonna is a trans girl/woman and has been physically threatened by several students. What would you do if you were Breonna? How would you feel? What would you want from others?

Questions to Consider

1. Watch the following short films and motion pictures. Then identify the stages of racial or ethnic identity development portrayed by the characters using any of the racial or ethnic identity development models discussed in this chapter. The characters in these short videos and films display various stages of racial or ethnic identity development.

   - "A Conversation with My Black Son" (5 min.; "Conversation," 2015)

   - "A Conversation About Growing Up Black" (5 min.; Brewster & Peltz, 2015)

   - "A Conversation with White People on Race" (5 min.; Stephenson & Foster, 2015)

   - "A Conversation with Police on Race" (7 min.; Gandbhir & Peltz, 2015)

   - "A Conversation with Black Women on Race" (6 min.; Stephenson & Brewster, 2015)

   - "A Conversation with Latinos on Race" (7 min.; Brewster et al., 2016)

   - "A Conversation with Asian-Americans on Race" (7 min.; Gandbhir & Stephenson, 2016)

- "A Conversation with Native Americans on Race" (6 min.; Stephenson & Young, 2017)

- *I Am Not Your Negro* (2016)

- *Just Mercy* (2019)

- *Imitation of Life* (1959)

- *Forrest Gump* (1994)

- *Driving Miss Daisy* (1989)

- *Do the Right Thing* (1989)

- *Malcolm X* (1992)

- *Queen & Slim* (2019)

- *Get Out* (2017)

- *Fences* (2016)

- *If Beale Street Could Talk* (2018)

Adapted from Whittlesey (2001), Richard (1996).

2. List three counseling strategies or methods that you frequently use with students. Is the strategy culturally appropriate? Is there research to support its use with students of varying racial, ethnic, and cultural backgrounds?

3. How do you define *liberation* and *empowerment*? Research the terms to compare your definition to others' definitions. How might using these terms to describe your counseling approach change your programming and work?

4. Describe a time when you felt empowered to make or demand a change. What did you do? What skills did you use? Then, with colleagues, discuss how you can use your experiences to help students or parents feel more empowered.

5. How would you respond to a problematic student who claims, "You don't care; you are just like the other people in this school"? What will you say? What will you do to retain the student's trust and confidence? How would you approach a demanding parent who has the same claims?

CHAPTER 4

Consultation

He who opens a school door, closes a prison.

—Victor Hugo

Consultation is a very powerful process that is indirect in its approach but has the capacity to affect large numbers of students. I am a firm believer that antiracist and social justice–focused school counselors should spend a significant amount of time working as school-based consultants. For it is in this role that school counselors work to change or alter teachers', parents', or other educators' faulty thoughts, assumptions, and racist (conscious and unconscious) ideas about students and communities. It is also through consultation that school-based consultants can provide professional development for school personnel to implement creative, antiracist and culturally appropriate approaches to working with students. This chapter offers a short overview of what consultation is, the impact of culture and race on consultation, and how consultation can be used to advocate for equity. The chapter ends with an introduction to school culture and its impact on the consultation process.

DEFINING CONSULTATION?

Consultation has been defined as "a method of providing preventively oriented psychological and educational services in which consultants and consultees form cooperative partnerships and engage in a reciprocal, systematic problem-solving process to enhance and empower consultees, thereby promoting students' well-being and performance" (Zins & Erchul, 2002, p. 625). Consultation has three participants: the consultant, the consultee, and the client or problem (see Figure 4.1).

FIGURE 4.1   The Consultation Process

The consultants are the skilled professionals that understand both the consultation process and the consultees and their problems. The consultee typically brings the problem to the consultant and initiates the consultation process. Consultees are often teachers, parents, or administrators. The client is typically a student or a problem related to a particular student or group of students, parents, or teachers. In schools, consultation involves adults (e.g., consultant–teacher, consultant–parent) attempting to change or alter a student problem. The client or student is not directly involved in consultation.

Over the last forty years, several models and modes of school-based consultation have been explored and established. For instance, Kurpius (1978) introduced four modes that may occur between the counselor and consultant: prescription, provision, initiation, and collaboration. The mediation mode was introduced by Baker in 1981. More recently, issues related to advocacy and empowerment (e.g., Holcomb-McCoy & Bryan, 2010), multiculturalism (e.g., Ingraham, 2000), feminism (e.g., Hoffman et al., 2006) and cultural competence (Fung et al., 2012) in consultation have been addressed in the literature but not in an exhaustive manner.

SCHOOL-BASED CONSULTATION

Consultation has been a major function within the school counselor's role, beginning in the years when counselors provided "guidance" services (Baker et al., 2009). The consultant or school counselor provides direct service to the consultee, who delivers direct service to the client system, which is typically the student, the classroom, or the students' family. Consultees, namely teachers and parents, are drawn to school counselors for the purpose of problem solving, making school-based consultation a critical function for school counselors and the function that has the greatest capacity to impact hundreds of students and even an entire school community.

RACE, CULTURE, AND EQUITY IN CONSULTATION

Counselors will undoubtedly encounter issues related to race/racism, culture, and equity when consulting with parents and teachers. School-based teacher consultation has the potential to promote equity in many areas, most notably regarding disproportionality in school discipline, low expectations of students, bias in the classroom, lack of representation in advanced courses or tracking (e.g., honors programs, gifted and talented programs), and cultural responsiveness in the classroom. However, in existing research and training, the potential for understanding cultural and racial issues in consultation has received limited attention. Most of the literature written on cultural issues in consultation have been published in school psychology journals and books, whereas little research on school counselor consultation to dispel inequities has been found in the literature. Clearly, when consulting with educators and parents, school counselors need to understand the power of environmental and societal factors on the client (e.g., child), the consultee, and the consultation process.

SOCIAL JUSTICE CONSIDERATIONS AND THE CONSULTATION PROCESS

In the classic consultation article, Gibbs (1985) suggested that the culturally skilled consultant should not be "colorblind." Although the intent of colorblindness may be to remove bias from the process, it can serve to deny the existence of differences in students' and consultees' perceptions of society arising from membership in culturally diverse groups. Overall, school-based consultants are ineffective if they ignore the influence of culture on their behavior, their consultee's behavior, and their client's behavior.

CULTURAL DIFFERENCES

Cultural differences have been found to be significant factors in the counseling relationship, causing difficulties in establishing trust and rapport. The same has been purported to be the case in consultation. For instance, Gibbs (1985) indicated that Black teachers responded differently to outside consultants than white teachers. She found that white teachers were quicker to trust a consultant and embrace the goals and tasks of consultation (instrumental style). Black teachers, on the other hand, were more interested in building a relationship of trust with the consultant. Gibbs purported that Black consultees preferred an interpersonal (relationship orientation) rather than an instrumental (task orientation) consultant style. As a result of her observations, Gibbs recommended that consultants who work with Black consultees or teachers would fare better if they focused on relationship building before the problem at hand. The research on Gibbs' model, nevertheless, has been contradictory. Duncan and Pryzwansky (1993), for instance, found that Black teachers in their study preferred the instrumental rather than the interpersonal style of consultation.

It is important to remember that school-based consultants should avoid identifying cultural differences as the problem (e.g., blaming a student's immigration status as the reason for a student's misbehavior). When cultural factors are viewed as the problem, the participants in the consultation are more likely to feel powerless in the problem-solving stage. Therefore, demographic variables such as race, class, religion, or marital status of the parent should never be perceived as the source of a student's or parent's problem. The following vignette provides an example:

> Sean, an 11-year-old white sixth-grader, has been referred to the counselor because of his lying and behavioral problems in class. Ms. Rogers, Sean's mother, is single with four children, ages 17, 16, 11, and 7. The counselor decides to consult with Ms. Rogers about Sean's problem behavior. After discovering that Ms. Rogers is single, the counselor assumes that Sean's problems stem from his mother's marital status. "If Sean had a father in the home, he would be better behaved." The problem, according to the counselor, is the mother's marital status rather than what is happening in Sean's classroom.

The counselor in the above vignette made a mistake by blaming Sean's problem on a cultural difference or a demographic characteristic (e.g., the marital status of his mother). It is quite possible that Sean's problem behavior is related to Sean's feelings about school or classwork, his peer relationships, or the teacher's classroom management. The counselor should gather more information about Sean's behaviors and feelings before making a conclusion.

CONSULTATION STRATEGIES

The strategies used in consultation can be roughly divided into two types: those that focus on the presentation of new information or ideas as the primary change agent and those that focus on the relationship between the consultee and the consultant as the source of change.

THE PROBLEM WITH PRESENTING ONLY INFORMATION

Many school-based consultants view the consultant–consultee relationship as important only to the extent that it facilitates the dissemination of knowledge regarding appropriate instructional and parenting practices. Such consultants generally adhere to behavioral or cognitive-behavioral theories and use psychoeducational approaches to alter student behavior. This approach can create several problems if cultural factors are not taken into account. Parents from culturally, economically, and racially diverse backgrounds may be suspicious of behavior modification techniques that use terminology such as *aversive conditioning, behavior control, extinction*, and *stimulus–reward*. For many parents, these terms infer intrusive treatments and possibly damaging interventions.

Consultation based solely on education and imparting information may also fail to consider the importance of psychosocial influences such as family structure, cultural value systems, interactional patterns, and adaptive coping strategies on behavior and functioning in culturally diverse families. For example, many culturally diverse families traditionally involve extended families such as grandparents to a greater extent in family decision making and child-rearing practices.

In addition to differences in family structure, consultation may be influenced by the adaptive coping strategies of many culturally diverse groups. These coping strategies (e.g., suspicion of outsiders, group unity) are necessary for dealing with hostile environments and are often misdiagnosed as pathological if not examined within the appropriate cultural context. There is literature documenting the misclassification of Black and Latinx/Hispanic children as having behavior problems (Oswald et al., 1999).

Consultants who work with parents should be cautious in assuming that referrals involving racially diverse students have been accurately diagnosed due to biased assessments and faulty assumptions. A consultant's attempts to change what are assumed to be maladaptive behaviors may lead to ineffective interventions not addressing the true source of difficulty or, most importantly, to resistance and hostility from parents. The child in the following vignette provides an example:

> Anthony Hill, a 5-year-old Black male kindergartner, was brought to the counselor because of his biting, hitting, and screaming episodes in class. Because his behaviors disrupted class, he was sent to the principal's office for at least an hour per day. After many attempts to change Anthony's behavior through contracts and punishments, the child study team gives Anthony a nonclassified disability label. As a follow-up, the child study team recommended that the counselor consult with Ms. Hill (Anthony's mother) about disciplining him at home. The counselor/consultant met with Ms. Hill and discovered that she works at night and her aunt looks after Anthony at night. The counselor also discovered that Ms. Hill and her aunt have set limited boundaries for Anthony and that he gets very little sleep because he stays up watching TV with his older cousins. The counselor concludes that Anthony may not have a disability; rather, his behavior is the result of lack of sleep. The counselor advocates for Anthony to be reevaluated and continues parent consultation focusing on setting boundaries at home.

THE BENEFITS OF DEVELOPING THE RELATIONSHIP

Consultants working toward social justice assume that the establishment of a warm and supportive relationship is a prerequisite to a significant change in the behavior of teachers or parents. Both consultants and consultees may enter into the consulting relationship with preconceived and inaccurate expectations of each other that are based on both conscious and unconscious perceptions. Asian cultures, for instance, traditionally view relationships to be hierarchical and value deference to authority figures. Parents adhering to such cultural values may, therefore, expect the consultant to provide advice and direction, whereas a parent with more Westernized values may expect more of an egalitarian relationship. Blacks have been reported to present passive resistance in helping alliances because of their anticipation of racial prejudice and discrimination by white American counselors. This resistance often leads to early termination, passive behavior, and discontent with the services provided (Locke, 1998).

The consultation relationship may also be influenced by the consultant's attitudes and beliefs. For example, Kalyanpur and Rao (1991) identified three qualities that were related to low-income Black mothers' negative perceptions of outreach consultants. First, consultants' perceived lack of respect for them and their failure to trust them were cited as significant barriers to fostering a collaborative relationship with the mothers. Second, the consultants' focus on the mothers and their children's deficits while ignoring their strengths also undermined the consultation relationship. The third factor leading to an impaired relationship between the mothers and the consultants involved a lack of appreciation toward the mothers' parenting styles, which were often blamed for children's behavioral problems at school. In the following example, the counselor neglects to build on the parent's strength and positive attributes:

> Marian, an experienced school counselor, meets with Sharon, a single mother of two children at Marian's middle school. Marian is meeting with Sharon to discuss Sharon's oldest son, Trevor. Trevor is failing four out of his six classes. This is new behavior for Trevor; in the past, he maintained a *C* average in all of his courses. Marian starts the consultation session by stating, "Well, I'm glad you could finally come in. You were late the last time and I thought you were going to be late again." She then proceeds to tell Sharon what she perceives as the problem: "Trevor is failing his courses and I believe you just need to discipline him more. Create a structured study space for him and make sure he gets his work in. If you would give him structure, he would do better."

THE POWER OF ADVOCACY

In many ways, consultation can be regarded as a special form of advocacy that attempts to mediate and promote the actions of at least two other parties. For counselors in schools, consultation consists of going outside the counseling office and entering the classrooms and other elements of the school and community. For social justice–focused school counselors, consultation is often used as an advocacy tool. Advocating for the use of culturally responsive practices in teaching, learning, and parenting can have a powerful impact on student success.

A common consultation/advocacy scenario might involve a teacher who is having difficulties with a student with a behavioral or learning problem. The teacher, not trained in special education, is frustrated with the student's attitude and performance in class. The teacher tries several strategies and interventions and finds that nothing is working satisfactorily. In a school where consultation and advocacy are practiced, the counselor as consultant can provide the teacher with new information on behavioral techniques and with assistance from experts in special education and meet with her to develop modified classroom strategies and accommodations that better meet the needs of the student.

QUESTIONING DOMAINS

One of the most important aspects of consultation is the consultant's ability to ask the right questions to get the right information from the consultee. This process of questioning is critical because if the problem is misidentified, then the interventions will not get to the root of the real problem. There are three domains of questions that should be addressed during consultation from social justice and antiracist perspectives. Those domains are

- student domain,

- consultee (e.g., teacher, parent) domain, and

- environmental and cultural domain.

The student domain consists of questions regarding the student's characteristics, behaviors, and perceptions. Sample questions would include the following: What does the student do that concerns you? How is the student progressing academically? Does the student have friends? Describe the student's behavior in class. Describe the student's strengths.

The consultee domain consists of questions regarding the consultee's behavior, skills, perceptions, and characteristics. Sample questions would include the following: What classroom interventions have you (the teacher) tried? What do you do when the student misbehaves? What do you like about the student? How might your beliefs and attitudes affect your response to the student? How are you culturally or racially different from the student? Does your culture (e.g., belief systems), racial background, or other factors have an impact on your perceptions of this student?

The environmental and cultural domain consists of questions that cover cultural and environmental variables that could be influencing the problem. Sample questions include the following: What do the other students do when this student misbehaves? What family issues might be influencing the student's problem? What classroom factors might be influencing the student's behavior? What role does the student's culture play in this problem?

Counseling Snapshot

Jim, a high school biology teacher, comes to you, the school counselor. Jim is having problems with a ninth-grade student who is openly gay. According to Jim, the student is belligerent, defiant, and talks too much in class. Jim tells the counselor that the student talks too much about his sexuality in class and that he annoys the other students. He says that he warned the student that he would send him to the office the next time he spoke out in class. The student has not changed his behavior and Jim wonders if he should have him taken out of his class.

Develop a list of questions that you would ask Jim based on the three domains of consultant questions.

ASSESSING SCHOOL CULTURE

School-based consultants working from an antiracist and social justice framework should be genuinely concerned about the school environment in which teachers, parents, and students must resolve their problems. For this reason, assessing a school's culture is a critical component of school-based consultation. An assessment of a school's culture gives the consultant an idea of the context in which a problem is occurring, and it helps the consultant determine how a problem can be resolved within a given environment.

The field of education lacks a clear and consistent definition of *school culture*. The term has been used synonymously with a variety of concepts, including *climate, ethos,* and *saga.* School culture involves the values, beliefs, and norms that lay the foundation for a school's climate, programs, and practices. School culture can also be defined as the historically transmitted patterns of meaning that include the norms, values, beliefs, ceremonies, rituals, traditions, and myths understood, maybe in varying degrees, by members of the school community. This system of meaning often shapes what people think and how they act. Unfortunately, one of the continuing problems includes prevalent underlying erroneous and harmful beliefs about Black and Brown students. Low expectations and negative stereotypes (e.g., deficient intelligence, lazy, criminals) are often reflected in common educational practices, such as assigning Black students to special education classes at disproportionately higher levels. Thus, for many students of color, these overall negative perceptions of their racial and cultural group create a damaging climate that can evolve into self-degrading, self-hating feelings and behaviors.

Creating a racist-free school culture, in which all students are expected to achieve, should be a goal of all school counselors. School counselors must be able to identify characteristics of white supremacy that manifests within the norms and standards of schools' organizational structures. These structures need to be named and adjusted to ensure a racist-free environment. The characteristics are damaging to both people of color and white people in that they elevate the values, preferences, and experiences of one racial group above all others. Organizations that are led by people of color or have a majority of people of color can also demonstrate characteristics of white supremacy culture. Below are characteristics of an antiracist school culture that counselors can use as a guide to helping school leaders and teachers conceptualize a racist-free, socially just, and equitable learning environment.

1. Establish a school mission statement with a commitment to antiracism and social justice. School leaders, including school counselors, communicate commitments to social justice, antiracism, and equity. Core values are clear. Terms such as *structural racism*, *white supremacy*, and *microaggressions* should be explicitly taught, discussed, and defined within the context of the local school community and history.

2. Establish a schoolwide understanding of micro and macro aggressions. These should be avoided.

3. Practice a culture of *microaffirmations*, which are small acts that foster inclusion, listening, comfort, and support for people who may feel isolated or invisible in an environment.

4. Allocate financial resources to promoting antiracism, social justice, and equity.

5. Review and change school curriculum (including school counseling curriculum) and materials to reflect a commitment to antiracism, social justice, and equity.

6. Ritualize meeting spaces—use humanizing ways to begin and close meetings. Closing rituals such as process checks, which include patterns of participation and facilitator moves, bring a reflective and purposeful closing tone.

7. Redistribute decision-making structures to reflect the organization's diversity. Structure school meetings to flatten positional hierarchy, especially in cultures that put a strong emphasis on titles and positions.

8. Establish norms that create "brave spaces"; norms should reflect a culture of curiosity, listening, and vulnerability.

9. Recruit, hire, and retain a diverse faculty and staff. Establish mentoring processes to ensure effective onboarding of new members of the school community.

10. Engage in storytelling: Storytelling helps to build intentional personal and professional relationships around shared values and identity.

11. Establish lines of accountability with the school community.

In teacher consultation, school counselors must be ready and prepared to examine the classroom culture; this includes an examination of effectiveness and preparation of teachers in promoting academic achievement for an increasingly diverse student population. Though all faculty should be aware, white faculty may, consciously or unconsciously, resist looking into how race and racism both privilege them within schools and influence their behaviors with students. Because teachers can make some students feel insignificant through their selection of educational material and teaching style, the cultural differences between them and their students must be explored. In cases where these faculty are white, assumptions about race and its influence on their classroom teaching are often left unexplored. When white teachers resist confronting such assumptions, they can simultaneously abandon the needs of their racially minoritized students, reinforce white racial knowledge, and dismiss the effects of racism to maintain white innocence. The result of this cyclical, highly cemented process suggests that there is a relationship between racial consciousness and a white faculty member's ability to employ behaviors in their classroom that promote equitable educational outcomes for racially minoritized students.

To create schools that support student success, school counselors must transform school cultures in ways that result in the elimination of harmful institutional practices and policies. Teacher consultation provides the means for creating school culture change. Social justice–focused school counselors assess their school's culture and work to make it more positive and conducive to student success. More importantly, antiracist and social justice–focused school counselors believe that school cultures can change!

Goldring (2002) provides a useful framework for consultation that divides school culture into three levels:

Level I: Things that can be observed—the way time and space are arranged, meetings are organized, budgets decided, communication and conflict managed, and celebrations held (e.g., discipline policies, course schedules, parent involvement)

Level II: The values everyone believes in—felt through behaviors and relationships of staff or symbols that represent the school. Staff (e.g., teachers, counselors, administrators) diversity is a symbol of a school's commitment to equity, diversity, and inclusion.

Level III: Collected assumptions gathered by a group over time—these assumptions determine who is accepted in a group, the extent of sharing between members (e.g., how college information is distributed to students), and so forth.

Creating school cultures that help students become resilient is a critical aspect of school counseling. *Resiliency* is the ability to bounce back from persistent stress and crisis. Building caring support systems is one way in which resiliency is fostered and cultivated. Denbo (2002) indicated that schools that promote resilience have the following characteristics:

- promote close bonds

- value and encourage education

- use high-warmth, low-criticism styles of interaction

- set and enforce clear boundaries (rules, norms, and laws)

- encourage supportive relationships with many caring others

- promote the sharing of responsibilities, service to others, and required helpfulness

- provide access to resources for meeting the basic needs of housing, nutrition, employment, health care, and recreation

- set high and realistic expectations for success

- encourage goal setting and mastery

- encourage development of prosocial values (such as altruism) and life skills (such as cooperation)

- provide opportunities for leadership, decision making, and other meaningful ways to participate

- support the unique talents of each individual

SOURCE: Denbo (2002, p. 56). Reprinted with permission from Charles C. Thomas Publisher.

Counselor in Action

What is the culture of your school? Think about your school in terms of Goldring's three levels of school culture. List things that can be observed (e.g., rituals, ceremonies, celebrations, master schedules), important values that everyone believes in, assumptions that are inherent in school policies, and so forth. What changes need to be made in your school's culture? Who and what groups of people set the tone for the culture of your school?

Antiracist and social justice–focused school counselors, teachers, and administrators work together to promote these characteristics to create school cultures that nurture and promote resilience among students. As with good counseling, building resilience is rooted in developing meaningful and respectful relationships with students. Antiracist and social justice–focused school counselors are also actively involved in the assessment of school culture. For more information on creating an antiracist organizational culture, school culture assessment, and other resources, see the list below:

- Racial Justice Assessment Tool (Western States Center, 2015)

- Multicultural School Climate (Marx & Byrnes, 2012)

- *Changing School Culture for Black Males* by Dr. Jawanza Kunjufu (2013)

- *Everyday Antiracism: Getting Real About Race in School* by Mica Pollock (2008)

- *Schooltalk: Rethinking What We Say About and To Students Every Day* by Mica Pollock (2017)

- *Radical Care: Leading for Justice in Urban Schools* by Rosa L. Rivera-McCutchen and Jamaal A. Bowman (2021)

- *Ratchetdemic: Reimagining Academic Success* by Christopher Emdin (2021)

- Advancing the Mission: Tools for Equity, Diversity and Inclusion (JustPartners, Inc., & The Annie E. Casey Foundation, 2009)

Also see the Resources section at the end of this book for sample school culture assessment items.

Questions to Consider

1. How much time do you spend per week consulting with teachers? How much time do you spend with parents? Is this more or less than what you desire? How much time do you believe you should spend consulting? Why?

2. What are the three most prevalent issues or problems that bring teachers to you for help? What types of interventions or resolutions are used to resolve the problems? What would you like to do in the future to help teachers overcome these problems?

3. You determine that a teacher is biased against Black male students. How would you approach this topic with the teacher? Role-play how you would discuss this topic in consultation.

CHAPTER 5

Connecting Schools and Communities

Education is for improving the lives of others and for leaving your community and the world better than you found it.

—Marian Wright Edelman

The key to increasing student success is to increase community and family involvement in schools. Schools that partner with families, parents, and community-based groups have observed increased youth antiracism action (Aldana et al., 2019). Although research (e.g., Sheldon & Jung, 2015) has indicated that family and community involvement increases student success and achievement, some schools are still slow to embrace real, authentic community partnerships.

Over the past two decades, the participation of professional school counselors in the development and implementation of school–family–community (SFC) partnerships has also been endorsed and strongly encouraged as a means to remedy uneven student outcomes and to enhance social capital among community members (Bemak, 2000; Bryan & Holcomb-McCoy, 2004; Bryan et al., 2019; Griffin & Steen, 2010; Holcomb-McCoy, 2004). Most advocates for SFC partnerships believe that school counselors, if involved in SFC partnerships, may better meet the personal, social, academic, and career needs of larger numbers of students. In addition, it is believed that school counselors have the necessary skills (e.g., consultation, collaboration) to carry out tasks related to promoting, developing, and implementing SFC partnerships.

For school counseling programs with antiracist and social justice orientations, school counselors recognize the benefits of connecting schools and communities and, therefore, spend a considerable amount of time working with parents and community-based groups and organizations. They realize that with solid SFC partnerships, there is a higher likelihood of equitable student success, better attendance, more completion of homework, more positive attitudes and behaviors among students (and parents!), higher graduation rates, and greater enrollment in higher education. At the same time, antiracist school counselors understand that schools, including teachers and school leaders, typically expect parents to engage with the school system in ways consistent with white, middle-income parenting and behavioral norms and in ways that are deferential to the school's agenda. Herein lies the areas of SFC partnerships that must change.

AVOIDING THE BLAME GAME AND RACIST NARRATIVES

I have worked with many schools that have a culture of blaming and demeaning parents and communities, particularly Black/Brown and low-income communities. When working with an elementary school staff, I asked them to analyze data regarding parent participation in the parent–teacher organization, teacher conferences, and volunteering. The data showed that the same parents participated across all three parent activities. Essentially, only 2% of the parents in the entire school were actively involved in school-related activities and events. After examining parent data, we examined the amount of interaction between the school and its local community organizations, agencies, families, and so forth. There was only one community organization that was visible in the school—child protective services. The same was true about the uneven communication with parents. Black and Brown parents in this school received more negative communications from teachers than white and Asian students. It was apparent that the school staff had done very little to connect positively to the community it served. During our dialogue about the data, the following comments were made:

- "The parents and community don't care about education because they don't come to the school! They only come to the school to complain."

- "We've done all we can do to get more involvement!"

- "If only we had more parental involvement, then we could do our jobs better!"

These types of statements shift the accountability away from school professionals and onto parents and community. Connecting schools, families, and communities require that school professionals, parents, and community members share the responsibility of educating children. The common cause among educators and community members is to tackle systemic inequities by joining with those who have been excluded, marginalized, or oppressed by schooling. Through authentic, meaningful, ongoing, and reciprocal learning and thinking about inequities (i.e., problem posing), all stakeholders can take action against the inequitable structures.

SFC also requires that educators and parents refrain from blaming one another for their challenges. They must collaborate and schools must develop policies that acknowledge the power of family and parent involvement, activities that systematically infuse parents' and community members' perspectives, knowledge, and skills into school life, and ongoing evaluation to assess and improve the partnership. Three primary roles of the school include

1. giving parents equitable and equal access to information to support their children's education,

2. coordinating community programming that meets the needs and issues that students and their families encounter, and

3. recognizing the rights of parents—and their fundamental competence—to share in decision making.

This chapter provides an equity framework for reciprocal partnerships and guidelines for developing SFC partnerships by looking at the five principles of effective SFC partnerships as suggested by the Education Alliance at Brown University: policies, leadership, communication, community, and evaluation.

EQUITY FRAMEWORK FOR RECIPROCAL PARTNERSHIPS

Ballard (1999) states that equity means removing "all barriers to learning . . . for all those experiencing disadvantage" (p. 2). As such, all equity efforts in schools must be grounded in dismantling the status quo (e.g., policies, practices, programs, resources, communications) so that all students and families are served equally and equitably. Essentially, equity means ensuring that all students have access and opportunities for success. In response to the need for SPC partnerships grounded in equity, Teemant et al. (2021) proposes that educators view equity as

- a relational, inclusive, and values-driven change process;

- inherently grounded in community with all of its social, cultural, historical, and political realities; and

- requiring a systems-thinking approach.

Antiracist and socially just schools, therefore, cannot occur when school counselors work in isolation and only in the school. In practice, school counselors must intentionally decide to work together with school stakeholders (i.e., the community) for a common cause—to tackle systemic inequities. School stakeholders are framed as agents of equity and are perceived by school counselors as "required thought partners" in the change process, thus all stakeholders must have voice regarding the scope and content of school counseling programs. The change process is guided by the values of mutual respect, democratic participation (e.g., power sharing), critical consciousness (e.g., naming privilege or marginalization), and sustainability (e.g., accountability to commitments). These values represent a starting point for work with community members. As partnerships develop over time, trust deepens and shared perspectives take shape. Figure 5.1 includes a depiction of Teemant et al.'s equity framework for SFC partnerships.

FIGURE 5.1   Equity Framework for Reciprocal Family, Community, and School Partnerships

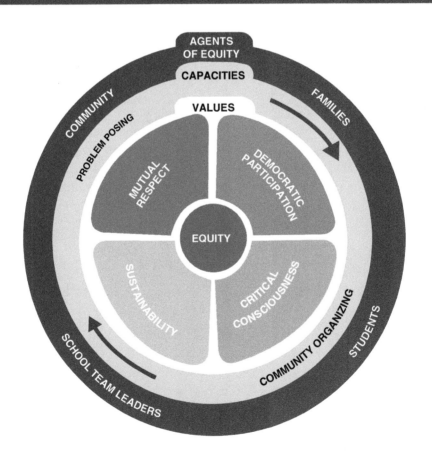

SCHOOL COUNSELING TO CLOSE OPPORTUNITY GAPS

Describe your relationships, hierarchies, structures, and patterns of communication with community groups, including parents and families from all communities represented in your school. Have you engaged in authentic discussions with community members in which addressing systemic inequities and racism have been at the core of the conversation? If not, why not? If yes, how did it go?

FIVE PRINCIPLES OF EFFECTIVE SFC PARTNERSHIPS

1. POLICIES

School communities rely on policies to guide their actions and inform their decisions. As such, specific policies regarding family involvement should be written to spell out the expectation that schools will institute, embrace, and support programs and activities that engage families and communities in children's education. Other critical policies (e.g., policies related to curriculum development, assessment, school climate) should be reviewed to integrate diverse parents' perspectives. Policies should reflect the attitude, mission, and philosophy of the school and its community. They should be developed collaboratively with parents and community members to be certain they represent the concerns of community groups, families, and foster families. See the example of an SFC policy below:

To support the mission of Mission Oaks Elementary School to educate all students effectively, schools and parents must work together as knowledgeable partners. The administration will support, through the California Department of Education, assistance in developing a strong comprehensive parent involvement program at Mission Oaks. The efforts should be designed to

- help parents develop skills to meet the basic obligations of family life and foster conditions at home that emphasize the importance of education and learning.

- promote two-way (school-to-home and home-to-school) communication about school programs and students' progress.

- involve parents, with appropriate training, in instructional and support roles at the school and in other locations that help the school and students reach stated goals, objectives, and standards.

- provide parents with strategies and techniques for assisting their children with learning activities at home that support and extend the school's instructional program.

- involve parents in school decision making and develop their leadership skills in governance and advocacy.

- provide parents with skills to access community and support services that strengthen school programs, family practices, and student learning and development.

■■■ Thinking About Your School

How does your school's mission statement demonstrate a commitment to family and community partnerships?

What family involvement policies currently exist in your school? What policies should be developed?

What other policies exist that should be reviewed and revised with family and community input?

How are parents, teachers, and community members involved in writing school policies?

How is information gathered from diverse groups of parents to guide policy development (i.e., do you use surveys, interviews, etc.)? Does your process of information gathering work?

How are parents involved in school leadership teams or councils? How could their roles be strengthened and improved? How are parents who typically don't participate involved? Are parent groups representative of all cultural, racial, and linguistic groups in the school's community?

Do family partnership policies result in higher achievement and a stronger school community? How is this assessed?

How do school policies reinforce state and district family involvement policies?

2. LEADERSHIP

School leadership has moved well beyond the authoritative model in which the principal and other school leaders make all the decisions. School counselors working from an antiracist and social justice framework are leaders in the school, yet they understand that leadership must be shared with parents and the community to build a genuine sense of collaboration. Social justice–focused school counselors encourage and seek out the participation of nontraditional school leaders from families and the community. These nontraditional leaders would include clergy, small business owners, transportation workers, police officers, grandparents, uncles, aunts, godparents, and community stakeholders.

For successful SFC partnerships, it is also important that an administrator or individual with power and resources assure staff that adequate funding exists to support SFC programs, that space and equipment needs are met, that there is regular training and development for staff and community members, and that all members of the community are invited to play meaningful and appropriate roles in the school.

■ ■ ■ Thinking About Leadership

What is your philosophy of leadership and what impact does it have on your school counseling program? What impact does it have on your work with parents?

Do you consider yourself a leader in your school? Why or why not?

What is your principal's philosophy of leadership and what impact does it have on the school? What impact does it have on you?

What is your principal's view of how parents should be involved in the school and in their children's education?

How and when does your principal talk about family partnerships? Do they support teachers in discussing family partnerships regularly (e.g., at grade-level meetings)? Does the principal place expectations on teachers in that regard?

Does the school's budget include a line item supporting SFC partnerships?

Does the school have a staff member dedicated to coordinating family involvement? Is the school counselor involved in coordinating SFC involvement? Why or why not?

Are racially and culturally diverse parents and community members involved in the planning, implementation, and evaluation of partnership activities?

Are racially and culturally diverse parents and community members included at curriculum meetings, professional development workshops, and staff retreats?

3. COMMUNICATION

Clear lines of communication build relationships between schools and families. Frequent, thoughtful, and diverse methods of communicating provide the strongest signals of genuine collaboration. Homes and schools hold critical information about children that must be shared. Families need to know what their children are learning and how to best support that learning at home. Teachers need to know about children's personalities, learning styles, and developmental history.

Families and schools should establish an expectation that communication will occur frequently and take many forms, including face-to-face meetings, regular written communications by email, telephone, and special methods of contact when events warrant it. In addition to building pathways of information about children and their learning, schools should pay special attention to communicating in a culturally sensitive manner with clear and thorough information about the basics, such as school events, day-to-day logistics (e.g., child pick-up routines, the daily schedule, homework expectations), and how parents can access community resources to support their parenting.

In the area of teacher–parent communication, sociologist Hua-Yu Sebastian Cherng (2016) found that race, ethnicity, and immigration status factor strongly. In his study, teachers were more likely to reach out to parents of Black and Latinx students about behavioral problems. And teachers were less likely to reach out to parents they perceived as uninterested and uninvolved.

In addition to means of communication, schools should pay close attention to how educators communicate with parents. Giles (2005) contends that there are three basic narrative patterns underlying the relationships between parents and educators: (a) the deficit, (b) *in loco parentis*, and (c) relational. In the *deficit* narrative, educators consider working-class and low-income parents to be deprived, deviant, or at-risk and have low expectations for their involvement in their children's education. The *in loco parentis* narrative shares the assumption that parents are not capable of contributing to their children's education and development, but the educators assume that they can compensate for the parents' deficits themselves. In other words, there is a sense among educators that they can educate students in spite of their families rather than in concert with them. And finally, there is the *relational narrative*. In this narrative, educators work *with* parents rather than *for* them. Educators working within this narrative expect parents to bring knowledge and strengths to improving the school and parents expect educators to do the same.

■ ■ ■ Thinking About Communicating with Parents and Families

How does your school communicate with parents and families? What is the rationale behind each method of communication? What are the gaps?

How well do teachers and other staff know their students' families?

How specifically does the school communicate with parents about learning and academics?

How are parents involved in decisions about their children's learning?

How are parents greeted when they come into your school? Are parents of different cultural groups greeted differently? How quickly do they receive answers to their questions?

How are families involved in suggesting and supporting home-school communications?

How would the community, parents, and staff each describe the culture of your school?

4. THE COMMUNITY

Developing a SFC initiative targeting families of color and low-income families requires broad-based outreach with the help of representatives from all community stakeholder groups. Truly successful schools extend invitations to the community to participate and keep the community fully informed on school activities, progress, and performance. Participation can involve the sharing of experience from other contexts (commercial, service agency work), the exchange of ideas and information, connections to critical financial and material resources, valuable perspectives that can inform school mission and goals, and the reinforcement of the critical notion that the school and community are working toward common objectives.

Keeping the community fully informed about what is happening at the school leads to a sense of openness and honesty, illustrates the achievements of the school and the challenges that lie ahead, and builds support for annual budgets and new initiatives. A primary reason for schools to invest in creating community partnerships is to build the capacity of others to support the school and to nurture potential leaders.

In addition to working with community stakeholders, it is also important for social justice–focused counselors to identify the formal and informal power structures in the community, including the top players or most powerful community members, their connections, and their positions on education issues. Social justice–focused counselors should reach out to local politicians and state legislators with mailings and briefings about school–community initiatives. It is possible that they will support the initiatives for their own political gains. Here are sample selection criteria for SFC partnership committees.

Criteria for Selection of School–Family–Community Committee Members

1. Identify and involve people whose support is absolutely critical, such as your school principal or chief administrator. If they do not actively support your initiative, it will never get off the ground. Also involve school faculty who will be directly affected by any changes in prevention programming. Gottfredson et al. (2000) found that school activities "initiated, selected, or planned by 'insiders' (i.e., persons within a school organization) tend to be more accepted by school staff; impulses to resist adoption or implementation sometimes triggered by programs imposed upon a school are less likely to be evoked" (p. 2).

2. Identify influential community leaders. These are people who can command attention, make decisions, involve others in positions of leadership, and provide access and influence. For example, a well-connected parent activist can rally a community around an issue.

3. Identify members from diverse backgrounds, including different religious, racial/ethnic, language, age, and socioeconomic groups. If you have difficulty recruiting a diverse team, invite stakeholders and community members who are strong advocates for particular causes or concerns (e.g., NAACP [National Association for the Advancement of Colored People] member).

4. Find people who have a strong interest in helping the school and community address problems. Passion and commitment will ultimately drive your initiative. Identify members who share your zeal and who will go the extra mile to get things done because they truly care about kids and believe in the potential of prevention.

5. Involve members whose positions, expertise, and skills match the purpose of your initiative. Initially, you may want to involve key stakeholders who can help you build community support. As your plan evolves and becomes more concrete, you will need to involve people who can help you implement your prevention strategies and, ultimately, institutionalize your efforts:

   a. If curriculum implementation is the focus of your work, make sure to involve teachers, curriculum coordinators, parents, nurses, and guidance counselors.

   b. If changing community norms is your focus, involve grassroots activists and community citizens.

   c. If service coordination is the focus, involve school counselors and psychologists, health care and social service providers, and teachers.

d. Involve students—and listen to them! Students know what's going on. They bring their own perspectives on strategies that will be most effective and can help you get participation from the student body.

Based on information from Epstein et al. (2002).

■ ■ ■ Thinking About Community Partnerships

What partners has your school invited to the table to participate in essential school matters? Who is missing?

How does your school support community partners? How do each of the partners contribute? How do they benefit from participating in your school's efforts?

What technical support is needed to sustain partnerships (a meeting convener, regular email updates, conference calls, etc.)?

How are nontraditional or harder-to-reach groups from the community contacted and involved?

Who are the naysayers in the community who could become better informed about the school and invited to participate?

How are the energies of different partners assessed? Are these partners being used to their best and most efficient advantage?

5. EVALUATION

In a comprehensive and systematic way, the school should revisit goals, assess progress, and make adjustments in its family- and community-involvement programs. Evaluation efforts might focus on the satisfaction of the partners in terms of their roles, accomplishments resulting from family and community involvement (especially those relating directly to student achievement), lessons learned, and new elements to add.

Evaluation methods should be broad-based (including both qualitative and quantitative methods such as interviews, focus groups, and surveys), collecting information from the key players as well as parents and community members in general. Although basic information can be helpful, such as the number of parents who attend meetings, it is also important to look deeply into important issues, such as how parent leaders have emerged and what strategies have worked to develop more diverse parent participation. Careful consideration should be given to how the original vision of family and community involvement has changed, what the new expectations are, and how programs and policies will support new directions.

■■■ Thinking About Evaluation

What kind of evaluation has been conducted to assess the effectiveness of the family and community involvement program?

How thorough is the evaluation and what components could be added?

How are the lessons of evaluation used?

How are parents and community members involved in the evaluation design and implementation? How are they involved in the interpretation of results and the development of recommendations for change?

How do these changes specifically relate to student achievement?

BARRIERS TO SCHOOL–FAMILY COLLABORATIONS

Families have a variety of reasons for not becoming involved in schools, and those reasons should be considered before dismissing noninvolved parents as uncaring or uninterested. These obstacles can range from inconvenient meeting times to feeling unwelcome in the school. Social justice–focused school counselors are skilled and creative when planning SFC partnership activities and are aware of the obstacles that keep parents from participating and attending school events.

The results from a national survey conducted by the Department of Education (Hanson & Pugliese, 2020) indicated distinct differences in parent participation based on economic background, race, and educational background of the parent (see Table 5.1). The survey also found that in the 2018–2019 academic year, school communication with parents, as reported by parents, most commonly occurred through schoolwide newsletters, memos, emails, or notices. This type of communication, addressed to all parents, was reported for 89% of students in kindergarten through Grade 12. Receiving emails or notes specifically about the student was reported for 66% of students, and receiving phone calls about a specific student was reported for 40% of students. However, there are still gaps in communication based on race and language. For instance, 68% of parents who both speak English received emails from the school, whereas only 57% of parents who do not speak English received emails.

TABLE 5.1   Percentage of Students in Kindergarten Through Grade 12 Whose Parents Reported Participation in School-Related Activities 2018-2019

STUDENT, PARENT, AND SCHOOL CHARACTERISTIC	ATTENDED A GENERAL SCHOOL MEETING	ATTENDED A PARENT-TEACHER CONFERENCE	ATTENDED A CLASS EVENT	VOLUNTEERED AT SCHOOL
STUDENT'S RACE/ETHNICITY				
White	90	76	85	49
Black	88	77	76	35
Hispanic	87	73	72	35
Asian or Pacific Islander	83	73	70	41
Other, non-Hispanic	90	79	83	45
HIGHEST EDUCATION LEVEL OF PARENTS/GUARDIAN				
Less than high school	82	68	61	25
High school/GED	82	71	69	28
Vocational/technical college or some college	88	75	79	38
Bachelor's degree	92	78	86	54
Graduate degree	94	80	90	58
STUDENT'S GRADE LEVEL				
Kindergarten-Grade 2	94	90	83	57
Grade 3-5	93	88	86	49
Grade 6-8	89	72	80	36
Grade 9-12	80	54	70	32
POVERTY STATUS				
Below poverty threshold	83	75	66	28
At or above poverty threshold	90	75	82	46

SOURCE: U.S. Department of Education, National Center for Education Statistics (2019).

Likewise, 68% of white parents received emails from the school whereas only 61% of Hispanic/Latinx parents received emails. While this data gives school counselors clues as to the gaps in communication, it doesn't tell the entire story. To ensure inclusive, antiracist, and equity-driven SFC partnerships, school counselors must talk to parents of all backgrounds and find out how to authentically increase engagement with them.

Creative planning for overcoming relationship barriers with parents is essential to a social justice–focused school counseling program. School counselors should be well-equipped with ideas for connecting with hard-to-reach and untrusting parents. First and foremost, school counselors working from a social justice perspective should approach every meeting with a parent or community member with a positive attitude and welcoming disposition. Developing a strong working relationship with community members is the basis for SFC partnerships. For instance, starting a meeting with community members and parents with the following statement would not be appropriate: "OK, let's get started quickly because I have to be out of here by 4:00." Although the counselor really needs to leave by 4:00, making this the first statement sends a message to the group that the committee, including the parents and community members, is not very important. A better statement would have been, "I am so happy that we are getting this chance to meet. I know we have common goals and desires for the students at this school and I look forward to us working together. I have another meeting that starts after 4:00 and I must leave by then, but I want you to know that I am committed to working with you." The following are a few ways to overcome obstacles to parent attendance and participation in school activities.

IDEAS FOR OVERCOMING OBSTACLES TO PARENT ATTENDANCE AND PARTICIPATION IN SCHOOL ACTIVITIES

- Provide multiple times for parents to participate in school activities.

- Inform parents of a school event in multiple ways and in different languages (e.g., send a save the date flyer, personal letters inviting parents, reminders written by students, or emails and text messages).

- Arrange for Lyft, Uber, car pools, or buses; provide information about public transportation; or arrange parent meetings near public transportation stops.

- Provide childcare and other supports for parents and families.

- Arrange informal social events for parents and staff to become better acquainted.

- Conduct parent advocacy training.

- Encourage parents to express their viewpoints and perspectives.

- Consult with staff on ways to welcome parents.

- Do not discount or degrade anything that a parent says.

- Learn the cultural norms and customs of parents, then plan school events accordingly.

- Have clear goals and purposes for meetings.

 ## Counseling Snapshot

Ms. Brown is a seventh-grade counselor at Riverdale Academy and she is the school liaison with the Family Resource Center (FRC). FRC is a community-based organization that provides services and support for Riverdale Academy's highly diverse student body and families. The school counselor works closely with the FRC and assists with the assessment of the community's needs. Being school based, the FRC serves as a positive connection between families from diverse racial and cultural backgrounds and the school staff. The FRC successfully communicates to families the importance of supporting their children's learning.

To increase communication with families, the FRC provides the following: a monthly roster of afterschool enrichment classes, in different languages, to decrease the number of children returning to an empty home after school; a library of culturally diverse books for parents on topics such as child development, CPR, school readiness activities; playgroups for parents and children not yet of school age; and other youth-development programs for parents and children in the community. The FRC's afterschool activities provide critical support for families and contribute to improved student success. The FRC has successfully drawn families into the school community while building strong relationships between the school and its families.

Although parents' barriers are often cited in the literature as the main reason for failed SFC partnerships, counselors and other educators are often resistant to developing closer relationships with parents and community members. Counselors will often say, "When do I have the time to create partnerships?" "My principal wants me to do other work, not partnerships!" or "I would if I had some help." Bryan (2005) recommends that counselors play the role of facilitator, advocate, and collaborator to increase SFC partnerships. She states that it is not enough to simply build partnerships; school counselors must also see their role in SFC partnerships as critical and integral to their school's ability to close opportunity gaps. Resources to help school counselors strengthen SFC partnerships can be found online at the following websites:

- **National Standards for Family–School Partnerships, National PTA**
  (https://www.pta.org/home/run-your-pta/National-Standards-for-Family-School-Partnerships)

- **Center on School, Family, and Community Partnerships** (https://www.sfcp .jhucsos.com)

- **Maximize Your Impact through School–Family–Community Partnerships, American School Counselor Association** (https://videos.schoolcounselor .org/maximize-your-impact-through-school-family-community-partnerships)

- **What the Research Says on Engaging Native Families, Education Northwest** (https://educationnorthwest.org/resources/what-research-says-engaging-native-families)

- **Strategies to Support Black Students, Teachers, and Communities in Schools, Education Northwest** (https://educationnorthwest.org/news/ strategies-support-black-students-teachers-and-communities-schools)

- **Building Strong Partnerships with Families, Highline Public Schools** (https://vimeo.com/135506454)

- **Family–School Relationships Survey, Panorama Education** (https://www .panoramaed.com/family-school-relationships-survey)

The following examples highlight school counselors who are building SFC partnerships. To assess your beliefs about the role of counselors in SFC partnerships, see the Resource section at the back of the book.

Counseling Snapshot

Mrs. Alvarez is the counselor at Avondale Elementary School, a school in a predominately low-income Latinx inner city community. More than three years ago, Mrs. Alvarez initiated a meeting with various community organizations (e.g., churches, social service agencies, community activists, and politicians) to discuss Avondale's low test scores, low attendance rates, and overall negative school culture. This was the type of initiative that would have alarmed most school officials; however, from this meeting, a committee (the Avondale Elementary School Community Organization) was formed to work on and focus on school improvement.

The committee, with the help of Mrs. Alvarez and administrators, opened an after-hours community center in the school building that offered childcare, adult literacy classes, GED classes, tutoring, parent services, and other needed resources. Mrs. Alvarez and her principal worked out an innovative school counselor schedule that allowed for Ms. Alvarez to work at the center on Wednesdays. Within one year, there was a 50% increase in test scores, more parents were volunteering to help in the school, teachers' morale had improved, and 42 residents had earned their GED.

The school counseling department at Grand Hill High School developed a consortium with a grassroots community organization for the purpose of getting more parents involved in the education of their students. The grassroots organization, Parents Empowered, consists of community parents, school reform advocates, and community activists who want schools to respect and include parents in school change efforts. The school counselors attend the group's meetings and make reports regarding Grand Hill's student needs and issues. Also, the counselors act as consultants to the group regarding school improvement plans and school data. The principal at Grand Hill encouraged the counselors to collaborate with Parents Empowered because he believes that the school must support and validate parents' empowerment and organized efforts outside of school.

Questions to Consider

1. Describe recent efforts that you and your school's leadership have made to connect with parents and community members from diverse racial and cultural groups. How were the efforts received? If they were received negatively, what did you do?

2. What are some barriers that keep you from working on SFC partnerships? How can you overcome these barriers?

3. How do teachers in your school relate to parents? Walk around your school and make note of how school personnel talk to parents. How do school personnel talk differently to parents of different cultural and racial groups? What can you do to change uneven messaging to different parent groups?

4. How would you, as a school counselor, respond to a high school parent who said the following: "I didn't like college application night. It's weird. I always feel like they think we—parents from the east-end community—don't care about our kids and don't show, but it's actually because they act like we don't understand and they only offer it one night and we're busy. The parents who show up are the ones who have jobs during the day. They make it a certain way and then wonder why people don't show up."

Collecting and Using Data

*Most of the world will make decisions by either guessing or using their gut.
They will be either lucky or wrong.*

—Suhail Doshi, chief executive officer, Mixpanel

*D*ata, *data-driven, evidence-based, accountability.* These have become buzzwords in education. For school counselors, these words are commonplace (Hatch, 2014). During public emergencies (such as COVID-19), data-driven decision making is necessary. School leaders want to know what the data can tell them about when to reopen schools, how to prevent learning loss, how to gauge dropout risk, how to encourage re-enrollment, where to deploy teachers to manage class sizes, and how to meet the needs of students when they return to school. And, as the quote above suggests, making data-informed decisions lessens the amount of guessing and increases the chances of being right.

Although data and accountability have become a cornerstone of school counseling programs, counselors are still using data in ways that don't necessarily change unjust systems. One of the central lessons from research on data usage in schools is that assessments, student tests, and other forms of data are only as good as how they are used. Existing research suggests that how data are used depends on individual factors such as one's beliefs and knowledge, including political views and racist ideas. To complicate matters further, data (e.g., assessments, test scores) are rarely used in isolation, so other systems and policies can negate the power of data-driven programming.

To motivate and encourage data use, the American School Counselor Association (ASCA) now recognizes counseling programs that use data to create impact and change. The Recognized ASCA Model Program (RAMP) is annually presented to schools and school counseling programs from around the country. Yet school counselors still struggle with data. These statements and questions are not uncommon among school counselors:

- "What data would I collect?"
- "What type of data do they want?"
- "Data doesn't *really* measure all that we do."
- "Where will we get this data?"
- "When will I have the time to collect and analyze data?"

Antiracist and social justice–focused counselors rely on data to promote systemic and programmatic changes within schools and counseling programs. Essentially, antiracist and social justice–focused school counselors use data to identify opportunity gaps for intervention planning and then use data again to determine the effectiveness of those interventions.

There is one caution, however: There are inappropriate uses of data, too. Data should never be used as a tool for blame or to leverage personal or political gain. Data, in the most effective schools, are used to guide programming and instruction but never to exclude students from opportunities. For instance, using test scores (e.g., data) to determine which students should be excluded from special programs is not the best use of data from a social justice perspective. Likewise, using data to promote one group of students as smarter than other groups of students is not a good use of data. A common interpretation of data is that the racial differences in outcomes are attributable to students' characteristics or home environments. In other words, the data are interpreted to mean that Black students are suspended at higher rates (or less likely to take honors courses) because they confront out-of-school challenges—not because of anything that schools do. Instead, data should be used to illustrate the uneven, limited access to opportunities by specific groups of students. Antiracist and social justice–based school counselors believe that schools should be held accountable to these data trends. If data are interpreted using deficit-based thinking, the data analysis is corrupt and may inadvertently mischaracterize or harm students.

Data are important tools for beginning a school's vision of becoming an equitable, antiracist, and social justice–focused learning environment. Having an equity- and social justice–based approach to data analysis means maintaining an awareness of potential distortion and taking proactive steps to use data to counteract it. Antiracist and social justice–focused school counselors adopt an equity mindset in the collection, interpretation, and use of education data. For instance, in addition to examining data on your school or classroom, you may break that data down by race. Maybe as a school, your attendance rate is above the state average—but it is below average for Black students, particularly Black girls. To see these trends, you must collect the data.

Schools and school districts collect all kinds of data, mostly for routine reporting and compliance purposes. Types of school data might include discipline data, standardized tests data, attendance data, social-emotional data, teacher evaluation data, and parent/community data. And many schools are beginning to utilize data in more advanced ways to better allocate resources, measure student success, and improve the efficiency of programming, such as school counseling programs.

What data do you need to examine a particular policy? If attendance data is stagnant and plays little to no role in changing your practices, don't give as much time to gathering or analyzing it. Part of selecting what data to use involves determining what data to intentionally omit. Assess what specific information is necessary to change your practices and stop collecting data you don't need.

In sum, data should be used primarily to validate the need for improvement, to monitor data-driven decisions, and to reveal inequities in access, attainment, and opportunity within the school community.

WHAT IS ACCOUNTABILITY?

In this era of educational reform, greater emphasis is being placed on making school personnel accountable for bringing all students to high levels of academic performance. All school personnel and educational policy makers are responsible for establishing responsive policies and initiating new strategies to enhancing student success and learning. Ensuring the success of every student falls upon school counselors in addition to teachers and school administrators.

Webster's (n.d.) dictionary defines *accountability* as "the state of being accountable; liability to be called on to render an account; the obligation to bear the consequences for failure to perform as expected." The recent movement in education focuses on the accountability of schools to students, parents, and communities. Parents and other community members are now able to access information regarding schools' educational progress. And if schools do not make progress, then parents are given other options to educate their children.

According to the ASCA National Model, accountability is an important and integral component of a comprehensive school counseling program. The model requires counselors to demonstrate the effectiveness of their work in measurable terms such as determining impact over time, performance evaluations, and undertaking a program audit (Stone & Dahir, 2004). The goal of the National Model is for counselors to become more accountable to school and community stakeholders and to align their programs with standards-based reform. By using data to guide their programs and to illustrate effectiveness, school counselors become accountable to students, parents, communities, and their colleagues.

USING DATA TO UNCOVER INEQUITIES

Data can be useful in determining and uncovering inequities in schools. To detect inequities and unjust practices, school counselors must first consider important and critical questions regarding their programs or schools: What do I want to know about my school's ability to educate students? What questions do I have about my students? What questions do I have about my school community? Asking difficult questions and developing a sense of inquiry is the first step to using data to promote social justice. Sample questions that might evolve include the following: What percentage of each racial, ethnic, gender, and language group is reading at their grade level? What percentage of our students go on to four-year colleges and universities? How many students are sent to the office daily from Ms. Lee's class? What is the breakdown of grade point averages by gender? What is the breakdown by race? What is the breakdown by ability?

TYPES OF DATA

Once the questions are developed, the counselors then need to gather the data to answer their questions. There are three types of data typically discussed in schools:

- achievement
- attainment or access
- school culture data

Achievement data include those from PSAT, SAT, ACT, state tests, grades, and performance tests; *attainment* or *access data* include promotion and retention rates, gifted and talented patterns, special education identification rates, postsecondary patterns, transition patterns, and enrollment patterns; and *school culture data* include data regarding attendance, student–faculty relationships, student relationships, staff relationships, leadership styles, respect for diversity, suspensions and expulsions, dropout rates, and staff attitudes and behaviors.

Data can be either qualitative or quantitative. Quantitative methods are those that focus on numbers and frequencies rather than on meaning and experience. Quantitative methods (e.g., experiments, questionnaires, psychometric tests) provide information that is easy to analyze statistically. Quantitative methods are associated with the scientific and experimental approach and are criticized for not providing an in-depth description. Qualitative data, on the other hand, are typically in the form of words, pictures, or objects. Researchers who desire qualitative data are concerned with describing meaning rather than with drawing statistical inferences. Qualitative methods for gathering data include interviewing people about their experiences, observing people, or gathering peoples' written descriptions of their experiences. For instance, Ms. Collins, an elementary counselor, wanted to know more about students who were suspended and expelled. She decided that she needed school culture data regarding who was suspended in the past six months, and she needed data regarding the number of reasons for the suspensions (quantitative data). In addition, she wanted to know the staffs' and students' perceptions of the suspension policies (qualitative data). She then collected the names and grades of suspended students from the secretary (quantitative). She also retrieved the suspension forms, which included reasons for suspensions, from the Central Office (qualitative and quantitative). Finally, she interviewed and surveyed teachers, administrators, students, and parents regarding the school's suspension and expulsion policy (qualitative).

In many cases, school districts will have collected an abundance of data that a counselor can easily retrieve. School or district reports, accreditation reports, and information on websites contain data that a counselor might need to answer a particular question. If the data don't exist, counselors can generate their own data or ask an individual within the district's research or accountability office for assistance. Whenever possible, counselors should collect at least two or three kinds of evidence or data to help answer a question. For instance, Ms. Collins in the previous example collected data from both teachers and students, and she used existing data that was collected by her school and the district. Possible data elements include the following:

- Grades, including reading and math levels

- Academic assessments and student-level achievement data

- Graduation data (graduation rates)

- Retention rates

- Enrollment in rigorous courses (e.g., Advanced Placement courses, honors courses)

- Special education status, placement, accommodations (e.g., individualized education programs [IEPs], 504s)

- Postsecondary enrollment (e.g., college attendance rates)

- Demographic data (e.g., gender, race/ethnicity, grade, free/reduced lunch status, address, language spoken at home, medical information)

- Attendance

- Discipline or office referrals

(Continued)

- Suspension/expulsions

- Gifted and talented placement

- Enrollment in remedial courses

- Parent involvement

- Student transportation needs

- Other program participation (e.g., Title I, Upward Bound, extended learning, after-school programs, sports/athletics, school clubs)

In order to collect qualitative data to understand the trends of quantitative data, school counselors can use online qualitative methods, such as online interviews and online focus groups, or versions of traditional methods, using internet venues instead of face-to-face interactions (Lobe et al., 2020). With our ever-growing digital societies, and moreover with the COVID-19 pandemic, school counselors have become familiar with various platforms (e.g., Zoom) and applications (e.g., Google Forms) to transmit at least some of their daily interactions, surveys, and communication online.

ANALYZING DATA

Again, whenever possible, data should be disaggregated by race/ethnicity, gender, and other demographic variables (e.g., income, neighborhood) that might illuminate inequities in student success, attainment, or access. If a school is racially and ethnically homogeneous, then data should still be disaggregated by cultural groupings (e.g., gender, socioeconomic status) and school/class characteristics (e.g., teacher, courses taken, grades). Table 6.1 shows data from a high school in a predominately Latinx community. Although the data could not be disaggregated by race/ethnicity, gender and socioeconomic status is clearly a factor when discussing students' postsecondary aspirations. See Tables 6.1 and 6.2 for examples of disaggregated data.

After you've collected data and identified some trends, the next step is interpretation or analysis. If you see disparities, ask why they're present in your school. It's a difficult question, and the answer will depend on your unique context. That said, you can improve interpretation by using two practices: avoiding deficit-based thinking and using qualitative data. Deficit-based thinking in interpretation means attributing differences in education outcomes among racial groups to student deficiencies while ignoring the impact(s) of systemic racism on those students. By failing to address systemic issues, deficit-based thinking tacitly accepts them—and expects more of students with fewer resources.

TABLE 6.1   College-Going Rate by Gender (Predominately Latinx School)

YEAR	MALES	FEMALES	NUMBER IN SENIOR CLASS
2018	21	75	110
2019	15	68	100
2020	13	79	121
2021	12	85	119

TABLE 6.2   School X Percentage of Suspensions by Ethnic Group, 2003–2006

YEAR	AFRICAN AMERICAN	LATINX	WHITE	ASIAN
2017	12	9	11	0
2018	10	6	6	0
2019	10	4	6	1
2020	8	4	4	0

Take SAT scores as an example: Black and Latinx/Hispanic students tend to score below the national average. Deficit-based thinking might conclude that Black and Latinx/Hispanic students need to spend more time studying to close this gap. That would ignore phenomena such as intergenerational systemic racism, which has privileged white perspectives in curricula, produced racially segregated schools, and caused Black and Brown students to internalize negative stereotypes. Avoiding deficit-based thinking means understanding these systems of oppression and taking the time to look beyond the student to explain trends in your data.

Qualitative data are an important type of data to collect to help with making deep analyses of trends. Relying only on quantitative data often leaves out students' contexts and lived experiences. Interviews, surveys, and focus groups can be implemented in person or virtually and allow students to describe their experiences; this can often help explain trends in your data or spark ideas for new investigations.

To assist with the analysis of data, there are several statistical programs (e.g., SPSS, Excel) that can help with simple statistical procedures such as percentages and frequencies. Counselors should inquire about statistical resources within their own school districts because many districts have research personnel that are highly skilled statisticians and data analyzers.

SHARING DATA

Tables, graphs, and pictographs (e.g., pie charts) are excellent ways to organize data for analysis, interpretation, and sharing. Some data may need to be represented in narratives, videos, or in their existing formats (e.g., course schedules, course syllabi). See Figure 6.1 for an example of a bar graph that illustrates days absent by grade and gender. Data are typically shared with others by examining proportions of each subgroup represented in a particular group, curriculum area, program, test range, or so forth. For instance, a counselor may show data that reflect the number of students by ethnic group that are in a special magnet program. Also, data that reflect change or growth over time should be shared with others. A school counselor may, for instance, show data reflecting a math achievement gap between white and Latinx students over a three-year period.

When presenting data, counselors should be sure that the audience can understand the key points or highlights of the data. Data presentations should be easy to understand, and the goals for presenting the data should be clear. Counselors must be ready to facilitate a dialogue about the data and be willing to initiate discussions that are often taboo in the school setting. It is common (and a good thing!) for issues related to racism, discrimination, and bias to arise when examining achievement or attainment gaps. Time and a safe environment should be provided for dialogue. Counselors should be prepared to encounter denial about what the data illustrate. Statements such as "Disaggregating data is racist" and "I understand the data, but that's just the way things are" are common denial statements that must be addressed in order to move forward.

■ ■ ■ Thinking About Data Analysis

See Figure 6.2, which graphs placement patterns of fifth-grade students in a gifted program by race. This is a one-year snapshot. What patterns or trends do you see? What contrasts are shown?

School Counseling Program Evaluation

Data can be used to evaluate school counseling programs and activities. School counselors can also use evaluation techniques to assess the extent to which stated goals and objectives are being achieved. Evaluation allows counselors to answer questions such as the following:

- Are we doing for our students what we said we would?

- Are students achieving what we set out for them to achieve?

- How can we make improvements to our interventions and programs?

FIGURE 6.1   Number of Students Who Are Absent More Than 10 Days/Month by Grade and Gender

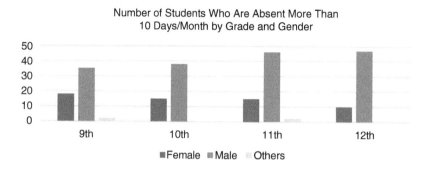

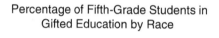

FIGURE 6.2   Percentage of Fifth-Grade Students in Gifted Education by Race

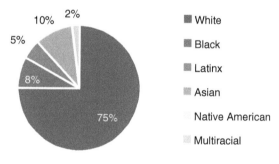

NOTE: The fifth-grade class is 55% white, 20% Black, 15% Latinx, 8% Asian, and 2% Multiracial.

For many years, school counselors collected data that described the frequency of counselor activities (e.g., how many students the counselor saw during a month) but there was little data to illustrate what impact school counseling interventions were having on students. In one school district, the counselors were very efficient when asked to keep a record of how many groups they worked with or how many classrooms they visited. When asked how much those groups influenced student achievement or student attendance, they had no idea. Thus, the primary purpose of implementing program evaluation is to assess the impact of counseling interventions on students.

PROCESS EVALUATION

An important type of evaluation for school counselors is *process evaluation*. Process evaluations are geared toward fully understanding how a particular intervention is

CHAPTER 6 · COLLECTING AND USING DATA   117

implemented. In other words, how does an intervention produce the results that it does? Process evaluations are useful if school counselors have implemented an intervention for a long time, if students seem to have lost interest in the intervention, or if the counselor would like for others to replicate the intervention. Process evaluation involves assessing the intervention, examining the methods used, exploring the school counselor's performance, and determining the adequacy of equipment and facilities. The changes made as a result of a total school counseling program process evaluation may involve immediate small adjustments (e.g., a change in how one particular unit is presented), minor changes in design (e.g., a change in how students are assigned to groups), or major design changes (e.g., dropping the use of a particular counseling activity or intervention).

In theory, process evaluation occurs on a continuous basis. At an informal level, whenever a counselor talks to another counselor or an administrator, they may be discussing adjustments to their program or interventions. More formally, process evaluation refers to a set of activities in which administrators or evaluators observe counseling activities and interact with counselors and students in order to define and communicate more effective ways of addressing counseling goals. Process evaluation can be distinguished from outcome evaluation on the basis of the primary evaluation emphasis. *Process evaluation* focuses on a continuing series of decisions concerning program improvements whereas *outcome evaluation* focuses on the effects of a program on its intended target audience (i.e., the students).

RECOGNIZED ASCA MODEL PROGRAM (RAMP)

To exemplify the importance of data-driven school counseling programs, the ASCA has initiated special recognition of school counseling programs that embrace accountability and the ASCA National Model. These programs—including RAMP—are guided by the collection, analysis, integration, and dissemination of data. RAMP recognition is granted to prekindergarten–Grade 12 schools with school counseling programs that evaluate their program and identify areas for improvement. The most recent version of the RAMP application involves submitting 10 sections or components that include a statement of philosophy, a mission statement, three school counseling program goals, competencies and indicators, management agreements for each counselor, an advisory council list, calendars, classroom guidance curriculum action plans and lessons, classroom guidance curriculum results reports, small group counseling responsive services, closing-the-gap results reports, and a program reflection. In addition to these documents, each of the first 11 components requires a narrative that provides the rationale for the information submitted. The use of data is central to the RAMP process. School counselors are required to review their data to identify three program goals that align with the school counseling mission statement and target specific gap issues (e.g., behavior, attendance, achievement). RAMP applicants also must identify interventions to evaluate the impact of classroom guidance curriculum lesson plans, small group interventions, and closing-the-gap interventions and report results that include process, perception, and outcome data.

There is little literature or research indicating whether RAMP programs address and fix structural racism or deep inequities in schools. The link between data-driven school counseling programs and the creation of antiracist learning environments has not been established by research nor directly addressed by the ASCA. However, Table 6.3 provides a checklist for antiracist and social justice–focused school counselors in their work on RAMP applications.

TABLE 6.3 Integrating Antiracism, Social Justice, and Equity to RAMP

RAMP APPLICATION SECTION	MODIFICATIONS/ADDITIONS BASED ON ANTIRACISM AND A SOCIAL JUSTICE FOCUS	YES	NO
Section 1: Vision and Mission Statement	Describe the future world in terms of equitable student outcomes, particularly across racial/ethnic, gender, economic, and other demographic groups. Include language signaling antiracist learning environments and language pertaining to inclusive, justice-focused schooling.	☐	☐
Section 2: Annual Student Outcome Goals	Each student outcome goal should address an inequity based on race/ethnicity, gender, income, sexual orientation, and so on. Attach student outcome goals to policy change(s).	☐	☐
Section 3: Classroom and Group Mindsets and Behaviors	Include the following as a student social skills standard: *Cultural and racial awareness, sensitivity, and responsiveness to issues of racism, sexism, homophobia, ableism, ageism, classism, and so on.* Include antiracism as a social skill. Include the following: *Lead efforts to challenge policies, procedures, practices, traditions, customs, or other behaviors perpetuating intentional or unintentional racist, unjust, and oppressive behaviors and unequal and inequitable student outcomes.*	☐	☐
Section 4: Annual Administrative Conference	Include community member(s) representing diverse communities in the administrative conference.	☐	☐

(Continued)

TABLE 6.3 (Continued)

RAMP APPLICATION SECTION	MODIFICATIONS/ADDITIONS BASED ON ANTIRACISM AND A SOCIAL JUSTICE FOCUS	YES	NO
Section 5: Advisory Council	Include the following: *Advisory council membership represents and includes diverse representation across race, gender, income, language, and so on.* Include the following: *Advisory council meetings must be accessible to all school community members, including meeting time, language translators, meeting place, and so on.*	☐	☐
Section 6: Calendars (Annual and Weekly)	Include in-school and out-of-school activities that align with equity, antiracist, and social justice goals.	☐	☐
Section 7: Lesson Plans	Include required lessons on issues such as ethnic/racial identity development, racism, justice, classism, acceptance of other cultures, and so on.	☐	☐
Section 8: Classroom Instruction	Utilize culturally responsive techniques and strengths-based/asset-based strategies in classroom lessons. Ensure that all students, regardless of background, participate in lessons; show evidence of all students' participation. Use classroom materials that represent diverse perspectives, racially diverse authors, and so forth.	☐	☐
Section 9: Small Groups	Ensure that small groups have diverse representation; give racial, ethnic, gender, and various other breakdowns of group participants. Ensure that small group outcomes align with equity, social justice, and antiracist principles (e.g., racial/ethnic identity). Utilize small-group counseling techniques that are culturally responsive and asset-based (not deficit-based).	☐	☐
Section 10: Closing the Gap	Disseminate opportunity gap results to diverse groups in the community. Connect opportunity gaps to policy change. Advocate for policy change and show evidence of advocacy efforts.	☐	☐

Counseling Snapshot

Jasper, a middle school counselor, was planning to implement an in-person social and emotional learning (SEL) group for sixth-graders; however, due to the pandemic lockdown, he implemented the group via Zoom. For the year, Jasper has implemented nine SEL groups using a curriculum he developed to promote prosocial behaviors, lessen anxiety, and address culturally diverse students' coping strategies during the COVID-19 pandemic. Students and teachers have raved about his groups, but he has no data to illustrate that it is helping students exhibit better social skills or less anxiety.

After consultation with his supervisor about program evaluation, Jasper decided to collect data related to his SEL group. His overall objective for the students was this: "As a result of participation in the SEL group, 90% of the participating students' will report less anxiety and increased satisfaction with school." Jasper collected information via online school satisfaction surveys disseminated to participating students. He also conducted interviews with students to determine students' levels of anxiety. For teacher feedback, he had teachers complete a short questionnaire about students' behavior in virtual classes.

Counselor in Action

Data at your high school reveal the following:

- A majority of the students who drop out in ninth grade are girls with low socioeconomic status. A majority (52%) of the girls who drop out identify as English language learners (ELLs) and as Latinx students.

- A majority of the students who drop out in tenth grade are boys with low socioeconomic status. A majority of the boys who drop out identify as ELLs and Latinx.

- Latinx students are under-identified in honors and Advanced Placement courses. While Latinx students make up 56% of the student population, they are underrepresented (5%) in honors/college track courses.

Describe possible interventions that a school counseling program might utilize to create equity and address the opportunity gap at your high school. Identify data points that you will address through your counseling program.

Developing Program Assessment Tools

Selecting the most appropriate means of determining whether students have achieved stated counseling objectives can take much thought. Traditionally, most assessments of students in the United States have been accomplished through the use of formalized tests. This practice has been criticized in recent years because such tests may not be accurate indicators of what the student has learned (e.g., a student may simply guess correctly on a multiple-choice question). Alternative approaches, which more fully involve the student in the evaluation process, have been praised for increasing student interest and motivation. This section looks at three assessment concepts: alternative assessment, performance assessment, and authentic assessment.

Standardized testing was initiated to enable schools to set clear, justifiable, and consistent standards for its students and teachers. Such tests are currently used for several purposes beyond that of classroom evaluation. They are used to place students in appropriate-level courses; to guide students in making decisions about various courses of study; and to hold teachers, schools, and school districts accountable for their effectiveness based on their students' performance.

ALTERNATIVE ASSESSMENTS

To encourage students to use higher-order cognitive skills and to evaluate students more comprehensively, several alternative assessments have been introduced. Generally, alternative assessments are nonstandardized evaluation techniques that use complex thought processes. Such alternatives are almost exclusively performance-based and criterion-referenced. Examples of alternative assessments include open-book exams, take-home exams, and collaborative testing.

PERFORMANCE-BASED ASSESSMENTS

Performance-based assessment is a form of testing that requires students to create an answer or product or demonstrate a skill that displays their knowledge or abilities. Many types of performance assessments have been proposed and implemented, including projects or group projects, essays or writing samples, open-ended problems, interviews or oral presentations, science experiments, computer simulations, constructed-response questions, and portfolios.

AUTHENTIC ASSESSMENTS

Authentic assessment is usually considered a specific kind of performance assessment, although the term is sometimes used interchangeably with performance-based or alternative assessment. The authenticity in the name derives from the focus of this evaluation technique to directly measure complex, real-world, relevant tasks. Authentic assessments can include writing and revising papers, providing oral analyses of world events, collaborating with others on a debate team, and conducting research. Such tasks require the student to synthesize knowledge and create polished, thorough, and justifiable answers. The increased validity of authentic assessments stems from their relevance to classroom material and applicability to real-life scenarios.

Whether or not specifically performance-based or authentic, alternative assessments achieve greater reliability through the use of predetermined and specific evaluation criteria. Rubrics are often used for this purpose and can be created by one counselor or a group of counselors involved in similar assessments. (A *rubric* is a set of guidelines for scoring and generally states all of the dimensions being assessed, contains a scale, and helps the grader place the given work on the scale.) Creating a rubric is often time-consuming, but it can help clarify the key features of the performance or product and allows for more consistency. Following is an example of an assignment and a rubric for assessing students' written responses.

An elementary school counselor completed a unit on bullying with fifth-grade students. She instructed the students to write a one-page paper explaining the following:

What is bullying? What should you do at school when a bully bothers you? How can students help stop bullying at school? Why do people bully others? Give examples to illustrate your points.

- A *4* paper addresses the questions asked of the student. The paper clearly shows an appropriate awareness of bullying. It is well-organized and contains details and insights to engage the reader.

- A *3* paper addresses the questions asked of the student; however, it contains vague or inarticulate language. It is missing some details and examples.

- A *2* paper does not fully address the questions asked of the student, which causes the paper to be rambling and disjointed. The paper demonstrates an incomplete or inadequate understanding of conflict resolution.

- A *1* paper barely addresses the questions. Awareness of the topic is missing. The general idea may be conveyed, but details, facts, examples, or descriptions are lacking.

Counselor in Action

Collect data regarding your school, students, policies, and so forth. Possible data sources might include your school's college-going rate, students' test scores, attendance rates, suspension rates, percentage of students in special education (by race and gender), and percentage of students in gifted and talented programs or courses (by race and gender). After retrieving and reviewing your data, respond to the following questions:

1. How is student performance described?

2. How are different groups of students performing? Which groups are meeting the targeted goals? What don't the data tell you about students? What other data do you need to get a better picture of what is going on?

3. What stakeholders might you need to talk to in order to better understand the assessment of students from diverse backgrounds?

4. What are the implications of the following actions?

   a. developing or revising school policies

   b. revising school counselor practices and strategies

   c. reading literature

   d. visiting other schools

   e. revising, eliminating, or adding programs

   f. initiating dialogues with experts

   g. implementing professional development

SOURCE: Adapted from Johnson (2002).

Questions to Consider

1. What types of data do you collect now? Discuss how that data can be used to highlight inequities or to illustrate your program's effectiveness.

2. Who or what office in your district collects, analyzes, and disseminates data? Where is it located? How can you access that data? Visit the person or the office and retrieve more information about your district's data.

3. Review the data in Figure 6.2. What does the data tell you? What types of patterns and trends do you see? What types of programs might you initiate based on the data? What additional data would you want?

4. New Town Elementary School (prekindergarten–Grade 5) opened in 2010. The school counselor, Chelsea Jones, joined the school in 2020. Chelsea has been a school counselor for 10 years and took the job at New Town as a chance to help turn it around. New Town Elementary School was one of the lowest-performing schools in the state on the four mandated state tests (assessments of math and literacy in Grades 3 and 5). According to U.S. Census data, New Town's neighborhood is the second-poorest area in the state. Here is a brief list of New Town's key characteristics: 745 students; prekindergarten–Grade 5; 85% African American, 15% Latinx; 90% free/reduced lunch; 95% of the parents did not graduate from college.

Discuss the following:

a. What additional data do you require to help you develop an understanding of the students' and community's needs?

b. What systems and data protocols will you put in place?

CHAPTER 7

Challenging Racism and Bias

But there is no neutrality in the racism struggle. . . . One either allows racial ineq-uities to persevere, as a racist, or confronts racial inequities, as an antiracist. There is no in–between safe space of "not racist." The claim of "not racist" neutrality is a mask for racism.

—Ibram Kendi, historian, author of *How to Be an Antiracist*

Racism and white supremacy continue to have dire impacts on the lives and outcomes of Black and Brown students in educational spaces. Thus, challenging and disrupting all forms of oppression, including racism, is key to developing an antiracist and social justice–focused school counseling program. Actually, I argue that school counselors cannot create equitable programs unless racism and bias are named, identified, and removed. This is often the most difficult aspect of social justice and antiracist school counseling because it requires counselors to swim upstream against everyday norms.

To challenge and disrupt racism and bias, let's quickly define these terms. What is racism? First, *race* is a socially constructed and fluid measure of phenotype. Globally, race has been used to include and exclude specific groups from equal participation, resources, and opportunity. In the U.S., race has been used systematically to oppress specific groups—from the first Africans to arrive in the U.S. to more recent Spanish-speaking immigrants from Central and South America. *Racism*, which is based on *race*, is the process used to include and exclude groups. Soloranzo et al. (2002) define racism as having three fundamental premises: (1) one group believes itself to be superior (i.e., white people), (2) the group that believes itself to be superior has power to carry out their racist ideas and behavior, and (3) racism affects multiple racial/ethnic groups. Thus, Soloranzo et al. frame racism as institutional power that Black and Brown people have never significantly possessed; that racism maintains the status quo and perpetuates racist ideologies rooted in white supremacy.

Bias is similar to racism but does not include institutional power. *Bias* is

> a tendency, inclination, or prejudice toward or against something or someone. Some biases are positive and helpful—like choosing to only eat foods that are considered healthy or staying away from someone who has knowingly caused harm. But biases are often based on stereotypes, rather than actual knowledge of an individual or circumstance. Whether positive or negative, such cognitive shortcuts can result in prejudgments that lead to rash decisions or discriminatory practices. (Psychology Today, 2021)

Based on the definitions above, racism and bias are ingrained in the social fabric of our society, which in turn makes biased and racist behavior ordinary and natural to people, particularly those in the dominant culture (Kendi, 2019). In schools, it's no different. Racism and bias are embedded in school practices and policies, which influence education outcomes. For instance, students of color with the same tests scores as white and Asian students are less likely to be placed in advanced classes. Why is this true? Is the problem the students or the systems and policies? In another example, schools in which white students are in the majority are more than twice as likely to offer a significant number of Advanced Placement (AP) classes as schools where Black and Latinx students are in the majority. These embedded racial inequities produce unequal opportunities for educational success.

It's imperative, therefore, that school counselors interrogate and challenge "typical" and "ordinary" practices in schools, including school counseling activities. School counseling is a ripe space for biased and racist practices because school counselors are often called on to maintain the status quo. Often, the status quo consists of education spaces in which Black and Brown students and their families are constructed as the problem and pathologized based on their race. Antiracist school counseling assumes that the problem is not in the student, it's in the policies and structures that hinder student opportunities for success. Using the example above, an antiracist school counselor would ask, "What are we doing to ensure that Black and Brown students are enrolling in advanced classes?" Herein lies the core of the antiracist and social justice school counselor's work—first not accepting the status quo, then changing it.

How to Be an Antiracist School Counselor

Antiracism is not a new term but it has received more attention in recent years due to the increase of public and horrific hate crimes and racist events. For instance, the Unite the Right rally in Charlottesville; the murders of nine Black parishioners at Emmanuel African Methodist Episcopal Church by a white nationalist; and the murders of George Floyd, Breonna Taylor, and countless other unarmed Black and Brown people by police officers have indicated that racism and hatred undergird our society. Thus, to be an antiracist school counselor is to actively challenge and disrupt racist and hateful ideas, behaviors, and policies. As professor Ibram Kendi (2019) states, "and the only way to undo racism is to consistently identify and describe it—and then dismantle it" (p. 9).

Although it sounds simple to say that one is an antiracist, it's not that easy. Being an antiracist school counselor means that one is not doing business as usual. Singh (2019) suggests that there are different pathways for becoming an antiracist but we can all be racist and/or antiracist. For example, Singh suggests that becoming an antiracist as a white person means taking responsibility for your power and privilege and cultivating a desire for understanding and growth. Becoming an antiracist as a person of color means recognizing that there are important economic differences between people of color, that colorism within racial groups creates oppressive behavior, that intersectionality of multiple identities are at play, and that internalized white supremacist views (i.e., internalized oppression) are prevalent among people of color.

Antiracist school counselors take individual action and collective action with others who also commit to dismantling racism and bias in schools and communities. Antiracist school counselors spend time examining how racism is a part of school structures and school counseling programs. This is probably the most difficult aspect of being an antiracist school counselor—admitting that you and your program have perpetuated racist beliefs and ideas. It's only through this discomfort and difficulty that one grows and changes for the better. Below are initial steps to becoming an antiracist school counselor.

Initial Steps to Becoming an Antiracist School Counselor

1. **Develop an understanding of racism** and the forms of racism (e.g., structural, systemic). Read diverse scholars' definitions of racism from many disciplines, including education, sociology, history, cultural studies, and so forth.

2. **Assess your expectations of students for norms that align with white European norms and values.** Modify those expectations and center your expectations with racially and culturally diverse norms. For instance, do you expect students to seek you out for information or do you seek them out to share information?

3. **Assess how school counselors have perpetuated racism and white supremacy through their work** (intentionally and unintentionally). For

(Continued)

(Continued)

instance, school counselors have acted as gatekeepers of information and accessibility in the college preparation process. School counseling, in general, has been centered on whiteness. Instead, center Black, Indigenous, and other voices of color in school counseling programming.

4. **Review policies and practices that impact racial disparities in your school**. Review discipline policies, gifted and talented identification processes, special education identification policies, suspension and expulsion policies, and so on.

5. **Acknowledge racialized stress and trauma**. Broach issues of race and racism in the counseling process (see Day-Vine et al.'s [2007] Broaching Race Framework).

6. **Understand how racism influences education and all aspects of Black and Brown students' lives**, including health, economics, housing, and so on. Disproportionality of COVID-19 deaths by race mirrors disproportionality of lower education outcomes by race.

7. **Utilize counseling approaches that empower and liberate**. Draw from students' strengths (see Chapter 3).

GUIDELINES FOR CHALLENGING RACISM AND BIAS

Given the fact that racism and bias are embedded in the fabric of our country, it's not surprising that racial and hate incidents occur in schools regularly. Most educators and students have heard comments about "those people" or jokes about students' nationality ("spic" jokes, "trailer trash" jokes) or cruel comments about an individual's physical characteristics. According to a 2019 report by the Southern Poverty Law Center (SPLC), hate crimes surged after the presidential election of Donald Trump, who used racist, xenophobic, and coarse language throughout his campaign. SPLC also found that more than two-thirds of the 2,776 educators who responded to their questionnaire witnessed a hate crime or bias incident in their school during the fall of 2018. And most of those hate crimes seemed to be motivated by racism. Hate in schools involve incidents that perpetuate stereotypes, bias, and racism and contradict social justice and antiracism. Bias reinforces oppressive attitudes and creates an environment of unjust policies and inequitable practices. Clearly, counselors who work from an antiracist and social justice framework do not silently accept or tolerate racism or bias. Ignoring racism and bias will not make it go away, and silence sends the message that you are in agreement with such attitudes and behaviors. Social justice–focused and antiracist school counselors make it clear that they do not tolerate any actions that demean, devalue, or dehumanize any person or group.

BE AWARE OF YOUR OWN ATTITUDES, STEREOTYPES, AND EXPECTATIONS

We have all been socialized to believe many myths and generalizations. None of us remains untouched by the discriminatory messages in our society. However, only a few of us are honest about our biased, prejudiced, and racist thoughts. Social justice–focused school counselors do not avoid discussions about bias, prejudice, racism, or any topic related to people's differences. To confront bias and racism, social justice–focused school counselors are not defensive when their biased behavior is pointed out to them. For example, let's say that a student calls a counselor racist. The counselor does not get angry; instead, the counselor validates the student's opinion and initiates an open discussion with the student about his perceptions and concerns. The counselor does not discount the student's accusation. To determine and understand your assumptions and stereotypes about different groups, complete Exercise 7.1.

ACTIVELY LISTEN TO AND LEARN FROM OTHERS' EXPERIENCES

Counselors working from a social justice framework never trivialize or deny people's concerns; they make an effort to see situations through others' eyes. Parents from culturally and racially diverse backgrounds will often perceive situations and activities at the school very differently from school personnel. Their varying views of what happens in a school are likely due to parents' diverse experiences with schools and school personnel. In many cases, students and their parents will use their experiences with discrimination and oppression to frame their understanding of what happens in schools. Counselors must be willing to listen and validate others' lived experiences as well as learn from what others tell them. The following example illustrates this point.

> Mr. Johnson, an African American father of a first-grade student, is very active in his daughter's schooling. He comes to the school regularly to talk to the staff and to pick up his daughter. Because the Parent–Teacher Organization (PTO) is lacking racial diversity, the counselor asks Mr. Johnson to attend the next PTO meeting because they will be discussing a new reading initiative. Mr. Johnson attends the meeting and is very vocal in his skepticism about the reading initiative. He believes the initiative encourages ability grouping and tracking (see Chapter 8 for a definition of these terms). The other PTO members were excited about the initiative and were angry that Mr. Johnson had a different view. Moreover, they resented that he was invited to the meeting, considering him to not be a part of their group. The PTO members became noticeably angry with Mr. Johnson and interrupted his statements repeatedly. Mr. Johnson became extremely upset and stormed out of the meeting: "You all don't want to hear from me!" The counselor voiced her

concerns about the group's treatment of Mr. Johnson. She then called Mr. Johnson and validated his concerns about the reading initiative. She invited him to come speak to the administrator about his concerns.

Exercise 7.1 Becoming Aware of Our Biases and Prejudices

I believe that . . .

1. African American students are _____.

2. Asian students can _____.

3. white students are _____.

4. Native American students tend to _____.

5. Latinx students tend to _____.

6. in school, girls tend to _____.

7. in school, boys tend to _____.

8. disabled students _____.

9. gay and lesbian students are _____.

10. if a school is predominately African American, it is _____.

11. if a school is predominately white, it is _____.

12. if I were offered a counseling position in an all-Latinx high school, I would _____ because _____.

13. if my children were zoned to attend a predominately African American school, I would _____.

14. if my children were zoned to attend a predominately white school, I would _____.

SOURCE: Holcomb-McCoy (2007). Reproduction authorized only for the local school site or nonprofit organization that has purchased this book.

The counselor in the preceding vignette understood that Mr. Johnson's perceptions of the reading initiative were likely based on his cultural and racial experiences. Because students of color have been historically oppressed by ability grouping and tracking, the reading initiative's grouping component was a red flag for Mr. Johnson.

The school counselor should be applauded in this case because she realized the value of Mr. Johnson's ideas and views and she persisted in having his voice heard by school personnel. Her actions also sent the message to the PTO that the school values all parents' concerns. The counselor and administrator later discovered that Mr. Johnson's views were closely aligned with other parents in the school community and acknowledged that his concerns about tracking were warranted.

ACKNOWLEDGE AND APPRECIATE DIVERSITY, DON'T JUST TOLERATE IT!

It is critical for counselors and other educators to acknowledge diversity and to point out the rich differences among staff and students. Acknowledging obvious differences is not the problem—placing negative value judgments on those differences is! Antiracist and social justice–focused counselors don't tolerate differences; they appreciate and celebrate differences.

BE AWARE OF YOUR OWN HESITANCIES TO INTERVENE

Counselors will often hear, experience, or witness racist and oppressive acts or statements in schools. What do you do? Do you hesitate? Do you feel nervous about intervening? A school counselor working from an antiracist and social justice framework might hesitate to intervene but will surely challenge the act or statement. Here are four simple steps to follow when challenging a person or group regarding an oppressive statement or act:

1. *Take a breath.* It takes courage to challenge racism and oppression because it will likely cause discomfort.

2. *Use reflection.* Reflect racist language back to the individual (e.g., "You said that Native people aren't really American. What do you mean by that?").

3. *Name the act.* Tell the individual exactly what they did and name the oppression they contributed (e.g., "Your statement about Latino males and drug possession was inaccurate and contributes to racist ideas about our Latino students.").

4. *Give information as to why the act was offensive or oppressive.* For example, a counselor might state, "Dave, your comment that girls should not be scientists is sexist because you are sending the message that it is not socially acceptable for girls to enter the science professions. You are not respecting girls' right to freely choose a career."

5. *Give direction and model good behavior.* Tell the person what they should do about it. For example, a counselor might say to Dave, "I've read a lot about gender bias in schools. I'll gladly share some information with you." Or a counselor may say to a colleague, "I've worked hard to learn to pronounce my students' names correctly. I'd be happy to help you learn them, too."

The key to challenging others' racist and biased comments and actions is to be as direct as possible. It is not a good idea to yell or to let one's anger take over. Yelling and screaming will only give the individual a chance to change the focus to *your* behavior rather than their oppressive behavior. You might want to ask the person for clarification, "Why do you say that?" "Are you saying that everyone should feel this way?" "Help me understand your attitude; I'm not understanding why you feel this way." Remember, most people make changes when they are pushed out of their comfort zones and are forced to evaluate why they are uncomfortable.

■■■ Thinking About Challenging Racism and Bias

Respond to the following items:

1. Joan, a middle school counselor, overhears a group of teachers making crude comments about a student's mothers. One teacher states, "Those women should be banned from our school. I think it is horrible that they are allowed to participate on the PTO. Who wants to plan a pizza party with a bunch of dykes?" What should Joan do?

2. Will and Karen are counselors at a high school with a science and math magnet program. The magnet program consists primarily of white and Asian students (96%) and the remainder of the student body is primarily Black and Latinx (95%). Each spring, Will and Karen make trips to promote the magnet program at middle schools with large numbers of white and Asian students. When you ask them why they do not visit some of the other middle schools in the district, they state that "students at the other middle schools would never be successful in our magnet program." How would you challenge them?

3. Denice, a counselor educator at a local university, is asked by a group of white parents to provide school counseling trainees for tutoring positions in their learning pod during the COVID-19 pandemic. The parents would like for the school counseling trainees to tutor their children for at least 10 hours per day. There are no parents of color in the group. In the local community, a majority of students of color do not have access to pods nor do they have access to Wi-Fi. What should Denice do? Should she let the parents know that she is uncomfortable with perpetuating uneven resources to students? Should she simply say no to the request or should she agree?

4. One of your white colleagues, Rick, continues to ignore Orrin in school counseling departmental meetings. Orrin is a Black counselor who was hired recently to fill a vacant position. Orrin is visibly frustrated at meetings and walked out early during the last meeting. You overhear Rick tell others in the department, "We're just hiring him because they want a Black person in this office." What would you do? What would you say to Rick? What would you say to Orrin?

EXPECT TENSION AND CONFLICT

Culturally and racially insensitive and biased issues are unlikely to change without some struggle and resistance. Antiracist and social justice–focused counselors understand that tension and conflict are positive forces that can foster change and growth. Therefore, antiracist and social justice–focused counselors do not avoid confronting bias and racism because they fear conflict. They learn to manage the tension and conflict.

ADVOCATE FOR STUDENTS

Antiracist and social justice–focused school counselors are advocates for racial and educational justice. Advocates are people within an organization, school, school district, and so forth who have serious ideas about what must change to address barriers and issues facing students. Advocates typically challenge bias and racism by utilizing data to support their arguments, empowering students and their families, collaborating with community stakeholders, analyzing systems, and lobbying decision-making bodies for policy change.

WORK COLLECTIVELY WITH OTHERS

Antiracist and social justice–focused counselors organize and support community efforts that combat racism, prejudice, and oppression. School counselors must decenter whiteness and work alongside community members. That means honoring the knowledge and power in the community. Be humble and listen. Social change is a long-term struggle and it's easy to get discouraged, but by working together, school counselors have the strength and vision to make a difference.

Antiracism and Social Justice Resources for Educators

To promote social justice and antiracism in schools, counselors and teachers need resources for planning schoolwide programs, classroom lessons, and group activities. Below is a list of organizations and websites that provide resources for educators:

1. American School Counselor Association, antiracism resources (https://www.schoolcounselor.org/Publications-Research/Publications/Free-ASCA-Resources/Antiracism-Resources)

2. American Counseling Association, antiracism toolkit (https://www.counseling.org/docs/default-source/resources-for-counselors/antiracism-toolkit.pdf)

(Continued)

(Continued)

3. American University, center for postsecondary readiness and success (https://www.american.edu/centers/cprs/)

4. Learning for Justice (https://www.learningforjustice.org/)

5. Learning for Justice, social justice standards (https://www.learningforjustice.org/frameworks/social-justice-standards)

6. ASCD, antiracism resources (http://www1.ascd.org/research-a-topic/building-racial-justice-and-equity-resources.aspx)

7. ASCD, how to be an antiracist educator (https://www.ascd.org/el/articles/how-to-be-an-antiracist-educator)

8. Culturally Responsive Education (CRE) Hub (https://crehub.org/)

9. Educators for Antiracism (https://www.edantiracism.com/)

10. UnboundEd, anti-bias toolkit (https://blog.unbounded.org/bias-toolkit/)

11. D.C. Area Educators for Social Justice: A Project of Teaching for Change (https://www.dcareaeducators4socialjustice.org/black-lives-matter/resources)

12. National Museum of African American History & Culture: Talking About Race (https://nmaahc.si.edu/learn/talking-about-race)

13. National Center for Children in Poverty (https://www.nccp.org/)

14. Teaching for Change: Building Social Justice Starting in the Classroom (https://www.teachingforchange.org/)

15. Center for Racial Justice in Education (https://centerracialjustice.org/)

16. Educators for Social Responsibility (https://creducation.net/intl-orgs/educators-for-social-responsibility-esr/#:~:text=Educators%20for%20Social%20Responsibility%20is,%2C%20democratic%2C%20and%20just%20world)

SOCIAL JUSTICE EDUCATION IN SCHOOLS

The main aim for a social justice–focused school counselor is to create an educational environment that encourages students to have public conversations about social justice and antiracism. According to sociologist Pierre Bourdieu, every youngster brings rich "cultural capital" to the classroom: subtleties of language, artistic preferences, unique knowledge bases, and links to resources (Fowler, 1997). Nevertheless, classrooms and schools often do not value, acknowledge, or use the cultural capital of some groups of students. This makes some students feel as if they have no acceptable way to express themselves and share their cultural capital in the school setting.

Schools can either cultivate social justice and its composite issues—appreciating diversity, promoting equity, advancing broad-mindedness, and encouraging voice and expression—or they can suppress it. The following scenarios illustrate counselor responses that devalue students' perspectives and alternative responses that recognize and honor the students' points of view.

SCENARIO 1: IGNORING WHAT STUDENTS SAY

In a high-performing school district, Malik's counselor introduced the concept of *community* through classroom lessons. The counselor asked the students to identify an individual who provided a valuable service to the people in their community. Malik, a bright Black student of Jamaican descent, eagerly raised his hand and said that his father's car detailer, Eric, cleaned his father's car and some of his father's friends' cars. He stated that he does a good job and was very helpful and nice. The counselor, who had been listing jobs on the board under the label "Important Services" did not list the occupation on the board. She thanked Malik and then moved on to another student. Malik's counselor had preconceptions about important community services and car detailing was not among these services.

Did Malik leave the session with a diminished view of the role and value of car detailing? Maybe or maybe not. However, what certainly occurred was the devaluing of Malik's perspective. In contrast, the counselor could have asked Malik to explain how car detailing is an important community service. After his explanation, she could then add the job to the board. With this response, the counselor would have honored and validated Eric's work and Malik's perspective.

SCENARIO 2: TRANSPOSING WHAT STUDENTS SAY

A sixth-grade newcomers group was engaging in a lively discussion about their new neighborhoods. The counselor asked the students to describe what they liked best about their neighborhoods. Juan, a Chicano student who had moved to the suburban community from a low-income community, said that he liked his new room and backyard but he missed his old neighborhood, especially sharing a room with his cousin and playing with his cousin and friends. The counselor thanked him for his contribution and then proceeded to explain to the group how fortunate Juan was to have a community that provided him with more space, safer living conditions, and good schools. By changing Juan's feelings about his former and current neighborhoods, his counselor essentially disregarded Juan's beliefs about the quality of community life in his former community.

Juan's counselor could have honored and validated Juan's views by asking more questions about what life was like in his previous neighborhood and by asking Juan whether it would be possible to recreate some of those advantages in his present neighborhood. The counselor could have reflected on Juan's relationship with his former friends and cousin, since his sense of belonging was fulfilled in his former neighborhood!

SCENARIO 3: MARGINALIZING WHAT STUDENTS SAY

While conducting a classroom guidance lesson on great leaders of the 20th century, Sharon, a tenth-grade Black student, offered Malcolm X's name as a great leader, adding that her parents had several of his books in their home. The counselor reiterated that she wanted "great leaders" and that Malcolm X was not a great leader. She suggested that Sharon refer to some library books for other ideas.

The counselor's response negated and devalued Sharon's idea of a great leader. The counselor also eliminated a possible learning moment and forestalled critical thinking on the topic. Sharon, however, learned a lot through this interaction but probably not about leadership nor about Black leaders and leaders during the Civil Rights period. Did Sharon learn that her parents don't know what they think they know? Or that certain library books dictate what is valued not only in the school but also in the larger society? Maybe or maybe not, but we do know that Sharon's perspective was devalued.

Instead, the counselor could have asked Sharon to explain the characteristics of Malcolm X that made him a great leader. The counselor's question directs attention to the definition of *greatness* and the value that society attributes to the cultural capital of certain leaders. Also, it reinforces that *greatness* is subjective and culturally defined.

Questions to Consider

1. Discuss a time when you heard a racist, biased, or prejudiced comment made by a colleague. What did you do? What do you wish you had done? How do you think the colleague would have reacted?

2. Describe and discuss a school policy that perpetuates racial inequities (e.g., school discipline policy, attendance policy, standardized test policy). As a school counselor, how might you advocate for a changed policy?

3. In a conversation with a fellow school counselor, the topic of critical race theory emerges. Your colleague believes Black people are being racist by talking about race all the time and she says, "Critical race theory is antiwhite; it's just another way for us to have to talk about race." She continues to talk and makes the following comment, "Why can't they [Black people] just get over it? Slavery was a long time ago." What would you say to her?

4. How do you move beyond performative advocacy—mere words and declaration about antiracism—to action?

CHAPTER 8

Coordinating Student Success and Support

Theory does not solve issues—only action and solidarity can do that—but theory gives you language to fight, knowledge to stand on, and a humbling reality of what intersectional social justice is up against.

—Dr. Bettina L. Love, professor and author

Central to high-achieving and justice-based schools is a school culture that supports students and provides services to enhance students' academic, career, and social/emotional development. Antiracist and social justice–focused school counseling programs address students' development and ensure that students thrive by offering equitable, culturally responsive, and strengths-based supports to all students. Also, antiracist and socially just student support systems are driven by policies that dictate equitable, antiracist, and equal resources for all students. This chapter includes an overview of student support that cultivates success for all students, regardless of cultural and racial background.

COLLABORATING WITH COMMUNITY ORGANIZATIONS AND SOCIAL SERVICE AGENCIES

When students struggle with academics, contributing factors often emanate from community or familial problems. For this reason, school counselors that work from an antiracist and social justice framework provide students and their families with the support they need to improve their condition. Although counselors are trained to provide an array of services to their students and families, sometimes the counselors' services during the school day are insufficient. Counselors must then turn to community resources to support their counseling programs. Most communities have an abundance of high-quality resources that are available to parents. The goal of collaborating with community agencies is to provide students and families with culturally responsive resources that will further empower the student's academic and social/emotional development. The typical community agencies that counselors refer students and their families to include community health agencies, mental health agencies, and social services (i.e., child abuse agencies, family service agencies, and private practitioners). Social justice–focused school counselors keep a record of which agencies offer the best services (based on feedback from students and parents). In addition, they seek out information regarding the agencies' ability to meet the needs of various racial and cultural groups. For instance, a counselor may discover that a popular family counseling agency in the school community has no bilingual therapists. As a result, the counselor does not refer her Spanish-speaking families to that agency until they hire bilingual staff.

To compile a list of agencies and organizations that assist families, school counselors should visit local agency and organization sites. While on these visits, counselors might note answers to the following questions:

- What is the name of the organization or agency?

- Where is the organization or agency located? Gather and review contact emails, phone numbers, social media sites, and so on. Is the organization accessible to your student population?

- What are the mission, vision, and core values of the organization? Who do they serve?

- What is the organization's fee structure?

- Who provides services (interns, licensed professionals, paid staff, volunteers, etc.)? Are the staff members racially and culturally diverse?

- How does a student or family access the organization's services? Ask the person you talk with to walk you through each step a client goes through from the moment they pick up the phone and call. Who answers the phone? What happens next?

- How does the organization accommodate clients who speak other languages?

- How does the organization address its clients' linguistic, cultural, and racial differences?

- Does the agency gather data to determine the effectiveness of its services? If so, what data do they have, and what does it say about their efficacy with diverse groups?

- Ask for an up-to-date annual report to review.

IMPLEMENTING SCHEDULING PRACTICES THAT PROMOTE RACIAL EQUITY

School counselors often perceive developing the master schedule as a task they would rather not do. However, scheduling is one of the most powerful tasks that counselors implement. A school's schedule lays out the plan for available classes, instructional time, student groupings, teacher assignments, and the physical location of classes. Most importantly, schedules influence students' educational trajectories. Research has indicated that scheduling practices advantage specific subgroups of students over others (Clay et al., 2021). Therefore, scheduling is one of the best school counseling levers for improving equity and access to advanced coursework and improving racial justice in schools. Below are essential initial steps to uncovering inequities via a schedule.

1. Audit the scheduling data and processes to understand how the current schedule is serving students and teachers. For example, are the schedules determined by teachers' preferences or the ability of students to take courses? In addition, determine which subgroups of students (e.g., English language learners vs. non–English language learners; special education students vs. non–special education students; Black students vs. white students) have access to which courses at which time.

2. In elementary schools, be sure to discuss the scheduling of special subjects (e.g., physical education, special education, library time) and staff schedules (e.g., paraprofessionals) in relation to when students need the most support.

3. The school leadership team, including school counselors, should define what an equitable schedule looks like in your school. Be sure to openly name the schedule as an equity tool.

4. Strategically place core and elective courses throughout the day to optimize possibilities for access.

Likewise, Johnson (2002) suggested that school counselors use the following questions/topics as a guide to analyzing the schedule:

- The types and numbers of courses offered. Are courses being offered that will prepare students to be competitive and provide eligibility for college? Are higher-level courses increasing over time and remedial courses decreasing? What is the ratio of vocational to academic classes?

- Other inquiries include monitoring the number of students in each section of a course at different points in time. For instance, what is the enrollment in geometry in September, November, February, and June? Are the numbers stable or dwindling? What do the numbers look like at the higher levels? Which teachers are teaching at different levels from year to year?

- School counselors can compare schedules from year to year and give a picture of the direction the school is moving in. This is important in schools that are increasing academic metrics and addressing equity issues.

- Counselors should also examine the schedule for trends that limit students' access to opportunities. For instance, the distribution of courses should be reviewed to ensure that higher-level classes are offered so that all students have a chance to take them. Other practices that should be examined include

  - distribution of teacher quality,

  - distribution of resources,

  - distribution of electives,

  - distribution of extracurricular activities, and

  - distribution of knowledge about opportunities for college or higher education.

Again, through scheduling, an antiracist and social justice–focused counselor advocates for more equitable course-taking across groups of students. Counselors working from a social justice perspective allot time to meet with each of their advisees regarding their schedules. These student conferences allow counselors and students to discuss future goals, student strengths, and student goals. Below is an outline of what might be addressed in a scheduling conference:

1. Current grades and courses

2. College and career goals

3. Students' strengths and areas of growth

4. Future class schedule: What courses will help the student attain goals? What courses might be challenging? Why? Discuss the supports that the student needs.

5. Devise a plan of action for the future (e.g., schedule for subsequent two semesters, a timeline for taking important tests such as PSAT/SAT, schedule for academic support).

Counselors should have information ready for students at the conferences. It's also a good idea for counselors to schedule the conferences in at least 30-minute intervals to discuss and build a relationship with the student. Counselors must be aware of some students' need for more time and plan accordingly. For example, Jordan, an eleventh-grade honors student, will be a first-generation college student. Because his family lacks information about the college application process, the counselor allots extra time for his scheduling conference so that they can discuss his schedule and college application deadlines. The same counselor also scheduled more time for a student failing all of her ninth-grade courses.

For students from families that lack college information, student conferences are a great time to provide information or inform students of where they can retrieve information. Although counselors have large student caseloads, scheduling should not be taken lightly because it is during this process that a counselor can make a difference between a student being college or career prepared and a student dropping out or not having the appropriate coursework for college or a career.

■ ■ ■ Thinking About the Master Schedule

If you are a school counselor, examine your school's schedule. Do you see any trends related to when courses are offered? For example, which teachers teach higher-level courses? Which teach lower-level courses? When can students receive support for their classes? When can students access school counseling services?

SAY NO TO GATEKEEPING

School counselors are often referred to as *gatekeepers*. *Gatekeeping* is a process of course selection and enrollment beginning in middle school and extending through high school, limiting student access to a challenging curriculum. Black and Latinx/ Hispanic students are more likely to report reluctance to use counselors because they perceive them as gatekeepers (Gandara & Bial, 2001; Ogbu, 2003). In addition, school counselors have been reported to place students of color and low-income students in noncollege track classes, effectively shutting these groups of students out of postsecondary educational opportunities. In essence, gatekeeping limits the opportunities for students to enroll in the courses necessary for college admission. Over twenty years ago, Hart and Jacobi (1992) called for school counselors to be advocates rather than gatekeepers. Antiracist and social justice–focused school counselors heed this call for "no gatekeeping" by providing more opportunities than blocking them.

SAY NO TO TRACKING

Counseling is often tied to the tracking of students. The term *tracking* refers to grouping students according to their perceived ability, IQ, or achievement levels. Once sorted and classified, students are provided with curriculum and instruction deemed suited to their ability and matched to spoken or unspoken assessments of each student's future. In many cases, school counselors use the tracking system to determine which students receive certain student services, emotional support, and college/career information.

Research has dramatically demonstrated that this practice has created as many problems as it was designed to solve. Tracking does not result in the equal and equitable distribution of effective schooling and services for all students. Instead, tracking allocates the most valuable school experiences—including challenging and meaningful curriculum, engaging instruction, and high teacher expectations—to students who already have the greatest academic, economic, and social advantages, whereas students who face the greatest struggles in school receive a curriculum based on lower expectations for their capacity to learn.

Over time, students assigned to the lower tracks move so much more slowly than those at the higher levels that differences that may have been real but not profound in the earlier grades become gigantic gaps in achievement, attitude, self-efficacy, and opportunity. Furthermore, the sorting of students into groups of haves and have-nots contradicts the concept of social justice and American values of schools as democratic communities that offer equal educational opportunity to all.

Untracking or de-tracking requires abandoning a strategy that sorts students according to individual weakness in favor of one that groups students for collective strength. It requires changing policies and methods for placing students in classes and programs. Methods for making decisions about student groupings or tracking typically include teacher recommendations, parent recommendations, student recommendations, test scores, and grades. These methods must be examined closely for inequities and biased practices that place groups of students at a disadvantage. For instance, if parent recommendations are weighted heavily in the gifted and talented identification process, students whose parents do not know about writing gifted placement recommendations are at a disadvantage. De-tracking also requires a shift from nurturing the ability of some children to cultivating effort, persistence, and pride in work in all children. It requires moving from a mindset that defines good education as a scarce resource, with the "best" education reserved for the most "deserving" students, to one that envisions a society in which good education and opportunities are abundant enough for all. Social justice–focused school counselors are committed to de-tracking and provoking a reconsideration of the purposes of education. In an era when knowledge is truly power, a redistribution of knowledge is both fair and necessary.

SAY NO TO RIGID DISCIPLINE POLICIES

One of the most detrimental systems of power in schools that contradicts the premise of increasing student support systems is student discipline policy and practice. Overregulation and zero-tolerance discipline practices disproportionately impact students of color and hinder the positive growth of students. Take, for instance, a recent case in which a 15-year-old student was punished for not completing her virtual school work during the COVID-19 lockdown. The student, who is a Black female on parole and has attention deficit hyperactivity disorder (ADHD), was particularly vulnerable during the pandemic. A judge ruled that due to her failure to submit schoolwork, she must be incarcerated based on the rationale that she is a threat to her community. These harsh punishments are common for Black and Brown students and for students with disabilities. Interestingly enough, students who are overregulated and surveilled are less likely to receive the supports that they often need, such as mental health support or additional academic support. In the case above, where were the necessary supports for the 15-year-old with ADHD?

According to a 2018 Government Accountability Office (GAO) report, Black students are overrepresented in every discipline category, particularly in suspensions, corporal punishments, and school-related arrests. Although Black students represent only 15.5% of all public school students, they accounted for 39% of suspensions. These suspensions continue to add up, resulting in lost instructional time for students. School counselors, from a social justice perspective, must work to change school cultures of high stakes and harsh discipline. Here are a few policies for antiracist, social justice–focused school counselors to examine:

1. Dress code policies (e.g., hair, clothing, etc.)

2. Language policies (e.g., speaking English only)

3. Policies on police presence in schools (e.g., school resource officer policies)

4. Virtual learning policies (e.g., camera policies, homework policies)

Antiracist Social and Emotional Learning (SEL) Support Systems

The primary goal of social and emotional learning (SEL) is to improve students' capacity to establish and maintain healthy relationships by establishing a safe, positive, and mutually beneficial environment. Schools with strong support systems are committed to SEL. Nevertheless, SEL cannot occur without a goal of being antiracist and social justice focused. Counselors must realize that racism and oppression impact the lives of students and the communities in which they live. Therefore, if school counselors aim to create safe, positive, healthy relationships in schools, they must also strive to build antiracist and justice-focused schools.

SEL has received much attention over the last decade (Schwartz et al., 2020; Van Velsor, 2009). And some of our favorite SEL terms—mindfulness, resilience, and grit—have become commonplace in counseling and education settings. Nevertheless, these frameworks and constructs are not necessarily aligned with an antiracist perspective. Mindfulness implores students to remain calm and take deep breaths when they feel themselves getting angry. Resilience encourages students to hold their heads high despite mistreatment. Grit tells students to persevere in the face of obstacles. Some educators believe that proficiency in these traits can guarantee a student's success. But what they overlook is that most Black and Brown students already possess these traits and, in most cases, these traits have not kept Black and Brown students safe from harm.

Antiracist and socially just school counselors are careful not to overuse these ambiguous terms and slogans as the foundation of their SEL work. These slogans are often ineffective solutions for a problem that stems from racist ideas, practices, and policies. It's impossible and insulting to tell Black and Brown students to take deep breaths when Black and Brown men and women die while stating "I can't breathe."

Though they are well intentioned, catch-all terms such as *grit* and *resilience* place the responsibility on students to endure an unjust system. And though the reality for Black students is that they may very well have to fight that fight their whole lives; that's even more reason for school counselors to design their programs and to act to open opportunities for students without placing the responsibility on them to change. An antiracist approach to SEL takes a view that recognizes and values the diverse social and emotional skills students bring with them to the classroom. Further, it relates students' individual social and emotional struggles to their lived experience with racial injustice and social inequity.

Restorative justice (RJ) presents an opportunity to do SEL better. RJ is a model and philosophy of conflict resolution that has roots in Maori traditions. It is premised on repairing harm when one's actions disrupt the community and is often considered an alternative to punitive school discipline. For more on RJ, the need for an antiracist approach to SEL, and additional information on antiracist teaching, see the following resources:

- Why We Can't Afford Whitewashed Social Emotional Learning, ASCD (https://www.ascd.org/el/articles/why-we-cant-afford-whitewashed-social-emotional-learning)

- Center for Restorative Justice at Suffolk University (https://www.suffolk.edu/cas/centers-institutes/center-for-restorative-justice)

- Resources to Support Antiracist Learning (https://ggie.berkeley.edu/school-challenges/antiracist-resources-for-educators/?_ga=2.122339915.1147096418.1591808542-1938306602.1591808542#tab__2)

Coordinating College Readiness and Preparation Interventions

Antiracist and social justice-focused school counselors spend significant time supporting students and their families through college and career readiness activities. Because disseminating information about colleges and careers is not enough, social justice–focused school counselors in middle and high schools engage students and their families in college-going activities (e.g., college tours, learning about postsecondary options). More specifically, antiracist and social justice–focused school counselors do the following to prepare all students, regardless of cultural or racial background, for college and careers:

- Create college-going cultures in their schools.

- Provide internships, apprenticeships, dual enrolment, and other opportunities for career and college exploration.

- Provide college preparation and admission activities that foster and support students' college aspirations.

- Assist all parents, guardians, and families in understanding their role in the college and career readiness process.

- Support students' decision making about college and careers.

- Help students realize the wide range of college and career options.

- Provide students with examples of successful college applications, college and career interviews, and career/job applications.

- Maintain professional networks with local college admission officers at diverse institutions.

School counselors can include college-going activities in many formats—individually, in small groups, in classrooms, or in large groups. The format can vary. The key is that students are getting early information and guidance about postsecondary options. Suggested college-going activities include the following:

- Arrange for students to enroll in dual-enrollment programs at local higher education institutions.

- Arrange panel presentations by former students, community leaders, media personalities, professional athletes, college alumni, or other role models explaining the advantages of a college education.

- Visit diverse local colleges and universities, including minority-serving institutions (e.g., historically Black colleges and university, Hispanic-serving institutions), for campus tours.

- Shadow a college student for a day.

- Complete mock college applications and career/job interviews.

- Research and prepare reports on individual colleges.

- Implement college fairs.

- Provide tutoring and mentoring programs.

- Offer elementary students tutoring on college campuses.

- Provide workshops (virtual and in-person) for parents and families on financial planning, strategies to pay for college, and the availability of financial aid.

COORDINATING TUTORING SERVICES

One of the most important student support services that antiracist and social justice–focused counselors can offer is tutoring services. One-on-one, adult-to-child, high-impact tutoring is one of the most effective and impactful instructional strategies known (Fryer & Howard-Noveck, 2017; Slavin et al., 2009). However, providing tutoring services can be a costly proposition. Many schools have developed tutoring programs in which adult volunteers and even teacher candidates implement the tutoring. From a social justice perspective, counselors should be at the forefront of coordinating high-quality tutoring services for those students who are lagging in academic development and need extra support to maintain or catch up in their grades. Social justice–focused counselors can play an active role in determining the diversity and preparation of tutors. Counselors should also attempt to ensure that the tutors provide culturally responsive tutoring.

ADVOCATING ON SCHOOLWIDE COMMITTEES

PARTICIPATING ON INDIVIDUALIZED EDUCATION PROGRAM (IEP) COMMITTEES

One of the most powerful and significant student support committees in a school is the individualized education program (IEP) committee, the committee that makes recommendations for student placement in special education. The issue of disproportionate placement of students of color in special education continues to be documented at the national level and in many state and local education agencies. *Disproportionate placement* generally refers to the representation of a particular group of students at a rate different than that found in the general population. Student placements can be considered disproportionate if they are overrepresented or underrepresented when comparing their presence in a particular class or category with their representation in the general population.

By far, the greatest attention in the literature has been given to the overrepresentation of students of color in special education. Students with disabilities may require services that provide them access to the same learning opportunities as students without disabilities. The Individuals with Disabilities Education Act (IDEA) supports states and localities in their efforts to aid children and youth with disabilities—and their families—in protecting their rights, meeting their individual needs, and improving their educational outcomes. According to the National Center for Education Statistics (NCES, 2016), 13% of students ages 3–21 enrolled in public schools were served under IDEA in the 2015–2016 school year, a total of 6.7 million individuals. The percentage served varied by race/ethnicity; it was highest for those who were American Indian/Alaska Native (17%), followed by those who were Black (16%), white (14%), of two or more races (13%), Hispanic (12%), Pacific Islander (12%), and Asian (7%).

However, some reports show that students of color are less likely than their white peers to be identified as needing special education services and to receive those services, despite demonstrating similar levels of academic performance and behavior—even when attending the same schools (Morgan et al., 2017). The U.S. Department of Education has indicated that racial bias is clearly playing a major role in the overrepresentation and underrepresentation of Black and Brown students in special education.

School counselors, from a social justice perspective, must advocate for equitable treatment of students on IEP committees. Social justice–focused counselors advocate locally and nationally for the best services for students with learning differences and they advocate for fair, unbiased decision-making regarding special education placements. Because the realities of disproportionality in special education suggest that race matters, counselors working toward social justice advocate for policies that state what is an unacceptable number of students of color in special education.

Antiracist and social justice–focused school counselors also work to empower parents and families to have a voice at IEP meetings. In many cases, parents and families are confused by the terminology used at IEP meetings, and they are unfamiliar with their rights and options. School counselors can act as parent advocates.

PARTICIPATING ON GIFTED AND TALENTED COMMITTEES

As is the case with special education committees, social justice–focused counselors also act as advocates on gifted and talented identification committees. For many years, educational professionals have been concerned about the underrepresentation of children from cultural, linguistic, and low-income backgrounds in traditional gifted programs (Ford et al., 2008). These children, many of whom show potential for superior performance in areas that are not easily assessed by traditional ability measures, have not been provided with opportunities that elicit their gifts and talents and encourage them to maximize that potential. The National Educational Longitudinal Study (NELS) of 1988 looked at eighth-graders throughout the nation and found that 65% of the public schools (serving 75% of all public school eighth-graders) had some kind of opportunity for gifted and talented students. The NELS study found that about 8.8% of all eighth-grade public school students participated in gifted and talented programs and that some minority groups were more likely to be served than others. Economically disadvantaged students were significantly underserved, according to NELS data. On the basis of this data, it is imperative that social justice–focused school counselors advocate for identification policies and criteria that make it more likely that a diverse group of students will be represented in gifted programs.

According to Ford (2010), there are three major paradigms fueling underrepresentation of Black and Brown students in gifted education—*deficit thinking, white privilege,* and *colorblind ideology.* She goes on to recommend that educators should do the following to combat underrepresentation: (a) place underrepresentation under the broader umbrella of the opportunity gap; (b) do not buy into deficit thinking about culturally and racially diverse students; (c) do not adhere to a colorblind philosophy and practices and ignore or discount social injustices and white privilege; (d) share the blame or responsibility for underrepresentation; (e) do not acquiesce to the status quo and be complacent with a business-as-usual attitude; and (f) provide substantive and ongoing preparation to work with both gifted and culturally diverse students.

The best identification practices rely on multiple criteria to look for students with gifts and talents. Multiple criteria involve

- multiple types of information, including, for example, indicators of students' cognitive abilities, academic achievement, and performance in a variety of settings; interests, creativity levels, and motivation; and learning characteristics and behaviors;

- multiple sources of information (e.g., parent recommendations, test scores, school grades); and

- multiple time periods to ensure that students are not missed by "one shot" identification procedures that often take place at the end of second or third grade.

We must also ensure that standardized measures use normative samples appropriate to the students being tested, taking into account factors such as race, ethnicity, language, or the presence of a disability.

The use of multiple criteria does not mean the creation of multiple hurdles to jump in order to be identified as gifted. Social justice–focused school counselors look for students with outstanding potential in a variety of ways and at a variety of time periods to ensure that no child who needs services provided through gifted education is missed. Data collected through the use of multiple criteria give us indicators of a student's need for services.

Questions to Consider

1. School counselors have been accused of keeping specific groups of students from gifted programming and college preparatory courses. Do you believe this is true? Why does this happen? Is it based on racist ideas? Is it based on stereotypes?

2. What student services and supports do counselors coordinate and offer at your school? Have those services been helpful to students? How do you know? Are those services based on deficit thinking about students? Explain.

3. What are your thoughts regarding the role of counselors in scheduling?

4. Dr. Bettina Love agrees to an extent that children need grit to be successful in life, but she believes measuring Black students' grit while removing no institutional barriers is deeply harmful. Stories that "remove [the history from] both sides of the water" cause outside perspectives to question whether Black students have grit and conclude that those who are "gritty enough" are an anomaly of endurance. Without recognizing the centuries of racism, boundaries, and policies Black people have had to battle against for years, this narrative of grit is unmeasurable and anti-Black. Do you agree or disagree with this notion of *grit*? Explain your answer.

CHAPTER 9

Doing the Right Thing

Developing an Antiracist, Social Justice–Focused School Counseling Program

True peace is not the absence of tension but the presence of justice.

—Dr. Martin Luther King, Jr.

When the East Lake Middle School principal asked Jennifer, the new school counseling chairperson, what her vision for the school counseling program would be after the pandemic lockdown and protests over George Floyd's murder, she was not sure how to respond. Jennifer realized that she hadn't thought about a vision or a plan for her program. She hadn't reflected on a vision, given the changing education landscape. Nor had she talked with the existing school counselors about what they would like to achieve in the next three years, five years, or 10 years at East Lake. They were merely going to continue what had always been done.

In the past, Jennifer developed yearly goals for her guidance supervisor, but she wrote these goals mostly for the benefit of central administration's expectations. Over the past three years, Jennifer's team discussed applying for ASCA's (American School Counselor Association) RAMP (Recognized ASCA Model Programs) recognition but never got around to submitting an application. However, their motivation for RAMP recognition was not a passion for racial equity. Sure, Jennifer and her team wanted to help students—she wanted them to succeed—but she had no guiding principles or philosophy for ensuring student success. Most of Jennifer's colleagues (i.e., teachers, specialists) had no idea what was in the school counseling plan, what counselors expected of students, or what their philosophy of counseling entailed. Her plans very rarely included clearly stated goals for student achievement, a vision for what she wanted for the total school, plans for changing school culture, or plans for challenging barriers to students' success. Yet, Jennifer's team followed the ASCA model in her district's stated guidance curriculum. And, Black and Latinx students at Jennifer's school continued to lag behind white students academically. There was evidence that East Lake's Black and Latinx students disliked school, distrusted the teachers, and were headed to lower postsecondary outcomes. Jennifer's case is not rare. There are many school counselors who are well-intentioned and do "ASCA-acceptable" work, but they work without fire, passion, or—simply put—without a philosophy for what they believe schools and school counselors must do to ensure social and racial justice for *all* students.

This book has offered a place for school counselors to begin their quest for an antiracist and social justice vision. The antiracist and social justice approach to school counseling is more about a paradigm shift in the way school counselors think about what they do. It's a shift from "I provide services that I think my students need" to "I provide services that are based on what I know students and their families need." It's a shift from "I treat all of my students the same regardless of their racial cultural background" to "When determining students' needs, I consider their racial and cultural experiences." It's a shift from thinking that racial and cultural differences are a problem to thinking that racial and cultural differences are an asset. It's a shift from assuming there are achievement gaps to assuming there are opportunity gaps based on unjust and racist policies, practices, and perceptions. And lastly, it's a shift from ignoring the implications of racism in the U.S. to acknowledging the implications of our country's and world's racist history (e.g., chattel slavery, colonialism). The antiracist and social justice approach, in essence, is a commitment to correcting injustices and setting out to provide opportunities for all students, regardless of their cultural and racial background. It takes courage, determination, and love to be an antiracist and social justice–focused school counselor!

Although developing an antiracist and social justice–focused school counseling program sounds like the logical, good thing to do, there is a price. Changing existing policies to those that bring about equity, opening our school doors to the marginalized and oppressed, and challenging racism and bias are all behaviors that will create tension and uneasiness among our colleagues. Change is difficult for everyone, but changing the landscape of schools, which has historically worked in favor of the dominant racial and income group, will surely cause resistance and backlash. A counselor and good friend of mine once told me, "Why should I change this AP (Advanced Placement) policy for more inclusion when it will only work against *my* child getting a spot in a class or a seat at a competitive university?" She was being very honest with me and reflected one reason why antiracist practice is so slow to occur in schools. We are even witnessing "antiracism backlash" in the debates to omit and erase slavery and other historical facts about systemic racism from school curricula (Dobbin & Kalev, 2016; Smith, 2021). However, if we want to do the right thing, we must put aside our selfish and personal gains and focus on the good of all. I believe that if we focus on the good of all, we will all reap the benefits. Remember, if we have better education for all, we will have more job opportunities for all, less poverty, less anger, and less frustration, which means less crime and violence in communities.

In this chapter, I will offer a way for you to begin reflecting on your vision for developing an antiracist and social justice–focused school counseling program. First, however, you will need to assess your personal beliefs and skills.

ASSESSING YOUR BELIEFS

To work from a social justice framework, you must tap into your beliefs about schools, school reform, student achievement, and social justice. Therefore, these questions should be discussed at length and reflected on before moving forward.

COUNSELOR BELIEF ASSESSMENT

Discuss each of the following questions either individually or in small groups. Be honest and reflect on your responses. Record your responses on your phone or a tape recorder and then go back and listen to your responses. You might be surprised at what you hear.

1. What are your beliefs about poverty? Using your experience and definition of poverty what are the top three conditions (or factors) that cause an individual, a family, or a group of people to be living in poverty?

2. Do you believe that the history of racism in the U.S. (e.g., colonization of the U.S., slavery) has an impact on current education racial inequities? Explain.

3. Explain and describe how racial disparities in health, education, housing, and criminal justice are connected. What do these connections mean in relation to your school counseling program?

4. What are your beliefs about racism? Do you believe that there is structural and systemic racism?

5. When you hear *white supremacy*, what do you immediately think of? How might your reaction impact your social justice and antiracism work?

6. In your opinion, what is the difference between *equity* and *equality*? How will you address equity and equality in your school counseling program?

7. How do you define *access*? Do your students have equitable and equal access to school counseling services—virtual support, in-person support, and so forth?

8. Describe how antiracism and social justice are the driving forces or guiding principles for your program.

9. Are all children positively influenced by your program? Who doesn't benefit from your services? Why not?

10. Reflect on equity. How do you define it? How do you know when your school counseling program has achieved it?

11. Do you believe that all students can achieve? What does *student success* mean to you?

12. Why do opportunity gaps exist? What is your responsibility in closing gaps?

13. What are your cultural and racial biases and prejudiced beliefs? How do these beliefs influence your decisions and practices?

14. Do you agree or disagree with the following statement? *I believe school counselors are partially responsible for the disparity in opportunities and access experienced by low-income and Black/Brown students.*

ASSESSING YOUR SKILLS

The more skills and strategies you have mastered, the greater will be your possibility for success as an antiracist, social justice–focused school counselor. The Skills Assessment Form lists the skills and strategies related to the topics in this book. Three levels of mastery are presented and defined here. Rate yourself on each skill or strategy for your mastery level.

Identification Mastery: You are able to identify the skill or strategy through observation. You are aware of cultural differences that might relate to the skill.

Basic Mastery: You are able to engage in the skill or strategy. You can use the skill or strategy with students from different cultural groups.

Teaching Mastery: You can teach others to implement this skill or strategy.

ASSESSING YOUR STUDENTS' NEEDS

After assessing your skills, assess the needs of your students by analyzing existing data at your school and at the district level. Keep ongoing records of school data and your notes regarding critical areas of concern. See Tables 9.1–9.3. for examples of data tables.

When reviewing the data, search for trends and patterns over at least a three-year period. For instance, in Table 9.1, over a three-year period, it is clear that there is a disparity in Native American, Latinx/Hispanic, and white students' access to Wi-Fi and internet service at home. As a school counselor, you would ask, "What effect does this trend have on students' ability to access information, complete homework, and participate in virtual learning? What other data would help me understand the problem better?"

Examine the data in Table 9.2. What are the districtwide trends in the identification of third-grade gifted and talented students? Do all third-graders have access to this special program? What factors are utilized to determine "giftedness"? Are those factors biased or racist? What is the identification process/protocol in second grade? What is the policy for identifying gifted and talented students? Is there inherent bias in the policy?

In Table 9.3, the wide disparity among grades distributed by math teachers is obvious. A school counselor should ask, "Are all students receiving equal opportunity in basic math?" This indicates a need for more data work and dialogue among teachers and administrators about what is the acceptable percentage of failing grades from one course.

SKILLS ASSESSMENT FORM

COUNSELOR SKILL	LEVEL OF MASTERY (I, B, T)	WHAT WILL YOU DO TO ACQUIRE THIS SKILL?
1. Ability to develop positive and authentic relationships with racially and culturally diverse people		
2. Ability to be culturally responsive to students		
3. Ability to discern whether a student's behavior is due to systemic racism rather than being pathological		
4. Ability to speak the language of students		
5. Ability to locate translators or bilingual counselors		
6. Ability to assess students' abilities and career development in a culturally appropriate manner		
7. Ability to determine when culture and race negatively influence a counseling relationship		
8. Ability to build trusting relationships with culturally and racially diverse students		

(Continued)

COUNSELOR SKILL	LEVEL OF MASTERY (I, B, T)	WHAT WILL YOU DO TO ACQUIRE THIS SKILL?
9. Ability to broach the topic of racism during the counseling process		
10. Ability to implement empowerment and strengths-based counseling		
11. Ability to interview students and their families in a culturally and racially sensitive manner		
12. Ability to assess a school's culture		
13. Ability to advocate for students during consultation		
14. Ability to challenge and disrupt teachers' and parents' culturally inappropriate and racist attitudes and behaviors		
15. Ability to develop and implement successful partnerships with culturally and racially diverse community organizations		
16. Ability to work with diverse parents using a relational narrative or style		
17. Ability to recognize when others' communication style is negatively influencing relationships with parents of culturally and racially diverse backgrounds		
18. Ability to advocate for policy change		
19. Ability to determine the types of data needed for critical equity questions		
20. Ability to disaggregate and analyze data for equity purposes		
21. Ability to present data to colleagues for equity purposes		
22. Ability to use data to advocate for school change		
23. Ability to evaluate school counseling interventions		

24. Ability to challenge others' racist and biased ideas		
25. Ability to integrate antiracist and social justice practices in college and career counseling curriculum.		
26. Ability to implement scheduling practices that promote equity and racial justice		
27. Ability to coordinate culturally responsive and antiracist tutoring and other student support services		
28. Ability to advocate for students and their families		
29. Ability to advocate for changing policies (e.g., discipline policies, special education, gifted/ talented identification) that further segregate students and create uneven opportunities		

TABLE 9.1   Percentage of High School Students With Access to Wi-Fi at Their Homes by Race

STUDENT IDENTIFIED RACE/ ETHNICITY	2017	2018	2019
Native American	5	5	3
Latinx/Hispanic	25	20	26
White	62	67	68

TABLE 9.2   Districtwide Percentages of Third-Grade Enrollment in Gifted and Talented Program by Race/Ethnicity

STUDENT IDENTIFIED RACE/ ETHNICITY	2018	2019	2020
Black	2	2	2
White	90	86	89
Latinx/Hispanic	3	2	2
Asian	5	8	5
Native American	0	0	0

NOTE: School demographics are 60% white, 25% Black, 10% Asian, 5% Latinx/Hispanic, and 1% Native American.

TABLE 9.3 Grade Analysis by Teacher for Basic Sixth-Grade Math

TEACHER	TOTAL # OF STUDENTS	A	B	C	D	F
A	30	4 (13%)	6 (20%)	10 (33%)	4 (13%)	6 (20%)
B	35	0	0	4 (11%)	4 (11%)	27 (77%)
C	33	5 (15%)	7 (21%)	5 (15%)	12 (36%)	4 (12%)
D	30	1 (3%)	3 (10%)	2 (7%)	8 (27%)	16 (53%)

VISION FOR MY SCHOOL COUNSELING PROGRAM

After reviewing your data and considering your notes on disparities, students' needs, and so on, it is time to think about how equity, antiracism, and social justice will influence your school counseling programming (e.g., time spent working with parents, time spent implementing counseling, time spent on coordinating services). For social justice–based and antiracist programming, it's critical to reflect on factors that contribute to the manifestation of racist ideas. According to psychologists Roberts and Rizzo (2021), seven factors contribute to American racism: categories, factions, segregation, hierarchy, power, media, and passivism. These factors can be utilized to reflect on the "tension areas" in an antiracist, social justice–focused school counseling program. Table 9.4 includes a table with brief definitions of each factor and considerations for your school counseling program.

The worksheet, My Vision for an Antiracist and Social Justice–Focused School Counseling Program, was developed to help you envision aspects of your school counseling program and its outcomes. It should help you organize your program's goals and activities around the six key functions and the factors that contribute to racism (see above). The resources section at the end of this book also includes an action plan template for developing an antiracist and social justice–focused school counseling program.

Share your worksheet and action plan responses with administrators, fellow counselors, parents, teachers, and other stakeholders in your community. Disseminate your plan widely so that your vision is clear to students, too!

CONCLUDING REMARKS

The most critical problem facing U.S. schools is the persistence of pernicious opportunity gaps. Fortunately, there is convincing evidence that opportunity gaps can be closed if certain components are present—leadership, accountability, data-driven programs, and parent involvement. Because of their unique position in

TABLE 9.4 Factors That Contribute to American Racism

FACTOR	DEFINITION	IMPLICATION FOR SCHOOL COUNSELING PROGRAMS
Categories	Humans tend to organize people into distinct groups; category labels promote the belief that category members share an essence that grants them their identity; categories are particularly negative and powerful when presented generically, for instance, "Girls do not like sports" rather than "This girl doesn't like sports."	Avoid labeling students by categories. Avoid overgeneralizing and including stereotypes in counseling materials. Avoid descriptive-to-prescriptive tendencies ("Members of a group should be treated this way.").
Factions	In-group loyalty to one's identity group, particularly for white Americans; feeling positivity in favor of one's group; white Americans show stronger ingroup preferences than Americans of color, who more often show preferences for the outgroup	Create opportunities for students of diverse backgrounds to interact and learn about each other and their histories. Create opportunities for racially diverse students to solve problems together—peer mentoring, peer conflict management, and restorative justice are important for students to lessen outgroup hostility.
Segregation	White people are often residentially segregated from persons of color; therefore, schools are racially segregated.	Advocate for policies that do not segregate and isolate communities and students (e.g., tracking, redlining).
Hierarchy	All societies are hierarchically ordered, and the U.S. is hierarchically ordered by race. White Americans make up the highest-status positions.	Ensure that the school counseling team and leadership are racially and culturally diverse. Use counseling materials that illustrate racially diverse people in different hierarchical roles (e.g., Black doctor, Latinx judge).
Power	White Americans hold high social status and social power, creating white social norms (e.g., standard English, who is advantaged, what is taught in schools).	Decenter traditional power structures and embrace various cultural norms in the school counseling program. Include parents and the community in the decision-making process of a program. "Unteach" the notion that whiteness is superior.

(Continued)

TABLE 9.4 (Continued)

FACTOR	DEFINITION	IMPLICATION FOR SCHOOL COUNSELING PROGRAMS
Media	Media shapes social cognition. The mis- and underrepresentation of racial minorities in the media influences' students perceptions of others.	Ensure that counseling media doesn't include pro-white biases about beauty, cognitive ability, and so forth. Ensure that media is used to advance racial diversity and equity.
Passivism	Passive racism is an apathy toward systems of racial advantage or a denial that those systems exist.	Acknowledge racism and racist systems, policies, and practices. Speak up about racist practices. Be an antiracist!

schools, school counselors can play a critical role in closing opportunity gaps by addressing the six key functions outlined in this book—counseling and intervention planning; consultation; connecting schools, families, and communities; collecting and using data; challenging racism and bias; and coordinating student success and support (the six Cs). Implementing school counseling with an emphasis on these functions is not simple, but it is attainable.

The process of discovering and challenging inequities in schools is difficult and time-consuming. Once you are aware of injustice and inequities, it can be burdensome and tiring. Remember, however, that your attention to social justice and antiracism will make a difference in our country's educational system. The key is that we change how we think about and do our jobs as school counselors. Good luck on your journey.

My Vision for an Antiracist and Social Justice–Focused School Counseling Program

1. My main goals for students are _____.

2. At this time, there are student inequities in my school (e.g., a disproportionate number of students of color in special education, a lack of girls in advanced math classes, a lack of English language learners represented in the gifted program). List these inequities below. Include data to support these statements. _____

3. My vision for students is _____.

4. Student achievement will be evident as a result of these school counseling activities: _____. (Describe at least five activities or interventions.)

5. To promote social justice, I will work with teachers and school personnel to _____ (e.g., communicate more effectively with low-income communities, advocate for new housing policies in my school community).

6. To promote antiracism and social justice, I will work with students to_____(e.g., enhance their racial identity development, identify their strengths, identify their goals).

7. To promote antiracism and social justice, I will work with teachers and other school personnel to_____ (e.g., enhance their racial identity development, identify their strengths, identify their goals).

8. To promote social justice, I will work with administrators to _____ (e.g., understand systemic oppression, understand data, promote the effectiveness of counseling interventions).

9. To promote social justice, I will work with parents _____ (e.g., to enhance their feelings of empowerment, to enhance their understanding of postsecondary options).

10. To promote social justice, I will work with communities to _____ (e.g., provide safety for children, provide resources for parents).

11. To promote social justice, I will collect and analyze these types of data _____ (e.g., college enrollment rates, access to special programs, grades, attendance rates).

12. To promote social justice, I will change the school's culture to

_____.

13. To promote social justice, I will challenge racism and bias in the following areas _____ (e.g., special education identification, postsecondary options, teachers' low expectations).

14. As a result of these interventions (e.g., individual work, group work, classroom guidance, schoolwide initiatives, community initiatives, parent initiatives), students will be able to (list student outcomes)

_____.

(Continued)

(Continued)

15. I want my school to become a place where

_____ .

_____ .

RESOURCES

Resource A

Assessing School Equity

In a small group (e.g., school-based leadership team, group of counselors), answer each of the following questions to assess whether or not your school is addressing equity.

- Which students actively participate in classes? Are teachers paying attention to, asking probing questions of, and encouraging all students?

- Who has access to technology and Wi-Fi? Why do some not have access?

- Are students being discouraged from speaking and writing in their native language and encouraged to give up their culture? Are students' names pronounced correctly by teachers and other educators in the school?

- Does the curriculum represent the contributions of all people (women and people of color, for example)?

- Are there accurate historical accounts of shameful periods of U.S. history (e.g., slavery, the treatment of Native Americans, the internment of Japanese Americans, anti-Semitism, and the eugenics movement)?

- Are there faculty role models for students? How does it affect students of color if most of the teachers they see are white?

- Do students talk with other students respectfully about important issues?

- Can students talk with each other about their problems? Can they talk with teachers?

- How much harassment and teasing (particularly of minoritized students) goes on in the school?

- Are there friendships in the school across cultural and racial groups?

- Are students of color in positions of leadership?

- Are students of color disproportionately disciplined, expelled, or suspended?

- How do people explain the disproportionate failure or success by students of color, language-minority students, and students from low-socioeconomic groups?

- When equity issues are raised, do teachers say, "We've already dealt with that" or "I don't see color"?

- Is it safe in your school or district to talk about sensitive issues such as racism, sexism, or homophobia? Are adults working to overcome their own biases?

- Do counselors understand how oppression and racism work in our society?

- Do educators from different racial backgrounds communicate with each other?

- Are there friendships among educators across racial lines?

- Are teachers of color respected? Are they in positions of leadership?

- Do bilingual teachers have as much power in the school as regular teachers?

- How do teachers feel about their jobs? How does teacher morale affect students' school experiences?

- How does the pressure at the state and district level to improve test scores affect the way educators relate to students?

- Is the atmosphere of the school one of respect for students? How do teachers talk about students in the faculty room? What are their expectations? What kind of relationships do they have with students?

- Are parents of students of color and English language learners present in school events and school board meetings? Are they represented on committees and on the school board? Do they feel they have a voice in the school and are respected members of the school community?

- Are language translators and ASL (American Sign Language) interpreters always present at school meetings?

- Do teachers have professional development about relating to parents of different cultural backgrounds? Do teachers make an effort to support all parents' participation in their children's education (especially recent immigrants, parents of color, and parents from low socioeconomic classes)?

- Which parents have the most influence in the school?

- Does the scheduling of parent–teacher conferences discriminate against parents who have to work during the day?

- Are schools connected to the community in which they reside?

- How does the assessment system being used affect the achievement of students from underrepresented groups?

- How does the emphasis on raising test scores affect students from underrepresented groups?

- Are high-stakes tests (including gifted/talented and Advanced Placement) available in languages other than English?

- How do counseling practices affect student self-perception and performance? How are tracking policies affecting students' success?

- Does professional development at the school provide opportunities for educators to talk about the biases they encountered growing up and how that affects them? Do they talk about how race, class, and gender bias affect teaching and learning? Are these issues treated in depth?

- Are teachers feeling empowered in planning and conducting their professional development?

- Are English language learners receiving adequate support for learning academic subjects or is an emphasis on increasing reading scores impeding their learning of other subjects?

- Are high-level math and science classes taught bilingually or with sheltered instruction (i.e., method of teaching English language learner students)?

- Do the most experienced teachers teach the classes with a disproportionately high number of white or affluent students?

- What is the racial/ethnic distribution of teachers in your school? What is the distribution within the district?

- How are resources allocated to different schools within the district? Do schools with the poorest students also have the least-experienced teachers and fewer resources?

- Do the district and school leadership emphasize equity and practice what they preach? Are administrators providing both intellectual and emotional support to teachers for changing unequal success rates? Do teachers of color report having difficulty with one or more administrators?

- Do administrators and school boards support teachers' attempts to implement new curriculum or pedagogical approaches that provide access to the curriculum for more students? Do they provide encouragement for risk taking?

SOURCE: Adapted/Reprinted from "the Discussion Areas for Equity" of the National Coalition for Equity in Education, Department of Education, University of California, Santa Barbara, University of California, Santa Barbara, CA 93106-7090 with the permission of the Director Julian Weisglass. http://ncee.education.ucsb.edu/ discussionareas.htm

Resource B

School Counselor Multicultural Competence Checklist

MULTICULTURAL COUNSELING

1. I recognize when my beliefs and values are interfering with providing the best services to my students.

2. I use strengths-based counseling with students.

3. I can identify the cultural basis of my communication style.

4. I can discuss how culture and race affect the help-seeking behaviors of students.

5. I know when a counseling approach is culturally appropriate for a specific student.

6. I know when a counseling approach is culturally inappropriate for a specific student.

7. I can identify culturally appropriate interventions and counseling approaches (e.g., indigenous practices) with students.

8. I can list at least three barriers that prevent ethnic minority students from using counseling services.

9. I know when my helping style is inappropriate for a culturally and racially diverse student.

10. I know when my helping style is appropriate for a culturally and racially diverse student.

11. I can give examples of how stereotypical beliefs about culturally and racially diverse persons impact the counseling relationship.

12. I know when my biases, racist ideas, and beliefs influence my service to students.

13. I know when specific cultural beliefs influence students' response to counseling.

MULTICULTURAL CONSULTATION

14. I know when my culture and race are influencing the process of consultation.

15. I know when the consultee's (e.g., parent, teacher) culture and race are influencing the process of consultation.

16. I know when the race or culture of a student is a problem for a teacher.

17. I initiate discussions related to race, ethnicity, and culture when consulting with teachers.

18. I initiate discussions related to race, ethnicity, and culture when consulting with parents.

UNDERSTANDING RACISM AND STUDENT RESISTANCE

19. I can define and discuss white privilege.

20. I can discuss how I (if European American or white) am privileged based on my race.

21. I can identify racist aspects of educational institutions.

22. I can define and discuss prejudice.

23. I can identify discrimination and discriminatory practices in schools.

24. I am able to challenge my colleagues when they discriminate against students.

25. I can define and discuss racism.

26. I can discuss the influence of racism on the counseling process.

27. I can discuss the influence of racism on the educational system in the United States.

28. I can help students determine whether a problem stems from racism or biases in others.

29. I understand the relationship between student resistance and racism.

30. I can discuss the relationship between student resistance and racism.

31. I include topics related to race and racism in my classroom guidance units.

32. I challenge others' racist beliefs and behaviors.

33. I can identify racist and unjust policies in schools.

UNDERSTANDING RACIAL AND ETHNIC IDENTITY DEVELOPMENT

34. I can discuss at least two theories of racial or ethnic identity development.

35. I can use racial and ethnic identity development theories to understand my students' problems and concerns.

36. I can assess my own racial and ethnic identity development in order to enhance my counseling.

37. I can help students explore their own racial identity development.

38. I can develop activities that enhance students' racial or ethnic identity.

39. I can discuss how racial identity may influence relationships between students and educators.

MULTICULTURAL ASSESSMENT

40. I can discuss the potential bias of assessment instruments frequently used in the schools.

41. I can evaluate instruments that may be biased against certain groups of students.

42. I use test information appropriately with culturally and racially diverse parents.

43. I advocate for fair testing and the appropriate use of testing of students from diverse backgrounds.

44. I can identify whether or not the assessment process is culturally and racially sensitive.

45. I can discuss how the identification stage of the assessment process might be biased against minority populations.

46. I use culturally appropriate instruments when I assess students.

47. I can discuss how assessment leads to inequitable opportunities for students.

MULTICULTURAL FAMILY INTERVENTIONS

48. I can discuss family counseling from a cultural/racial/ethnic perspective.

49. I can discuss at least two racial/ethnic groups' traditional gender role expectations and rituals.

50. I anticipate when my helping style is inappropriate for a parent or guardian from a different culture.

51. I can discuss culturally diverse methods of parenting and discipline.

52. I can discuss how class and economic level affect family functioning and development.

53. I can discuss how race and ethnicity influence family behavior.

54. I can identify when a school policy is biased against culturally diverse families.

SOCIAL JUSTICE ADVOCACY

55. I know of societal issues that affect the development of culturally and racially diverse students.

56. When counseling, I address societal issues that influence the development of culturally and racially diverse students.

57. I work with families and community members to orient them to the school.

58. I can define *social justice change agent*.

59. I am a social justice change agent.

60. I can discuss what it means to take an activist counseling approach.

61. I intervene with students at the individual and systemic levels.

62. I can discuss how factors such as poverty and powerlessness have influenced the current conditions of at least two racial/ethnic groups.

63. I advocate for students who are being subjected to injustices.

64. I can use data as an advocacy tool.

DEVELOPING SCHOOL–FAMILY–COMMUNITY PARTNERSHIPS

65. I can discuss how school–family–community partnerships are linked to student achievement.

66. I develop partnerships with families that are culturally different from me.

67. I develop partnerships with diverse agencies within my school's community.

68. I can define a school–family–community partnership.

69. I can discuss more than three types of parent involvement.

70. I encourage the participation of racially and culturally diverse parents in school activities.

71. I work with community leaders and other resources in the community to assist with student and family concerns.

UNDERSTANDING CROSS-CULTURAL INTERPERSONAL INTERACTIONS

72. I can discuss interaction patterns that might influence students' perceptions of inclusion in the school community.

73. I solicit feedback from students regarding my interactions with them.

74. I verbally communicate my acceptance of racially and culturally diverse students.

75. I nonverbally communicate my acceptance of racially and culturally diverse students.

76. I assess the manner in which I speak and the emotional tone of my interactions with culturally and racially diverse students.

77. I greet students and parents in a culturally acceptable manner.

78. I can identify culturally and racially insensitive topics and gestures.

MULTICULTURAL CAREER ASSESSMENT

79. I implement culturally sensitive career development activities in which materials are representative of all groups in a wide range of careers.

80. I arrange opportunities for students to have interactions with racially and culturally diverse professionals.

81. I assess the strengths of multiple aspects of students' self-concept.

82. I can discuss differences in the decision-making styles of students.

83. I integrate my knowledge of varying decision-making styles when implementing career counseling.

84. I integrate family and religious issues in the career counseling process.

85. I use career assessment instruments that are sensitive to students' cultural differences.

86. I can discuss how *work* and *career* are viewed similarly and differently across cultures.

87. I can discuss how many career assessment instruments are inappropriate for culturally and racially diverse students.

MULTICULTURAL SENSITIVITY

88. I develop close, personal relationships with people of other races.

89. I can live comfortably with culturally and racially diverse people.

90. I am comfortable with people who speak another language.

91. I make friends with people from other ethnic/racial groups.

Resource C
School Culture Assessment

Below are dimensions of a school's culture. To assess a school's culture, collect items and participate in the following activities. Take notes and then summarize what you found.

1. *Artifacts:* Collect school memorabilia, yearbooks, faculty and student handbooks, school website information, schedules, newsletters, memos, school newspaper, bulletin board items, and so forth. What themes do you see? What is valued in the school—academics, athletics, standardized tests, social justice, equity?

2. *Rituals:* What types of events and activities occur at the school on a regular basis—open houses, Parent–Teacher Association or Parent–Teacher Organization meetings, celebrations, morning and afternoon announcements, programs, websites, social media sites, weekend events, seasonal events (holiday parties, programs), faculty meetings, and so forth. Attend at least four of these events. If there are very few rituals, what effect does that have on the school?

3. *Communication:* Interview faculty, parents, and students about how groups interact and communicate with one another. How are parents greeted when they enter the office? Are they greeted on the phone? How does the school accommodate non–English-speaking students and parents? How has the school managed crises and/or emergencies (e.g., COVID-19)?

4. *Collaboration:* Interview teachers, administrators, and parents regarding how they work with one another. Is there collaboration among teachers across grades and subjects?

5. *Innovation:* How are new concepts and strategies introduced and received? What new programs or curricula are being implemented in the school?

6. *Decision making:* How are decisions made? Describe the process of decision making. Is it shared? How are crises handled?

7. *Leadership:* Who are the leaders in the school? Who has the strongest voice? Who has the weakest? Describe the administrators' leadership style. Do leaders openly discuss issues of equity, antiracism, and social justice?

Resource D

Assessing Beliefs About School–Family–Community Partnership Involvement

How involved do you believe school counselors should be in each of the following activities (a lot, some, not too much, none)?

1. Working with a team of school staff, families, community members, or professionals (e.g., school mental health team)

2. Locating community services and resources (e.g., mental health, nutrition, social services, and clothing) for students and their families

3. Collaborating with community agency professionals

4. Working with school staff, families, and community members to advocate for equity, access, and academic success for students

5. Teaching parents and students how to access services in the school and community

6. Involving parents, families, and community members in the delivery of guidance activities and services to students (e.g., career guidance)

7. Using school and student data to advocate for change in the school on behalf of students

8. Helping parents, families, and community members to organize support programs for students (e.g., tutoring and mentoring programs)

9. Implementing programs to help families and community members understand the school (e.g., parent and family seminars)

10. Coordinating school–community outreach efforts

11. Providing parent education workshops and seminars

12. Serving on advisory councils or committees in the community

13. Facilitating integration of community services within the school (e.g., mental health and social services housed in the school)

14. Implementing programs to help the school staff understand families and the community (e.g., in-service training on culturally diverse families)

15. Using data to show the benefits of school–family–community partnership programs for students

16. Teaching the staff how to build effective school–family–community partnerships

17. Conducting home visits to families

SOURCE: Adapted from Bryan & Holcomb-McCoy (2007).

Suggested Readings by Topic

Antiracism, Racism, Prejudice, and Oppression

The 1619 Project. (2019, August 14). *The New York Times.* https://www.nytimes.com/interactive/2019/08/14/magazine/1619-america-slavery.html

Alexander, M. (2011). *The new Jim Crow: Mass incarceration in the age of colorblindness.* The New Press.

Allport, G. W. (1954). *The nature of prejudice.* Doubleday.

Coates, T. (2015). *Between the world and me.* Spiegel & Grau.

Cokley, K. (2021). *Making Black lives matter: Confronting anti-Black racism.* Cognella Publishing.

Davis, A. Y. (2012). *The meaning of freedom: And other difficult dialogues.* City Lights Books.

DiAngelo, R. (2018). *White fragility: Why it's so hard for white people to talk about racism.* Beacon Press.

Dubar-Ortiz, R. (2014). *An indigenous peoples' history of the United States.* Beacon Press.

Fadiman, A. (1998). *The spirit catches you and you fall down.* Farrar, Straus, & Giroux.

Fanon, F. (1961/2005). *Wretched of the earth.* Grove Press.

Forman, J. (2017). *Locking up our own: Crime and punishment in Black America.* Farrar, Straus, & Giroux.

Freire, P. (2000). Pedagogy of the oppressed. Continuum.

Kendi, I. (2019). *How to be an antiracist.* One World.

King, R. (2014). *Mindful of race: Transforming racism from the inside out.* Sounds True Publishing.

Kivel, P. (2002). *Uprooting racism: How white people can work for racial justice.* New Society Publishers.

Lester, N. (2020). *No, I am not OK. Thanks for asking.* Learning for Justice. https://www.learningforjustice.org/magazine/no-i-am-not-ok-thanks-for-asking

Love, B. (2019). *We want to do more than survive: Abolitionist teaching and the pursuit of educational freedom.* Beacon Press.

Lynn, M., & Dixson, A. D. (2013/2021). *Handbook of critical race theory in education.* Routledge.

McCall, N. (1994). *Makes me wanna holler: A young Black man in America.* Vintage Books.

McIntyre, A. (1997). *Making meaning of whiteness: Exploring racial identity with white teachers.* State University of New York Press.

Metzl, J. M. (2019). *Dying of whiteness: How politics of racial resentment is killing America's heartland.* Basic Books.

Middleton, S., Roediger, D. R., & Shaffer, D. (2016). The construction of whiteness: An interdisciplinary analysis of race formation and the meaning of a white identity. University of Mississippi Press.

National Museum of African American History and Culture Releases "Talking About Race" Web Portal. (2020, May 31). *The Smithsonian National Museum of African American History and Culture.* https://nmaahc.si.edu/about/news/national-museum-african-american-history-and-culture-releases-talking-about-race-web

Oluo, I. (2018). *So you want to talk about race.* Seal Press.

Plous, S. (Ed.). (2003). *Understanding prejudice and discrimination.* McGraw-Hill.

Razack, S. H. (1998). *Looking white people in the eye: Gender, race, and culture in courtrooms and classrooms.* University of Toronto Press.

Simmons, D. (2019). *How to be an antiracist educator.* ASCD. https://www.ascd.org/el/articles/how-to-be-an-antiracist-educator

Singh, A. A. (2019). *The racial healing handbook: Practical activities to help you challenge privilege, confront systemic racism, and engage in collective healing.* New Harbinger Publications.

Steele, C. M. (2011). *Whistling Vivaldi: How stereotypes affect us and what we can do.* W. W. Norton & Company.

Steele, C. M. (1997). A threat in the air: How stereotypes shape intellectual identity and performance. *American Psychologist, 52,* 613–629.

Sue, D. W. (2016). *Race talk and the conspiracy of silence: Understanding and facilitating difficult dialogues on race.* Wiley.

Tatum, B. D. (2003). *Why are all the Black kids sitting together in the cafeteria? And other conversations about race.* Basic Books.

Wells, A. S., & Crain, R. L. (1999). *Stepping over the color line: African-American students in white suburban schools.* Yale University Press.

INTERSECTIONALITY

Cavendish, W., Samson, J. F., & Artiles, A. (2021). *Intersectionality in education: Toward more equitable policy, research, and practice.* Teachers College Press.

Chantler, K. (2005). From disconnection to connection: "Race," gender and the politics of therapy. *British Journal of Guidance and Counselling, 33*(2), 239–256.

Coates, R. D., Ferber, A. L., & Brunsma, D. L. (2018). *The matrix of race: Social construction, intersectionality, and inequality.* SAGE.

Collins, P. H., & Bilge, S. (2020). *Intersectionality (key concepts).* Polity Press.

Crenshaw, K. (2019). *On intersectionality: The essential writings of Kimberlé Crenshaw.* The New Press.

Hannon, M. D. (2017). Acknowledging intersectionality: An autoethnography of a Black school counselor educator and father of a student with autism. *Journal of Negro Education, 86*(2), 154–162.

López, D., Ochoa, D., Romero, M., & Parr, K. (2020). Integrating Latinx/Hispanic culture, traditions, and beliefs into effective school psychology practice. *Communique, 49*(4).

Pebdani, R. N. (2019). Changing how we approach multicultural counselor education: Using intersectionality, power, privilege, and oppression to frame lived experiences. *Rehabilitation Research, Policy, and Education, 33*(4), 214–220.

Williams, W., Karlin, T., & Wallace, D. (2012). Project Sister Circle: Risk, intersectionality, and intervening in urban schools. *Journal of School Counseling, 10*(17), 1–35.

MULTICULTURAL AND SOCIAL JUSTICE COUNSELING

Bashur, M. R., Codrington, J. N., & Liang, C. T. H. (2002). Client perspectives of multicultural counseling competence: A qualitative examination. *Counseling Psychologist, 30,* 355–393.

Chung, R., & Bemak, F. P. (2011). *Social justice counselling: The next steps beyond multiculturalism.* SAGE

Constantine, M. G. (2002). Predictors of satisfaction with counseling: Racial and ethnic minority clients' attitudes toward counseling and ratings of their counselors' general and multicultural counseling competence. *Journal of Counseling Psychology, 49,* 255–263.

Day-Vines, N., Cluxton-Keller, F., Agorsor, C., & Gubara, S. (2021). Strategies for broaching the subjects of race, ethnicity, and culture. *Journal of Counseling and Development, 99*, 348–357.

Day-Vines, N., Wood, S., Grothaus, T., Craigen, L., Holman, A., Dotson-Blake, K., & Douglass, M. J. (2007). Broaching the subjects of race, ethnicity, and culture during the counselling process. *Journal of Counseling and Development, 85*, 401–409.

Holcomb-McCoy, C. (2021). *Antiracist counseling in schools and communities.* American Counseling Association.

Lee, C. C. (2006). *Multicultural issues in counseling: New approaches to diversity.* American Counseling Association.

McClure, F. H., & Teyber, E. (1996). *Child and adolescent therapy: A multicultural-relational approach.* Harcourt Brace College Publishers.

Paniagua, F. (1994). *Assessing and treating culturally diverse clients.* SAGE.

Ponterotto, J. G., Casas, J. M., Suzuki, L. A., & Alexander, C. M. (2001). *Handbook of multicultural counseling.* SAGE.

Pope-Davis, D. B., Toporek, R. L., Ortega-Villalobos, L., Ligiero, D. P., Liu, W. M., & Russell, J. (1999). Professional and socio-cultural aspects of the counseling relationship. In C. Feltham (Ed.), *Understanding the counseling relationship* (pp. 183–199). SAGE.

Schwarzbaum, S. (2004). Low-income Latinos and drop out: Strategies to prevent dropout. *Journal of Multicultural Counseling and Development, 32*, 296–306.

Sue, D. W., Ivey, A. E., & Pederson, P. B. (1996). *Theory of multicultural counseling therapy.* Wadsworth Publishing.

Sue, D. W., Sue, D., Neville, H., & Smith, L. (2021). Counseling the culturally diverse: Theory and practice (8th ed.). Wiley & Sons.

Walker, R. (2020). *The unapologetic guide to Black mental health: Navigate an unequal system, learn tools for emotional wellness, and get the help you deserve.* New Harbinger Publications.

Migration and Acculturation

Alba, R., & Nee, V. (2003). *Remaking the American mainstream: Assimilation and contemporary immigration.* Harvard University Press.

The American Federation of Teachers. (2016). *Immigrant and refugee children: A guide for educators and school support staff.* Author.

Caplan, N., Whitmore, J. K., & Choy, M. H. (1991). *Children of the boat people: A study of educational success.* University of Michigan Press.

Edwards, L. M., & Black, J. (2017). *Stress related to immigration status in students: A brief guide for schools.* https://www.gsafewi.org/wp-content/uploads/Immigration-Related-Stress-A-Guide-for-Schools.pdf

Gonzalez, R. (2011). *Butterfly boy: Memories of a Chicano mariposa.* The University of Wisconsin Press.

Guerrero, D. (2017). *In the country we love: My family divided.* St. Martin's Press.

Jeffries, J. (2014). Fear of deportation in high school: Implications for breaking the circle of silence surrounding migration status. *Journal of Latinos and Education, 13*, 278–295.

Lieberson, S., & Waters, M. (1988). *From many strands: Ethnic and racial groups in contemporary America.* Russell Sage Foundation.

Massey, D. S., Durand, J., & Malone, N. (2002). *Beyond smoke and mirrors: Mexican migration in an era of economic integration.* Russell Sage Foundation.

Nayeri, D. (2020). *The ungrateful refugee: What immigrants never tell you.* Catapult.

Obiakor, F. E., & Afolayan, M. O. (2007). African immigrant families in the United States: Surviving the sociocultural tide. *Family Journal: Counseling and Therapy for Couples and Families, 15*(3), 265–270.

Peralta, D. (2016). *Undocumented: A Dominican boy's odyssey from a homeless shelter to the Ivy League.* Penguin Books.

Portes, A., & Rumbaut, R. G. (2001). *Legacies. The story of the immigrant second generation.* University of California Press and Russell Sage Foundation.

Rumbaut, R. G., & Russell Portes, A. (Eds.). (2001). *Ethnicities: Children of immigrants in America.* University of California Press and Sage Foundation.

Suárez-Orozco, C., & Suárez-Orozco, M. M. (2002). *Children of immigration.* Harvard University Press.

Waters, M. C. (1999). *Black identities: West Indian immigrant dreams and American realities.* Russell Sage Foundation.

Yeh, C. J., Kim, A. B., Pituc, S. T., & Atkins, M. (2008). Poverty, loss, and resilience: The story of Chinese immigrant youth. *Journal of Counseling Psychology, 55*(1), 34–48.

Yoon, E., Langrehr, K., & Ong, L. Z. (2011). Content analysis of acculturation research in counseling and counseling psychology: A 22-year review. *Journal of Counseling Psychology, 58*(1), 83–96.

COLLEGE AND CAREER READINESS

Bryan, J., Holcomb-McCoy, C., Moore-Thomas, C., & Day-Vines, N. (2009). Who sees the school counselor for college information? A national study. *Professional School Counseling, 12*(4), 280–291.

Byars-Winston, A. (2010). The vocational significance of Black identity: Cultural formulation approach to career assessment and career counseling. *Journal of Career Development, 37*(1), 441–464.

Castro, E. L. (2013). Racialized readiness for college and career: Toward an equity-grounded social science of intervention programming. *Community College Review, 41*(4), 292–-310.

Cottom, T. M. (2018). *Lower ed: The troubling rise of for-profit colleges in the new economy.* The New Press.

Delpit, L. (2012). *Multiplication is for white people: Raising expectations for other people's children.* The New Press.

The Education Trust–West. (2011). *Unlocking doors and expanding opportunity: Moving beyond the limiting reality of college and career readiness in California high schools.* Author.

Georgetown University Center on Education and the Workforce. (2017). *Career pathways: Five ways to connect college and careers.* Author. https://1gyhoq479ufd3yna29x7ubjn-wpengine.netdna-ssl .com/wp-content/uploads/LEE-final.pdf

Goldrick-Rab, S. (2016). *Paying the price: College costs, financial aid, and the betrayal of the American dream.* The University of Chicago Press.

Harris, P. N., Gonzalez, L. M., Kearney, B., & Ingram, K. (2020). Finding their SPARCK: College and career readiness groups for African American females. *Journal for Specialists in Group Work, 45*(1), 40–55.

Jack, A. (2020). *The privileged poor: How elite colleges are failing disadvantaged students.* Harvard University Press.

Majors, A. T. (2019). From the editorial board: College readiness: A critical race theory perspective. *The High School Journal, 102*, 183–188.

Mayes, R. D. (2020). College and career readiness groups for gifted Black students with disabilities. *Journal for Specialists in Group Work, 45*(3), 200–212.

Perusse, R., Poynton, T. A., Parzych, J. L., & Goodnough, G. E. (2015). The importance and implementation of eight components of college and career readiness counseling in school counselor education programs. *Journal of College Access, 1*(1), 29–41.

Prystowsky, R. J., Herrera, J., Crowley, C., Lowery-Hart, R., & Fannon, S. (2017). Grabbing third rails: Courageous responses to persistent equity gaps. *Liberal Education, 103*(2).

Rosen, R., & Dalporto, H. (2020). *Does technology-based advising promote equity in career and technical education?* MDRC.

Savitz-Romer, M. (2012). The gap between influence and efficacy: College readiness training, urban school counselors, and the promotion of equity. *Counselor Education and Supervision, 51*(2), 98–111.

Vespia, K. M., Fitzpatrick, M. E., Fouad, N. A., Kantamneni, N., & Chen, Y. (2010). Multicultural career counseling: A national survey of competencies and practices. *Career Development Quarterly, 59*(1), 54–71.

Williams, J. M., Bryan, J., Morrison, S., & Scott, T. R. (2017). Protective factors and processes contributing to the academic success of students living in poverty: Implications for counselors. *Journal of Multicultural Counseling and Development, 45*(3), 183–200.

Gender Diversity

Boykin, K. (1996). *One more river to cross: Black and gay in America.* Anchor Books.

Chappell, S. V., Ketcham, K., & Richardson, L. (2018). *Gender diversity and LGBTQ inclusion in K–12 schools: A guide to supporting students, changing lives.* Taylor & Francis.

Herek, G. M. (1992). Psychological heterosexism and anti-gay violence: The social psychology of bigotry and bashing. In G. M. Herek & K. T. Berrill (Eds.), *Hate crimes: Confronting violence against lesbians and gay men* (pp. 149–169). SAGE.

Kilman, C. (2013). The gender spectrum. *Learning for Justice.* https://www.learningforjustice.org/magazine/summer-2013/the-gender-spectrum

Lorde, A. (2014). *Sister outsider: Essays and speeches.* Crossing Press.

McQuillan, M. T., & Leininger, J. (2021). Supporting gender-inclusive schools: Educators' beliefs about gender diversity training and implementation plans. *Professional Development in Education, 47*(1), 156–176.

Mock, J. (2014). *Redefining realness: My path to womanhood, identity, love & so much more.* Atria Books.

Simons, J. D., Beck, M. J., Asplund, N. R., Chan, C. D., & Byrd, R. (2018). Advocacy for gender minority students: Recommendations for school counsellors. *Sex Education: Sexuality, Society and Learning, 18*(4), 464–478.

TedTalks. (n.d.). *Celebrating and de-constructing the gender spectrum.* https://www.ted.com/playlists/459/the_gender_spectrum

Ullman, J. (2017). Teacher positivity towards gender diversity: Exploring relationships and school outcomes for transgender and gender-diverse students. *Sex Education: Sexuality, Society and Learning, 17*(3), 276–289.

Socioeconomic and Social Class

American Psychological Association, Task Force on Socioeconomic Status. (2007). *Report of the APA task force on socioeconomic status.* Author.

Bell, L. E., & Van Velsor, P. (2018). Counseling in the gentrified neighborhood: What school counselors should know. *Professional School Counseling, 21*(1), 161–168.

Castleman, B., & Goodman, J. (2018). Intensive college counseling and the enrollment and persistence of low-income students. *Education Finance and Policy, 13*(1), 19–41.

Croizet, J. C., Autin, F., Goudeau, S., Marot, M., & Millet, M. (2019). Education and social class: Highlighting how the educational system perpetuates social inequality. In J. Jetten & K. Peters (Eds.), *The social psychology of inequality* (pp. 139–152). Springer.

Hochschild, J. L. (2003). Social class in public schools. *Journal of Social Issues, 59*, 821–840.

Liu, W. M. (2002). The social class-related experiences of men: Integrating theory and practice. *Professional Psychology: Research and Practice, 33*, 355–360.

Liu, W. M., & Ali, S. R. (2005). Addressing social class in vocational theory and practice: Extending the emancipatory communitarian approach. *The Counseling Psychologist, 33*, 189–196.

Liu, W. M., Ali, S. R., Soleck, G., Hopps, J., Dunston, K., & Pickett, T., Jr. (2004). Using social class in counseling psychology research. *Journal of Counseling Psychology, 51*, 3–18.

Liu, W. M., Soleck, G., Hopps, J., Dunston, K., & Pickett, T. (2004). A new framework to understand social class in counseling: The social class worldview and modern classism theory. *Journal of Multicultural Counseling and Development, 32*, 95–122.

McDonough, P. M. (1997). *Choosing colleges. How social class and schools structure opportunity.* State University of New York Press.

Stephens, N. M., Townsend, S., & Dittman, A. G. (2019). Social class disparities in higher education and professional workplaces: The role of cultural mismatch. *Current Directions in Psychological Science, 28*, 67–73.

Stern, E. M. (1990). *Psychotherapy and the poverty patient.* Haworth Press.

ENGLISH LANGUAGE LEARNERS

Baker, C., & Wright, W. E. (2017). *Foundations of bilingual education and bilingualism* (6th ed.). Multilingualism Matters.

Biever, J. L., Castano, M. T., Gonzalez, C., Navarro, R. E., Sprowls, C., & Verdinelli, S. (2005). Spanish-language psychotherapy: Therapists' experiences and needs. In S. P. Shohov (Ed.), *Advances in psychology research* (pp. 157–185). Nova Science Publishers.

Bruhn, R. A., Irby, B. J., Lou, M., Thweatt, W. T., & Lara-Alecio, R. (2005). A model for training bilingual school counselors. In V. Gonzalez & J. Tinajero (Eds.), *Review of research and practice* (pp. 145–161). Lawrence Erlbaum.

Burck, C. (2004). Living in several languages: Implications for therapy. *Journal of Family Therapy, 26*, 314–339.

Chávez-Moreno, L. C. (2020). Researching Latinxs, racism, and white supremacy in bilingual education: A literature review. *Critical Inquiry in Language Studies, 17*(2), 101–120.

Gándara, P., & Hopkins, M. (Eds.). (2010). *Forbidden language, English learners and restrictive language policies.* Teachers College Press.

Glodjo, T. (2017). Deconstructing social class identity and teacher privilege in the second language classroom. *TESOL Journal, 8*, 342–366.

Grosjean, F. (1982). *Life with two languages.* Harvard University Press.

Paris, D., & Alim, H. S. (2017). *Culturally sustaining pedagogies: Teaching and learning for justice in a changing world.* Teachers College Press.

Perez-Foster, R. (1998). *The power of language in the clinical process: Assessing and treating the bilingual person.* Jason Aronson.

Ramos-Sanchez, L. (2009). Counselor bilingual ability, counselor ethnicity, acculturation, and Mexican Americans' perceived counselor credibility. *Journal of Counseling & Development, 87*(3), 311–318.

Santiago-Rivera, A. L., & Altarriba, J. (2002). The role of language in therapy with the Spanish–English bilingual client. *Professional Psychology: Research and Practice, 33*, 30–38.

Seto, A., & Forth, N. L. A. (2020). What is known about bilingual counseling? A systematic review of the literature. *Professional Counselor, 10*(3), 393–405.

ETHNIC AND RACIAL IDENTITY DEVELOPMENT

Akos, P., & Ellis, C. M. (2008). Racial identity development in middle school: A case for school counselor individual and systemic intervention. *Journal of Counseling & Development, 86*(1), 26–33.

Benedetto, A. E., & Olisky, T. (2001). Biracial youth: The role of the school counselor in racial identity development. *Professional School Counseling, 5*(1), 66–69.

Gibbs, J., & Hines, A. (1992). Negotiating ethnic identity: Issues for Black–white biracial adolescents. In M. Root (Ed.), *Racially mixed people in America* (pp. 223– 238). SAGE.

Hays, D. G., Chang, C. Y., & Havice, P. (2008). White racial identity statuses as predictors of white privilege awareness. *Journal of Humanistic Counseling, Education and Development, 47*(2), 13–234.

Helms, J. E. (1993). *Black and white racial identity: Theory, research, and practice.* Praeger.

Kincheloe, J. J. (1999). The struggle to define and reinvent whiteness: A pedagogical analysis. *College Literature, 26,* 162–194.

Malott, K. M., Paone, T. R., Humphreys, K., & Martinez, T. (2010). Use of group counseling to address ethnic identity development: Application with adolescents of Mexican descent. *Professional School Counseling, 13*(5), 257–267.

Moss, L. J., & Singh, A. A. (2015). White school counselors becoming racial justice allies to students of color: A call to the field of school counseling. *Journal of School Counseling, 13*(5), 1–36.

Phinney, P., & Rotheram, M. (Eds.). (1987). *Children's ethnic socialization: Pluralism and development.* SAGE.

Ponterotto, J. G., & Park-Taylor, J. (2007). Racial and ethnic identity theory, measurement, and research in counseling psychology: Present status and future directions. *Journal of Counseling Psychology, 54*(3), 282–294.

Spencer, M. B., & Markstrom-Adams, C. (1990). Identity processes among racial and ethnic minority children in America. *Child Development, 61,* 290–310.

Tatum, B. D. (1992). Talking about race, learning about racism: The application of racial identity development theory in the classroom. *Harvard Educational Review, 62,*1–24.

Tatum, B. D. (1997). *Why are all the Black kids sitting together in the cafeteria?* Basic Books.

Thompson, C. E., & Carter, R. (2013). *Racial identity theory: Applications to individual, group, and organizational interventions.* Routledge.

Utt, J., & Tochluk, S. (2020). White teacher, know thyself: Improving anti-racist praxis through racial identity development. *Urban Education, 55*(1), 125–152.

Wijeyesinghe, C., & Jackson, B. (2012). *New perspectives on racial identity development: Integrating emerging frameworks* (2nd ed.). New York University Press.

References

Agency for Healthcare Research and Quality. (2017). *National healthcare quality and disparities report.* https://www.ahrq.gov/research/findings/nhqrdr/nhqdr17/index.html

Akbar, N. (1996). *Breaking the chains of psychological slavery.* Mind Productions and Associates.

Aldana, A., Bañales, J., & Richards-Schuster, K. (2019). Youth anti-racist engagement: Conceptualization, development, and validation of an Anti-Racism Action Scale. *Adolescent Research Review, 4*(4), 369–381.

Allport, G. W. (1954). *The nature of prejudice.* Doubleday.

American Counseling Association. (n.d.). *Anti-racism toolkit.* https://www.counseling.org/docs/default-source/resources-for-counselors/anti-racism-toolkit.pdf

American School Counselor Association. (2021). *Anti-racism resources.* https://www.schoolcounselor.org/Publications-Research/Publications/Free-ASCA-Resources/Anti-Racism-Resources

Anderson, C. (2016). *White rage: The unspoken truth of our racial divide.* Bloomsbury.

Anti-Defamation League. (2021). *What is racism?* https://www.adl.org/racism

Arredondo, P. (2005). Multicultural counseling to empower all families. In G. R. Walz & R. K. Yep (Eds.), *VISTAS: Compelling perspectives on counseling* (pp. 9–15). American Counseling Association.

Baca, L. M., & Koss-Chioino, J. D. (1997). Development of a culturally responsive group counseling model for Mexican American adolescents. *Journal of Multicultural Counseling and Development, 25,* 130–141.

Baker, S. B., Robichaud, T. A., Dietrich, V. W., Wells, S. C., & Schreck, R. E. (2009). School counselor consultation: A pathway to advocacy, collaboration, and leadership. *Professional School Counseling, 12,* 200–206.

Ballard, K. (Ed). (1999). *Inclusive education: International voices on disability and justice.* Falmer Press.

Bañales, J., Aldana, A., Richards-Schuster, K., Flanagan, C. A., Diemer, M. A., & Rowley, S. J. (2019). Youth anti-racism action: Contributions of youth perceptions of school racial messages and critical consciousness. *Journal of Community Psychology,* 10. https://doi.org/10.1002/jcop.22266

Barnard-Brak, L., McGaha-Garnett, V., & Burley, H. (2011). Advanced placement course enrollment and school-level characteristics. *NASSP Bulletin, 95*(3), 165–174.

Bell, D. (1992). Racial realism. *Connecticut Law Review, 24,* 363–379.

Bemak, F., & Chung, R. C. (2005). Advocacy as a critical role for urban school counselors: Working toward equity and social justice. *Professional School Counseling, 8,* 196–202.

Bemak, K. (2000). Transforming the role of the counselor to provide leadership in educational reform through collaboration. *Professional School Counseling, 3,* 323– 331.

Berkel, C., Murry, V. M., Hurt, T. R., Chen, Y. F., Brody, G. H., Simons, R. L., Cutrona, C., & Gibbons, F. X. (2009). It takes a village: Protecting rural African American youth in the context of racism. *Journal of Youth and Adolescence, 38*(2), 175–188.

Bohan-Baker, M., & Little, P. M. D. (2002). *The transition to kindergarten: A review of current research and promising practices to involve families.* Harvard Family Research Project.

Boyd-Franklin, N. (1989). *Black families in therapy: A multisystems approach.* Guilford Press.

Brewster, J., Foster, B., & Stephenson, M. (2016, February 29). A conversation with Latinos on race. *The New York Times.* [Video]. https://www.nytimes.com/video/opinion/100000004237305/a-conversation-with-latinos-on-race.html

Brewster, J., & Peltz, P. (2015, May 7). A conversation about growing up Black. *The New York Times.* [Video]. https://www.nytimes.com/video/opinion/100000003670178/a-conversation-about-growing-up-black.html

Brondolo, E., Brady Ver Halen, N., Pencille, M., Beatty, D., & Contrada, R. J. (2009). Coping with racism: A selective review of the literature and a theoretical and methodological critique. *Journal of Behavioral Medicine, 32,* 64–88.

Bryan, J. (2005). Fostering resilience and achievement in urban schools through school family–community–partnerships. *Professional School Counseling, 8,* 219–227.

Bryan, J., Griffin, D., Kim, J., Griffin, D. M., & Young, A. (2019). School counselor leadership in school–family–community partnerships: An equity-focused partnership process model for moving the field forward. In S. Sheldon & T. Turner-Vorbeck (Eds.), *The Wiley handbook on family, school, and community relationships in education* (pp. 265–287). Wiley.

Bryan, J., & Holcomb-McCoy, C. (2004). School counselors' perceptions of their involvement in school family community partnerships. *Professional School Counseling, 7,* 162–171.

Bryan, J., & Holcomb-McCoy, C. (2007). An examination of school counselor involvement in school–family–community partnerships. *Professional School Counseling, 10*(5), 441–454.

Carnevale, A. P., & Strohl, J. (2013). *Separate & unequal: How higher education reinforces the intergenerational reproduction of white racial privilege.* Georgetown University, Center on Education and the Workforce.

Casey-Cannon, S. L., Coleman, H. L. K., Knudtson, L. F., & Velazquez, C. C. (2011). Three racial and ethnic identity measures: Concurrent and divergent validity for diverse adolescents. *Identity, 11,* 64–91.

The Century Foundation. (2020). *TCF study finds U.S. schools underfunded by nearly 150 billion annually.* https://tcf.org/content/about-tcf/tcf-study-finds-u-s-schools-underfunded-nearly-150-billion-annually/

Chao, R. K., & Willms, J. D. (2002). The effects of parenting practices on children's outcomes. In J. D. Willms (Ed.), *Vulnerable children: Findings from Canada's national longitudinal survey of children and youth* (pp. 149–165). University of Alberta Press.

Chavous, T. M., Rivas-Drake, D., Smalls, C., Griffin, T., & Cogburn, C. (2008). Gender matters, too: The influences of school racial discrimination and racial identity on academic engagement outcomes among African American adolescents. *Developmental Psychology, 44*(3), 637–654.

Chenoweth, K., & Theokas, C. (2011). *Getting it done: Leading academic success in unexpected schools.* Harvard Education Press.

Cherng, H.-Y. S. (2016). Is all classroom conduct equal? Teacher contact with parents of racial/ethnic minority and immigrant adolescents. *Teachers College Record, 118,* 1–32.

Child Care Aware of America. (2014). *Parents and the high cost of child care.* https://www.childcareaware.org/wp-content/uploads/2016/12/costofcare20141.pdf

Clay, A., Chu, E., Davis, A., Deane, Y., Lis-Perlis, A., Lizarraga, A., Monz, L., Muhammad, J., Recinos, D., & Wolters, M. (2021). *About time: Master scheduling and equity.* Columbia University, Center for Public Research and Leadership. https://cprl.law.columbia.edu/sites/default/files/content/Publications/CPRL_2021_About%20Time%20Report_Final.pdf

Cokley, K. (2005). Racial(ized) identity, ethnic identity, and Afrocentric values:

Conceptual and methodological challenges in understanding African American identity. *Journal of Counseling Psychology, 52,* 517–526.

Cokley, K. (2006). The impact of racialized schools and racist (mis)education on African American students' academic identity. In M. G. Constantine & D. W. Sue (Eds.), *Addressing racism: Facilitating cultural competence in mental health and educational settings* (pp. 127–144). John Wiley & Sons, Inc.

Cokley, K. (2007). Critical issues in the measurement of ethnic and racial identity: A referendum on the state of the field. *Journal of Counseling Psychology, 54*(3), 224–234.

Colbert, R. D. (1996). The counselor's role in advancing school and family partnerships. *The School Counselor, 44,* 100–104.

The College Board. (2020). *2020 SAT suite of assessments annual report, total group.*

Connell, J. P., Spencer, M. B., & Aber, J. L. (1994). Educational risk and resilience in African-American youth: Context, self, action and outcomes in school. *Child Development, 65,* 493–506.

A conversation with my Black son. (2015, March 17). *The New York Times.* [Video]. https://www.nytimes.com/video/opinion/100000003575589/a-conversation-with-my-black-son.html

Craft, M., Hayes, S., & Moore, R. (2020). *Supporting the mental health well-being of high school students.* ACT Center for Equity in Learning. https://www.act.org/content/dam/act/unsecured/documents/R1798-mental-health-2020-01.pdf

Creanga, A. A., Berg, C. J., Syverson, C., Seed, K., Bruce, F. C., & Callaghan, W. M. (2015). Pregnancy-related mortality in the United States, 2006-2010. *Obstetrics Gynecology, 125,* 5–12.

Crenshaw, K. (2017). *On intersectionality: Essential writings.* The New Press.

Day-Vines, N. L., Wood, S. M., Grothaus, T., Craigen, L., Holman, A., Dotson-Blake, K., & Douglass, M. J. (2007). Broaching the subjects of race, ethnicity, and culture during the counseling process. *Journal of Counseling & Development, 85*(4), 401–409.

Denbo, S. J. (2002). Institutional practices that support African American student achievement. In S. J. Denbo & L. M. Beaulieu (Eds.), *Improving schools for African American students* (pp. 55–70). Charles C Thomas.

Dixon, A. (2006). Mattering to others: Implications for the counseling relationship. *Journal of Counseling and Development, 84,* 483–487.

Dixon, A. L., & Tucker, C. (2008). Every student matters: Enhancing strengths-based school counseling through the application of mattering. *Professional School Counseling, 12,* 123–126.

Dobbin, F., & Kalev, A. (2016). Why diversity programs fail. *Harvard Business Review, 94,* 52–61.

Duncan, C., & Pryzwansky, W. B. (1993). Effects of race, racial identity development, and orientation style on perceived consultant effectiveness. *Journal of Multicultural Counseling and Development, 21,* 88–96.

Education Trust. (1997). *The national guidance and counseling reform program.* Author.

Education Trust. (2001, May). *The other gap: Poor students receive fewer dollars.* Education Trust Data Bulletin. https://edtrust.org/resource/the-other-gap-poor-students-receive-fewer-dollars-gap/

Education Trust. (2020). *COVID-19 education equity guide: School funding.* Author. https://edtrust.org/resource/covid-19-education-equity-guide-school-funding/

EdWeek Research Center (2020). *Antiracist teaching: What educators really think.* https://www.edweek.org/leadership/anti-racist-teaching-what-educators-really-think/2020/09

Epstein, J., Sanders, M., Simon, B., Salinas, K., Jansorn, N., & VanVoorhis, F. (2002). *School, family and community partnerships: Your handbook for action* (2nd ed.). Corwin Press.

Ford, D. Y. (2010). Multicultural issues: Underrepresentation of culturally different students in gifted education: Reflections about current problems and recommendations for the future. *Gifted Child Today, 33*(3), 31–35.

Ford, D. Y., Grantham, T. C., & Whiting, G. W. (2008). Culturally and linguistically diverse students in gifted education: Recruitment and retention issues. *Exceptional Children, 74*, 289–308.

Fowler, B. (1997). *Pierre Bourdieu and cultural theory: Critical investigations.* SAGE.

Freire, P. (1970). *Pedagogy of the oppressed.* Herder and Herder.

Frey, W. (2018). *America's demographic future: Population aging with youthful diversity.* Brookings Institution Press.

Fryer, R. G., & Howard-Noveck, M. (2017). *High-dosage tutoring and reading achievement: Evidence from New York City* [NBER Working Papers 23792]. National Bureau of Economic Research Inc.

Fung, K., Lo, H., Srivastava, R., & Andermann, L. (2012). Organizational cultural competence consultation to a mental health institution. *Transcultural Psychiatry, 49*, 165–184.

Gandara, P., & Bial, D. (2001). *Paving the way to higher education: K–12 intervention programs for underrepresented youth.* National Postsecondary Education Cooperative.

Gandbhir, G., & Peltz, P. (2015, November 11). A conversation with police on race. *The New York Times.* [Video]. https://www.nytimes.com/video/opinion/100000004027684/a-conversation-with-police-on-race.html

Gandbhir, G., & Stephenson, M. (2016, April 5). A conversation with Asian-Americans on race. *The New York Times.* [Video]. https://www.nytimes.com/video/opinion/100000004308529/a-conversation-with-asians-on-race.html

Gates, H. L. (2019). *Stony the road: Reconstruction, white supremacy, and the rise of Jim Crow.* Penguin Books.

Geiser, S., & Atkinson, R. C. (2013). Beyond the master plan: The case for restructuring baccalaureate education in California. *California Journal of Politics and Policy.* https://escholarship.org/content/qt0gj789nd/qt0gj789nd.pdf

Gershenson, S., Hart, C., Hyman, J., Lindsay, C., & Papageorge, N. W. (2018, November). *The long-run impacts of same-race teachers* [NBER Working Paper No. w25254]. https://ssrn.com/abstract=3282954

Gibbs, J. T. (1985). Can we continue to be color-blind and class-bound? *The Counseling Psychologist, 13*, 426–435.

Giles, H. C. (2005). Three narratives of parent-educator relationships: Toward counselor repertoires for bridging the urban parent–school divide. *Professional School Counseling, 8*(3), 228–235.

Goldring, L. (2002). The power of school culture. *Leadership, 32*, 32–35.

Gopaul-McNicol, S. A., & Thomas-Presswood, T. (1998). *Working with linguistically and culturally different children: Innovative clinical and educational approaches.* Prentice Hall.

Gordon-Reed, A. (2009). *The Hemingses of Monticello: An American family.* W. W. Norton & Co.

Gottfredson, G., Gottfredson, D. C., Czeh, E. R., Cantor, D., Crosse, S. B., & Hantman, I. (2000). *National study of delinquency prevention in schools.* Gottfredson Associates. (Final report for the National Institute of Justice, U. S. Department of Justice, Grant # 96-MN-MV-008).

Green, A., & Keys, S. (2001). Expanding the developmental school counseling paradigm: Meeting the needs of the 21st century student. *Professional School Counseling, 5*, 84–95.

Griffin, D., & Steen, S. (2010). School, family, community partnerships: Applying Epstein's theory of the six types of involvement to school counselor practice. *Professional School Counseling, 13*, 218–226.

Groce, L. L., &. Johnson, L. V. (2021). School counselors igniting the hope of undocumented students in college access, *The Journal for Specialists in Group Work, 46*, 128–142.

Hango, D. W. (2007). Parental investment in childhood and educational qualifications: Can greater parental involvement mediate the effects of socioeconomic disadvantage? *Social Science Research, 36*, 1371–1390.

Hanson, R., & Pugliese, C. (2020). *Parent and family involvement in education: 2019*

(NCES 2020-076). *U.S. Department of Education*. National Center for Education Statistics. http://nces.ed.gov/pubsearch/pubsinfo.asp?pubid=2020076

Hart, P., & Jacobi, M. (1992). *From gatekeeper to advocate: Transforming the role of the school counselor*. The College Board.

Hartmann, W. E., & Gone, J. P. (2012). Incorporating traditional healing into an urban American Indian health organization: A case study of community member perspectives. *Journal of Counseling Psychology, 59*(4), 542–554.

Hatch, T. (2014). *The use of data in school counseling: Hatching results for students*. Corwin Press.

Helms, J. E. (1990). *Black and white racial identity: Theory, research, and practice*. Greenwood Press.

Hoffman, M. A., Phillips, E. L., Noumair, D. A., Shullman, S., Geiser, C., Gray, J., Homer, J., Paulk, D. L., Remer, R., Robinson, S., Rocha-Singh, I., Tinsley, D. J., Toporek, R., & Ziegler, D. (2006). Toward a feminist and multicultural model of consultation and advocacy. *Journal of Multicultural Counseling and Development, 34*, 116–128.

Holcomb-McCoy, C. (2004). Assessing the multicultural competence of school counselors: A checklist. *Professional School Counseling, 7*, 178–182.

Holcomb-McCoy, C. (2007). *School counseling to close the achievement gap: A social justice approach*. Corwin Press.

Holcomb-McCoy, C., & Bryan, J. (2010). Advocacy and empowerment in parent consultation: Implications for theory and practice. *Journal of Counseling & Development, 88*(3), 259–268.

Holcomb-McCoy, C., Harris, P.C., Hines, E.M., & Johnston, G. (2008). School counselors' multicultural self-efficacy: A preliminary investigation. *Professional School Counseling, 11*, 166–178.

Holcomb-McCoy, C., & Moore-Thomas, C. (2001). Empowering African American adolescent females. *Professional School Counseling, 5*, 19–25.

Holcomb-McCoy, C., & Myers, J. E. (1999). Multicultural competence and counselor training: A national survey. *Journal of Counseling and Development, 77*, 294–302.

Holt, S. B., & Gershenson, S. (2015). *The impact of teacher demographic representation on student attendance and suspensions* [Discussion paper]. The Institute for the Study of Labor.

Howard, T., & Terry, C. L. (2011). Culturally responsive pedagogy for African American students: Promising programs and practices for enhanced academic performance. *Teaching Education, 22*, 345–362.

Ingraham, C. L. (2000). Consultation through a multicultural lens: Multicultural and cross-cultural consultation in schools. *School Psychology Review, 29*(3), 320–343.

The Institute for College Access and Success. (2019). *Dire disparities: Patterns of racial inequitable funding and student success in public postsecondary education*. The Institute for College Access and Success.

Jernigan, M. M., & Daniel, J. H. (2011). Racial trauma in the lives of Black children and adolescents: Challenges and clinical implications. *Journal of Child & Adolescent Trauma, 4*, 123–141.

Johnson, R. (2002). *Using data to close the achievement gap: How to measure equity in our schools*. Corwin Press.

Jones, N. H. (2019). The 1619 project. *The New York Times*. https://www.nytimes.com/interactive/2019/08/14/magazine/black-history-american-democracy.html

JustPartners, Inc., & The Annie E. Casey Foundation. (2009, September 1). *Advancing the mission: Tools for equity, diversity and inclusion*. Author.

Kalyanpur, M., & Rao, S. S. (1991). Empowering low-income, Black families of handicapped children. *American Journal of Orthopsychiatry, 61*, 523–532.

Kendi, I. (2017). *Stamped from the beginning: The definitive history of racist ideas in America*. Bold Type Books.

Kendi, I. (2019). *How to be an antiracist*. One World.

Kini, T., & Podolsky, A. (2016). *Does teaching experience increase teacher effectiveness? A review of the research*. Learning Policy Institute.

Kiselica, M., & Robinson, M. (2001). Bringing advocacy counseling to life: The history, issues, and human dramas of social justice work in counseling. *Journal of Counseling and Development, 79*, 387–397.

Krogstad, J. M., & Gonzalez-Barrera, G. (2021). Key facts about U.S. immigration policies and Biden's proposed changes. *Pew Research Center*. https://www.pewresearch.org/fact-tank/2021/03/22/key-facts-about-u-s-immigration-policies-and-bidens-proposed-changes/

Kurpius, D. J. (1978). Defining and implementing a consultation program in schools. *School Psychology Review, 7*(3), 4–17.

Ladson-Billings, G. (1998). Teaching in dangerous times: Culturally relevant approaches to teacher assessment. *The Journal of Negro Education, 67*, 255–267.

Lapan, R. T., Gysbers, N. C., Stanley, B., & Pierce, M. E. (2012). Missouri professional school counselors: Ratios matter, especially in high-poverty schools. *Professional School Counseling, 16*(2), 108–116.

Larson, K. E., Pas, E. T., Bradshaw, C. P., Rosenberg, M. S., & Day-Vines, N. L. (2018). Examining how proactive management and culturally responsive teaching relate to student behavior: Implications for measurement and practice. *School Psychology Review, 47*(2), 153–166.

Lee, C. (1995). *Counseling for diversity: A guide for school counselors and related professionals.* Allyn and Bacon.

Lee, C. (2005). *Multicultural issues in counseling.* American Counseling Association.

Lee, C., & Richardson, B. L. (1991). *Multicultural issues in counseling: New approaches to diversity.* American Association for Counseling and Development.

Leithwood, K., Louis, K. S., Anderson, S., & Wahlstrom, K. (2004). *How leadership influences student learning.* The Wallace Foundation. https://www.wallacefoundation.org/knowledge-center/Documents/How-Leadership-Influences-Student-Learning.pdf

Leon, A., Villares, E., Brigman, G., Webb, L., & Peluso, P. (2011). Closing the achievement gap of Latina/Latino students: A

school counseling response. *Counseling Outcome Research and Evaluation, 2*, 73–86.

Lobe, B., Morgan, D., & Hoffman, K. A. (2020). Qualitative data collection in an era of social distancing. *International Journal of Qualitative Methods, 19*. https://doi.org/10.1177/1609406920937875

Locke, D. C. (1998). *Increasing multicultural understanding: A comprehensive model.* SAGE.

Long, M. C., Conger, D., & Iatarola, P. (2012). Effects of high school course-taking on secondary and postsecondary success. *American Educational Research Journal, 49*(2), 285–322.

Losen, D., Hodson, C., Ee, J., & Martinez, T. (2014). Disturbing inequities: Exploring the relationship between racial disparities in special education identification and discipline. *Journal of Applied Research on Children: Informing Policy for Children at Risk, 5,* Article 15. http://digitalcommons.library.tmc.edu/childrenatrisk/vol5/iss2/15

Losen, D., & Orfield, G. (2002). *Racial inequity in special education.* Harvard Education Publishing Group.

Love, B. (2019). *We want to do more than survive: Abolitionist teaching and the pursuit of educational freedom.* Beacon Press.

Mackay, H., & Strickland, M. J. (2018). Exploring culturally responsive teaching and student-created videos in an at-risk middle school classroom. *Middle Grades Review, 4*(1). https://scholarworks.uvm.edu/mgreview/vol4/iss1/7

Magnuson, K. A., & Waldfogel, J. (2005). Early childhood care and education: Effects on ethnic and racial gaps in school readiness. *The Future of Children, 15,* 169–196.

Malott, K., Paone, T. R., Humphreys, K., & Martinez, T. (2010). Use of group counseling to address ethnic identity development: Application with adolescents of Mexican descent. *Professional School Counseling, 13,* 257–267.

Manset, G., St. John, E. P., Simmons, A., Gordon, D., Musoba, G. D., & Klingerman, K. (2000). *Wisconsin's high performing/high poverty schools.* North Central Regional Laboratory.

Marshall, P. L. (2002). Racial identity and challenges of educating white youths for cultural diversity. *Multicultural Perspectives, 4*(3), 9–14.

Marx, S., & Byrnes, D. (2012). Multicultural school climate inventory. *Current Issues in Education, 15*(3), 1–15.

Merriam-Webster. (n.d.). Accountability. In *Merriam-Webster.com dictionary.* from https://www.merriam-webster.com/dictionary/accountability

Morgan, P. L., Farkas, G., Cook, M., Strassfeld, N. M., Hillemeier, M. M., Pun, W. H., & Schussler, D. L. (2017). Are Black children disproportionately overrepresented in special education? A best-evidence synthesis. *Exceptional Children, 83*(2), 181–198.

Morgan, P. L., Farkas, G., Hillemeier, M. M., Mattison, R., Maczuga, S., Li, H., & Cook, M. (2015). Minorities are disproportionately underrepresented in special education: Longitudinal evidence across five disability conditions. *Educational Researcher, 44*(5), 278–292.

Moule, J. (2012). Understanding unconscious bias and unintentional racism. *Other Lectures* [Video file]. Submission 17. https://digitalcommons.linfield.edu/lectures_other/17

Nance, J. P. (2017). Student surveillance, racial inequalities, and implicit racial bias. *Emory Law Journal, 66*, 765–837.

National Center for Education Statistics. (2016). *Status and trends in education of racial and ethnic groups, Indicator 13: High school course taking.* https://nces.ed.gov/programs/raceindicators/indicator_rcd.asp

Neville, H. A., & Carter, R. T. (2005). Race and racism in counseling psychology research, training, and practice: A critical review, current trends, and future directions. *The Counseling Psychologist, 33*(4), 413–418.

Neville, H. A., Tynes, B. M., & Utsey, S. O. (Eds.). (2009). *Handbook of African American psychology.* SAGE.

Norris, D. M., & Spurlock, J. (1992). Racial and cultural issues impacting on countertransference. In J. R. Brandell (Ed.), *Countertransference in psychotherapy with children and adolescents* (pp. 91–123). Aronson.

Ogbu, J. (1994). Racial stratification and education in the United States: Why inequality persists. *Teachers College Record, 96*, 264–298.

Ogbu, J. (2003). *Black American students in an affluent suburb: A study of academic disengagement.* Lawrence Erlbaum Associates.

Oswald, D. P., Coutinho, M. J., Best, A. M., & Singh, N. N. (1999). Ethnic representation in special education: The influence of school-related income and demographic variables. *Journal of Special Education, 32*, 194–206.

Pachter, L. M., & Coll, C. G. (2009). Racism and child health: A review of the literature and future directions. *Journal of Developmental Behavioral Pediatrics, 30*, 255–263.

Pahl, K., & Way, N. (2006). Longitudinal trajectories of ethnic identity among urban Black and Latino adolescents. *Child Development, 77*, 1403–1415.

Parham, T. A. (2002). *Counseling persons of African descent: Raising the bar of practitioner competence.* SAGE.

Parham, T. A., Ajama, A., & White, J. L. (2000). *Psychology of Blacks: Centering our perspectives in the African consciousness* (4th ed.). Psychology Press.

Parrett, W. H., & Budge, K. M. (2012). *Turning high-poverty schools into high-performing schools* (2nd ed.). ASCD.

Phinney, J. S. (1990). Ethnic identity in adolescents and adults: Review of research. *Psychological Bulletin, 108*, 499–514.

Phinney, J. S. (1992). The multigroup ethnic identity measure: A new scale for use with diverse groups. *Journal of Adolescent Research, 7*(2), 156–176.

Pitts, J. (2020, September). What antiracism really means for educators. *Learning for Justice.* https://www.learningforjustice.org/magazine/what-antiracism-really-means-for-educators

Ponterotto, J., & Casas, H. (1987). In search of multicultural competence within counselor education programs. *Journal of Counseling and Development, 65*, 430–434.

Pope-Davis, D. B., Reynolds, A. L., Dings, J. G., & Ottavi, T. M. (1994). Multicultural competencies of doctoral interns at university counseling centers: An exploratory investigation. *Professional Psychology: Research and Practice, 25,* 466–470.

Proweller, A. (1999). Shifting identities in private education: Reconstructing race at/in the cultural center. *Teachers College Record, 100,* 776–808.

Psychology Today. (2021). *Bias.* https://www.psychologytoday.com/us/basics/bias

Quintana, S. M. (1998). Development of children's understanding of ethnicity and race. *Applied & Preventive Psychology: Current Scientific Perspectives, 7,* 27–45.

Quinton, S. (2014, December). The race gap in high school honors classes. *The Atlantic.* https://www.theatlantic.com/politics/archive/2014/12/the-race-gap-in-high-school-honors-classes/431751/

Ratts, M. J., & Hutchins, A. M. (2009). ACA advocacy competencies: Social justice advocacy at the client/student level. *Journal of Counseling & Development, 87*(3), 269–275.

Richard, H. W. (1996). Filmed in black and white: Teaching the concept of racial identity at a predominantly white university. *Teaching of Psychology, 23*(3), 159–161.

Roberts, S., & Rizzo, M. T. (2021). The psychology of American racism. *American Psychologist, 76,* 475–487.

Rose, H., & Betts, J. R. (2004). The effect of high school courses on earnings. *The Review of Economics and Statistics, 86,* 497–513.

Saleem, F. T., Anderson, R., & Williams, M. (2019). Addressing the "myth" of racial trauma: Developmental and ecological considerations for youth of color. *Clinical Child and Family Psychology Review, 23,* 1–14.

Schwartz, H. L., Hamilton, L. S., Faxon-Mills, S., Gomez, C. J., Huguet, A., Jaycox, L., Leschitz, J. T., Tuma, A. P., Tosh, K., Whitaker, A., & Wrabel, S. L. (2020). *Early lessons from schools and out-of-school time programs implementing social and emotional learning.* RAND Corporation.

Schwartz, S. J., Syed, M., Yip, T., Knight, G. P., Umana-Taylor, A. J., Rivas-Drake, D., & Lee, R. M. (2014). Methodological issues in ethnic and racial identity research with ethnic minority populations: Theoretical precision, measurement issues, and research designs. *Child Development, 85,* 58–76.

Sellers, R. M., Rowley, S. A. J., Chavous, T. M., Shelton, J. N., & Smith, M. A. (1997). Multidimensional inventory of Black identity: A preliminary investigation of reliability and construct validity. *Journal of Personality and Social Psychology, 73,* 805–815.

Sheldon, S. B., & Jung, S. B. (2015). *The family engagement partnership: Student outcome evaluations.* Johns Hopkins Center on School, Family, Community Partnerships.

Singh, A. A. (2019). *The racial healing handbook: Practical activities to help you challenge privilege, confront systemic racism, and engage in collective healing.* New Harbinger Publications.

Slavin, R. E., Lake, C., Chambers, B., Cheung, A., & Davis, S. (2009). Effective reading programs for the elementary grades: A best-evidence synthesis. *Review of Educational Research, 79*(4), 1391–1466.

Slavin, R. E., Madden, N. A., Dolan, L. J., Wasik, B. A., Ross, S. M., Smith, L. J., & Dianda, M. (1998). Success for all: Achievement outcomes of a schoolwide reform model. In J. Crane (Ed.), *Social programs that work* (pp. 43–74). Russell Sage Foundation.

Smith, D. (2021, June). There's a concerted backlash: Ibram X. Kendi on antiracism under attack. *The Guardian.* https://www.theguardian.com/world/2021/jun/12/ibram-x-kendi-antiracism-backlash-interview

Soloranzo, D., Allen, W., & Carroll, G. (2002). Keeping race in place: Racial microaggressions and campus racial climate at the University of California, Berkeley. *Journal Chicana/o Latina/o Law Review, 23*(1), 15–111.

Southern Poverty Law Center. (2019). *Hate at school.* https://www.splcenter.org/sites/default/files/tt_2019_hate_at_school_report_final_0.pdf

Southern Poverty Law Center. (2021). *Costly and cruel: How misuse of the Baker Act harms*

37,000 Florida children each year. https:// www.splcenter.org/sites/default/files/ com_special_report_baker_act_costly_ and_cruel.pdf

Spencer, M. B. (2019). Developmental and intersectional insights about diverse children's identity. *Florida Law Review, 71,* 12.

Steele, C. M. (1997). A threat in the air: How stereotypes shape intellectual identity and performance. *American Psychologist, 52,* 613–629.

Stephenson, M., & Brewster, J. (2015, December 1). A conversation with Black women on race. *The New York Times.* [Video]. https://www.nytimes.com/video/opinion/100000004050379/a-conversation-with-black-women-on-race.html

Stephenson, M., & Foster, B. (2015, July 1). A conversation with white people on race. *The New York Times.* [Video]. https:// www.nytimes.com/video/opinion/100000003773643/a-conversation-with-white-people-on-race.html

Stephenson, M., & Young, B. (2017, August 15). A conversation with Native Americans on race. *The New York Times.* [Video]. https:// www.nytimes.com/video/opinion/100000005352074/a-conversation-with-native-americans-on-race.html

Stone, C. B., & Dahir, C. A. (2004). *School counselor accountability: A measure of student success.* Prentice Hall.

Stonerock, G. L., & Blumenthal, J. A. (2017). Role of counseling to promote adherence in healthy lifestyle medicine: Strategies to improve exercise adherence and enhance physical activity. *Progress in Cardiovascular Diseases, 59*(5), 455–462.

Sue, D. W., Arredondo, P., & McDavis, R. (1992). Multicultural counseling competencies and standards: A call to the profession. *Journal of Counseling and Development, 70,* 477–486.

Teachers College Columbia University. (2004). *A campaign for equity: 2004 Annual Report.* Author.

Teemant, A., Yoder, G., Sherman, B., & Graff, C. (2021). An equity framework for family, community and school partnerships. *Theory Into Practice, 60,* 28–38.

Terrell, Y. L., & Cheatham, H. E. (1996). Creating a therapeutic alliance: A multicultural perspective. In J. L. DeLucia-Waack (Ed.), *Multicultural counseling competencies: Implications for training and practice* (pp. 63–88). Association for Counselor Education and Supervision.

Theokas, C., & Saaris, R. (2013). *Finding America's missing AP and IB students.* The Education Trust.

Thomas, W. P., & Collier, V. (1997). *Virginia school effectiveness for language minority students.* NCBE Resource Collection Series, No. 9. National Clearinghouse for Bilingual Education, Washington, DC, Office of Bilingual Education and Minority Languages Affairs (ED).

Toporek, R. L., & Liu, W. M. (2001). Advocacy in counseling: Addressing issues of race, class, and gender oppression. In D. B. Pope-Davis & H. L. K. Coleman (Eds.), *The intersection of race, class, and gender in counseling psychology* (pp. 385–416). SAGE.

U.S. Department of Commerce, Census Bureau. (2018, December 6). *American community survey 2013–2017 5-year data release.* https://www.census.gov/newsroom/press-kits/2018/acs-5year.html

U.S. Department of Commerce, Census Bureau. (2019). American Community Survey (ACS). See Digest of Education Statistics 2020, Table 202.20.

U.S. Department of Education. (2000). *National Center for Educational Statistics, Digest of Education Statistics.* U.S. Department of Education.

U.S. Department of Education. (2018). *2015–16 Civil Rights Data Collection, School Climate and Safety.* Author. https://www2 .ed.gov/about/offices/list/ocr/docs/school-climate-and-safety.pdf

U.S. Department of Education, National Center for Education Statistics. (2019). *Parent and family involvement in education survey of the national household education surveys program.* Author.

U.S. Government Accountability Office. (2018). *K-12 education: Discipline disparities for Black students, boys, and students with disabilities.* U. S. Government

Accountability Office. https://www.gao
.gov/assets/gao-18-258.pdf

Urban Institute. (2019). *Segregated from the
start: Comparing segregation in early childhood and K–12 education.* Urban Institute.

Utsey, S. O. (1999). Development and validation of a short form of the index of race-
related stress (IRRS)-brief version.
*Measurement and Evaluation in Counseling
and Development Special Issue: Assessment
and Race, 32,* 149–167.

Utsey, S. O., & Ponterotto, J. G. (1996). Development and validation of the index of
race-related stress (IRRS). *Journal of
Counseling Psychology, 43,* 490–501.

Valentino, Rachel. (n.d.). *Will public pre-K really
close achievement gaps? Gaps in prekindergarten quality between students and across
states.* Stanford University.

Van Velsor, P. (2009). School counselors as
social-emotional learning consultants:
Where do we begin? *Professional School
Counseling, 13,* 50–58.

Wang, M., & Huguley, J. P. (2012). Parental racial
socialization as a moderator of the effects of
racial discrimination on educational success
among African American adolescents. *Child
Development, 83,* 1716–1731.

West, C. (1994). *Race matters.* Vintage.

Western States Center. (2015, April). *Racial justice assessment tool.* National Juvenile Justice
Network. https://www.njjn.org/uploads/
digital-library/AssessingOurOrganiza-
tions_RacialJustice%20(1)%20(1).pdf

White, J. (1980). Toward a Black psychology. In
R. Jones (Ed.), *Black psychology* (2nd ed.,
pp. 5–12). Harper Row.

Whittlesey, V. (2001). *Diversity activities for
psychology.* Allyn & Bacon.

Williams, J. L., Tolan, P. H., Durkee, M. I.,
Francois, A. G., & Anderson, R. E. (2012).
Integrating racial and ethnic identity
research into developmental understanding of adolescents. *Child Development Perspective, 6,* 304–311.

Wong, C. A., Eccles, J. S., & Sameroff, A.
(2003). The influence of ethnic discrimination and ethnic identification on African American adolescents' school and
socioemotional adjustment. *Journal of Personality, 71*(6), 1197–1232.

Zayas, L. H. (2001). Incorporating struggles
with racism and ethnic identity in therapy
with adolescents. *Clinical Social Work Journal, 29,* 361–373.

Zeichner, K. M. (2003). The adequacies and
inadequacies of three current strategies to
recruit, prepare, and retain the best teachers for all students. *Teachers College Record,
105*(3), 490–519.

Zins, J. E., & Erchul, W. P. (2002). Best practices in school consultation. In A. Thomas
& J. Grimes (Eds.), *Best practices in school
psychology—IV* (pp. 625–643). National
Association of School Psychologists.

Zutlevics, T. L. (2002). Towards a theory of
oppression. *Ratio, 15,* 80–102.

Index

microaggressions, 48, 85
mindsets and behaviors for student success, 6
minoritized students, 86
mothers, 19, 42, 54, 58, 70–71, 80, 82
multicultural counseling, 31
Multicultural School Climate, 88

NAACP (National Association for the
  Advancement of Colored People), 6, 100
NASSP (National Association of Secondary
  School Principals), 24
National Association of Secondary School
  Principals (NASSP), 24
National Center for Education Statistics.
  See NCES
National Center for Transforming School
  Counseling (NCTSC), 24
National Office of School Counselor Advocacy.
  See NOSCA
National Teacher and Principal Survey
  (NTPS), 16
Native American students, 6, 9, 11, 14–15,
  17, 132
NCES (National Center for Education
  Statistics), 13, 16, 103, 151
NCTSC (National Center for Transforming
  School Counseling), 24
New Town Elementary School, 125
NOSCA (National Office of School Counselor
  Advocacy), 24
NTPS (National Teacher and Principal
  Survey), 16

oppression, 6, 29–33, 48–49, 58, 60, 62–64,
  115, 127, 131, 133, 135
Orrin in school counseling departmental
  meetings, 134
outcomes of Black and Brown
  students, 127
overpolicing in Black and Brown
  communities, 5
overrepresentation and underrepresentation of
  students of color, 150–151

parent attendance and participation, 104
parent consultation, 81
parent recommendations, 146, 152
parents and community members, 95, 101–2,
  104–5, 107
parents and families, 95, 98, 104, 150–51
Parents Empowered, 107

parents in school change efforts, 107
Parent–Teacher Association (PTA), 34
Parent–Teacher Organization (PTO), 92, 131,
  133–34
partnerships, 40, 42, 91, 93–94, 105
performance, school counselor's, 118
place groups of students, 146
playgroups, 105
postsecondary options, 149, 165
poverty, 18–19, 23, 28, 32, 35, 50–52, 103,
  136, 157
power of school counselors, 8
pregnancy, 19, 70
preschools, 19–20
Process evaluations, 117–18
  total school counseling program, 118
process for identifying students for special
  education, 19
programs, school counselor education, 24
PTA (Parent–Teacher Association), 34
PTO (Parent–Teacher Organization), 92, 131,
  133–34

racial identity, 61–62, 64, 165
racial socialization, 62, 64
racism and bias, 28, 41, 127–28, 130, 165
RAMP (Recognized ASCA Model Program),
  6, 110, 118–20, 155
resilience, 87–88, 147–48
Resources to help school counselors strengthen
  SFC partnerships, 105
Resources to Support Antiracist
  Learning, 148
revising school counselor practices, 124
RJ (Restorative justice), 148

sample school culture assessment items, 88
Sam's parents, 69
SASS (Schools and Staffing Survey), 16
schedules, 21, 54, 87, 116, 143–44
  innovative school counselor, 106
  school's, 143, 145
scheduling, 143–45, 153

school culture, 28, 33, 77, 84, 86–88, 141
  negative, 106
  racist-free, 85
  transform, 86
school culture assessment, 88
school culture change, 86
school culture data, 112–13

A SAGE Publishing Company

Solutions YOU WANT | *Experts* YOU TRUST | *Results* YOU NEED

INSTITUTES

Corwin Institutes provide regional and virtual events where educators collaborate with peers and learn from industry experts. Prepare to be recharged and motivated!

corwin.com/institutes

ON-SITE PROFESSIONAL LEARNING

Corwin on-site PD is delivered through high-energy keynotes, practical workshops, and custom coaching services designed to support knowledge development and implementation.

www.corwin.com/pd

VIRTUAL PROFESSIONAL LEARNING

Our virtual PD combines live expert facilitation with the flexibility of anytime, anywhere professional learning. See the power of intentionally designed virtual PD.

www.corwin.com/virtualworkshops

CORWIN ONLINE

Online learning designed to engage, inform, challenge, and inspire. Our courses offer practical, classroom-focused instruction that will meet your continuing education needs and enhance your practice.

www.corwinonline.com

PLSN209A8

Visit www.corwin.com

CORWIN